C000235869

THE
DAUNTLESS
IN BATTLE

THE
DAUNTLESS
IN BATTLE

The Douglas SBD Dauntless Dive-Bomber in
the Pacific 1941–1945

PETER C. SMITH

Pen & Sword
AVIATION

AN IMPRINT OF PEN & SWORD BOOKS LTD
YORKSHIRE – PHILADELPHIA

First published in Great Britain in 2019 by
PEN AND SWORD AVIATION
an imprint of
Pen & Sword Books Limited
Yorkshire – Philadelphia

ISBN 978 1 52670 460 3

Printed and bound in England by TJ International,
Padstow, Cornwall, PL28 8RW

Typeset in Times New Roman 11/13.5 by
Aura Technology and Software Services, India

Pen & Sword Books Ltd incorporates the imprints of
Pen & Sword Aviation, Pen & Sword Maritime, Pen & Sword Military,
Wharncliffe Local History, Pen & Sword Select,
Pen & Sword Military Classics and Leo Cooper.

For a complete list of Pen and Sword titles please contact
PEN & SWORD BOOKS LTD
47 Church Street, Barnsley, South Yorkshire, S70 2AS, England
E-mail: enquiries@pen-and-sword.co.uk
Website: www.pen-and-sword.co.uk

Or

PEN & SWORD BOOKS
1950 Lawrence Rd, Havertown, PA 19083, USA
E-mail: Uspen-and-sword@casematepublishers.com
Website: www.penandswordbooks.com

Contents

Foreword

This edition of my book updates the original work which was published in 1997 in both the United Kingdom and the United States, and contains both additions and corrections to that volume, but this new edition also differs in that it concentrates on what the Douglas SBD Dauntless actual *did* than on its origins, specifications and preservations. Thus, this book is more action-orientated than being statistically-driven. This was a deliberate choice in response to reader requests, and so here the men are as important as the data. I have still incorporated much of the original documentation from both the Douglas company archives at Long Beach and the Official US Navy, Marine Corps and Army Air Force documentation held at various centres in the United States during my original research there between 1994 and 1997, but this has often been modified and added to in the light of subsequent research.

As before I wish to acknowledge the deep debt of gratitude I owe to the many organizations and individuals who offered unstinted help and assistance both then and since. I was fortunate that while conducting my original research trips I was afforded every facility and help by historians, archivists and curators alike, who had, without exception, both welcomed me and gave me valuable direction and advice. In a way I was fortunate that this done at the time it was, before the many onerous restrictions and unnecessary and even absurd limitations were imposed in the panic following the 9/11 attacks. Quite what exactly the naval battles of the Second World War have to do with twenty-first-century Islamist terrorism I have been unable to ascertain, but it certainly had a baneful influence on historical research facilities and openness.

I would therefore like to re-acknowledge my deep gratitude to the following for all they did to assist my searches. Don Hudson, and especially Pat McGinnis, both of the Douglas Aircraft Company (Boeing-McDonnell) at Lakewood, Long Beach, California, for their warm hospitality on my

FOREWORD

visits and for throwing open to me their extensive archives – an invaluable source; Hill Goodspeed of the Emil Buehler Naval Aviation Library, National Museum of Naval Aviation, Pensacola, Florida, for wise counsel and great help in researching their archives and for making my stay in Pensacola such a pleasant rewarding one; Ray Wagner, Archivist, of the San Diego Aerospace Museum, San Diego, California, for access to their archives (which includes the Ed Heinemann papers) and for his kindness to me on both my visits there over the years; Vernon Raymond Smith, Textual Research Reference Division, National Archives, College Park, Maryland, for his patience and dedication in producing for me all the various combat reports and war diaries of the US squadrons involved in the SBD's many battles.

Likewise to the following: Dr Steve Ewing, historian, USS *Yorktown*, Patriots Point & Maritime Museum, Mount Pleasant, Charleston, South Carolina, a mine of information and good ideas; Bill Tunnell, Executive Director, USS *Alabama* Battleship Memorial Park, Mobile, Alabama; T.J. Zalar, Curator, Lone Star Flight Museum, Galveston, Texas; Robert L. North, New England Air Museum, Windsor Locks, Connecticut; Danny J. Crawford, Head, Reference Section, History and Museums Division, Marine Corps Historical Center, Washington DC; Michael E. Starn, Aviation Specialist, Museums Branch, Marine Corps History and Museums Division, Quantico, Virginia, during my visit there; Paula Ussery, Curator, Admiral Nimitz Museum, Fredericksburg, Texas; James W. Robinette, Project Assistant, American Airpower Heritage Museum Inc., Midland, Texas; Dan Hagedorn, Reference Team Leader, Archives Division, Smithsonian Institution, National Air and Space Museum, Washington DC; Cindy J. Keller and Frank R. Mormillo, Planes of Fame Aviation Museum, Chino, California; the late Wendy Vandervort, Air Power History, Lexington, Virginia; M. Vincent Moller, Conservateur des Archives Centrales, Le Chef du Service Historique de la Marine, Marine Nationale, Vincennes, France; Jean Cuny, Historian, Soignolles-en-Brie, France, for invaluable help in unearthing little-known documents of the French Purchasing Commission in the USA.

Nick Williams, Historian, AAHS, Waverly, Iowa, for the generous loan and the permission to use some of his considerable documentation and some rare photographs accumulated during his own research into the A-24 forty years ago, but never used; Walter Walsh, Historian 27th Fighter Bomber Squadron, Desert Hot Springs, California, for records and eyewitness accounts held in his excellent archives; the late Arthur Pearcy, Historian and friend, Sharnbrook, Bedfordshire, for his guidance and wise words when things got tough; Thomas M. Alison, Curator, Aeronautics Department, National Air & Space Museum, Washington DC; Air Commodore T.J. MacLean de Lange, Rotorua, New Zealand, and to the veterans of No. 25 Squadron RNZAF for their kindness to me and their backing; Meg Campbell, Wellington, New Zealand; the late Colonel Elmer Glidden, Canton, Massachusetts, for his notes and memories; Ken R. Scadden, National Archives, Department of Internal Affairs, Wellington, New Zealand, for detailed documentation on No.25 Squadron RNZAF.

Richard K. Smith, Historian, Wilmington, North Carolina, for is pertinent views on various aspects of aircraft design and dive-bombers in particular and for his encouragement and example; Vice Admiral William I. Martin, USN, Alexandria, Virginia; Admiral Paul A. Holmberg, USN, Arlington, Virginia; David A. Wilson, Historian, Narrubundah, ACT, Australia, for documents on the 8th Dive Bomber Squadron in New Guinea; Captain Claude Huan, Historian, French Navy, Paris, for helping me decipher the various French combat reports and combat diaries; Teruaki Kawano, Military History Department, National Institute for Defense Studies, Tokyo, for once again guiding me through the Japanese combat reports and graciously assisting me to research at the Japanese archive centre there to assess the accuracy of various battle claims and reports.

Barbara Cooper, USS *Lexington* Museum on the Bay Association, Corpus Christi, Texas; Frank B. Mormillo, The Air Museum, Planes of Fame, Chino, California; Colonel Tom Barnes, Commemorative Air Force, Marietta, Georgia; The Curator, RNZAF Museum, Air Force World, Wigram AFB, Christchurch, New Zealand; Frank A. Tinker, Pearce, Arizona, for memoirs of 351 Fighter-Bomber Squadron; the late Richard H. Best, Santa Monica, California, for his detailed memories of the Dauntless and Battle of Midway; Barton N. Hahn and Simon Volpe. Special thanks to Dales Jenkins, who permitted me to freely quote from his thesis on the Midway battle. Thanks also to Guy Robbins for the Accident Report of Louis Lee Bangs and to Russell Hill of NARA, College Park, MD for VB-10's Aircraft Action Report. Anyone who conducts deep research into the battles fought by the Dauntless owes a deep debt of thanks to Mark Horan, tireless in his search for factual truth, and I add my acknowledgement to that long list. Natalie Navar, Archivist, Lawrence de Graaf Center for Oral* Public History (COPH), California State University Fullerton, Cal.; Group Captain David Duxbury, RNZAF Rtd, of the Air Historical Society of New Zealand, for his immense help and advice on information appertaining to No. 25 Squadron, RNZAF; David Homewood, Historian and Author, AHSNZ, for much

FOREWORD

help and advice; Barrett Tillman, historian, author, pilot and Dauntless restoration expert par excellence, for his kindness and patience; Guy Robbins for kind help and advice; Louisa Hormann, Archive Technician, Research Team, Air Force Museum of New Zealand, Auckland; George M Walsh, who has taken up his father's fight for the truth about many aspects of the Midway battle and provided help and advice; Dale Jenkins, historian and former US naval officer whom I had the pleasure of a long discussion with at the Athenaeum, Piccadilly, London on Midway and radar matters; Guy C. Robbins of navavrep for the Accident Report on Louis Lee Bangs; Royal Cheney, Library Research at the National Naval Aviation Museum, Pensacola, Florida; Russell Hill, Archives Specialist, NARA, College Park, Maryland, for the VB-10 Action Report; Craig Jones of the VB-10 Association, who offered help; Suzanne Isaacs, Community Manager, National Archives Catalog, National Archives at College Park, Maryland; Paul B. Brown, Textual Reference Operations, National Archives at College park, Maryland for assistance concerning Japanese Naval Communications, ca 1952-81 (Entry AI-9016), in Records of the National Security Agency (Record Group 457). Louisa Hormann, RNZAF Museum, Christchurch; Guy Robbins, VB-10 Association and last but by no means least, Richard Doherty, my indefatigable editor, for so much guidance.

I would like to extend my heartfelt and sincere thanks to everyone else who assisted me in tracking down the full story of the Dauntless aircraft in the Second World War. The list could be much longer, but many requested that they remain anonymous, while others, far too many, have now passed on. Their achievements, however, largely ignored and even scorned by many historians of air warfare, deserve recording, as do they. So sincere thanks to the pilots and navigators, designers and test pilots, mostly now passed on, whom I have interviewed or corresponded with down the years. To all these, and many others who have assisted my researches, my grateful thanks, plus the acknowledgement that any errors herewith are more likely to be mine than theirs.

Peter C. Smith
Riseley
Bedford
March 2019

A Note on Aircraft Names

It was not until 1 October 1939 that US Navy aircraft were officially allocated names, although Dauntless had been used unofficially before that date. The USAAF followed this practice even later, when the name Banshee was allocated to the A-24 in April 1942. In neither service did these names really have much currency among the aircrew themselves who, with the brashness of their youth, were mainly disdainful of using anything 'official'; so arose the many nicknames of the SBD, ranging from the 'Barge' to 'Speedy D.', always with a wry mockery relating to her performance. Army flyers never adopted the Banshee name at all, always referring to their mounts as A-24s, but often using names that were more derogatory, again because of the Douglas aeroplane's lack of speed – to which western air forces were hopelessly addicted over the virtue of accuracy. These young men were awaiting, vainly as it turned out, the over-hyped and heralded Brewster SB2A Buccaneer and Curtiss A-24 Shrike, which were also destined never to appear in combat.

So, nicknames abounded, the SBD being translated acronymically but far more accurately as 'Slow But Deadly' by many aircrew – and indeed the Dauntless was no racehorse. When a batch was tested by the British they were scornfully rejected[1] and the most experienced Royal Navy test pilot of his time, Eric 'Winkle' Brown, was equally lukewarm, dubbing the SBD a very pedestrian machine and amazed how such an aeroplane achieved so many victories against both ships and aircraft.[2] The US Army aviators applied other epithets to the Banshee, including 'Blue Rock Clay Pigeons'

---

1 In addition, the early retirement of the Royal Navy's only monoplane dive-bomber, the Blackburn Skua, left that service with only the obsolete 'wire-and-struts' biplanes of a bygone era, like the Fairey Swordfish and Albacore, with which to conduct dive-bombing.

2 Brown, Captain Eric Melrose RN, *Wings of the Navy – Testing British and US Naval Aircraft,* Hikoki, Manchester, 2013.

in bitter reference to their appalling loss rate. The Navy teams added their own variations to the Dauntless including 'The Barge', 'Clunk' and the like.

But if not the speediest of warplanes, the 'Deadly' part of one such title became very apt, for, as with most dive-bombers – few of which were very fast warplanes, although there were exceptions[3] – the SBD shared the one attribute that was to prove more valuable in combat than any other, the ability to actually *hit* the target it aimed at. US Army airmen and their leaders, like General George Churchill Kenney, became notorious for their boastful and bragging claims of sinking of Japanese ships by four-engine altitude bombing with Boeing B-17s and the like – since the days of General William Lendrom 'Billy' Mitchell and his one-sided 'demonstrations', it had been an article of faith that they would defeat the Japanese Navy singlehanded and this they clung to even though 90 per cent of their claimed direct hits turned out to be false, and very few warships were ever sunk by them. So much so that the Navy dive-bomber pilots got to referring their own near-miss bombs as 'Army Hits'![4]

The official designations therefore remained predominant, SBD being the composite of the aircraft's two main functions, S = Scout and B = Bomber, plus the manufacturers' designation, D = Douglas, followed by various mark numbers. On the Army side the lateness and reluctance with which they came to the dive-bomber caused them to range these aircraft in the A for 'Attack' bracket, plus their number. To this was added D = Douglas, followed by the plant of construction, E = El Segundo and T = Tulsa. In the Navy the Scout function needed range so the Dauntless carried a single 500lb bomb, while for striking the enemy the bomber toted a 1,000lb bomb. In the event both weapons were used, and both were far more potent that the Imperial Japanese Navy's 250lb bomb, the standard ordnance of their equivalent, the Aichi D3A1/2 'Val'.

3　Both the North American A-36 Apache and the Soviet Petlyakov Pe-2 Peshka were faster than many contemporary fighter aircraft.

4　The origin of this ironic term is credited to Lieutenant (j.g.) Robert Douglas Gibson of *Saratoga*'s VB-3 at the battle of the Eastern Solomons in 1942, after the USAAF claimed to the world's press that they had 'won' the Battle of Midway, when in truth they had failed to score a single hit.

List of Tables

LIST OF TABLES

Maps and Inserts

List of Illustrations

(NB: All photographs are from Official US Navy Sources and no longer under copyright.)

Chapter 1

Origins

The four major naval powers that emerged from the Washington Naval Treaty in the 1920s, the United Kingdom, United States, Japan and France, all acknowledged the development of air power during the Great War, but their adoption of it into a maritime warfare scenario differed considerably. Conversion of both existing and planned battleships and battlecruisers followed and by the outbreak of the Second World War in September 1939 the Royal Navy possessed seven aircraft carriers[1], the US Navy had commissioned seven;[2] the Japanese possessed five such ships;[3] and the French one.[4] The Italians, allocated the same tonnage as the French, scorned carriers as their seemingly dominant position in the central Mediterranean meant they felt that they could rely totally upon land-based air power to ensure *Mare Nostrum* became a fact as well as a boast.[5] All these navies were building new carriers at by 1939, with the Royal Navy, so often criticized for not being air minded, constructing no fewer than seven new ships;[6] the Americans had just one further ship under construction;[7] the Imperial Japanese Navy seven also;[8] while the French had plans for two new carriers.[9]

Hulls were one thing but the factors that turned out to be decisive were how these carriers were equipped and used. Here the divergence of the

---

1 *Argus, Hermes, Eagle, Furious, Courageous, Glorious* and the modern *Ark Royal*.
2 *Langley, Lexington, Saratoga,* and the modern *Ranger Yorktown, Enterprise* and *Hornet*.
3 the first completed carrier, *Hōshō*, along with the *Akagi, Kaga, Ryūjō,* and *Hiryō*.
4 *Béarn*.
5 The realities of war, especially the Taranto experience, led to a later change of heart, and two liners were selected for conversion to carriers, *Aquila* and *Sparviero*, but neither was ever completed for service.
6 *Illustrious, Victorious* and *Formidable, Indomitable, Implacable, Indefatigable* and *Unicorn*.
7 *Wasp*.
8 *Shōkaku, Zuikaku, Zuihō, Shōhō, Ryōhō, Jun'yō,* and *Hiyō*.
9 *Joffre* and *Painlevé*, neither of which was ever completed.

1

principal users differed even more widely. France's solitary carrier arrived late on the pre-war scene and, found to be too slow, was used mainly as an aircraft transport and not as a combat unit, although she did participate in the hunt for German raiders early in the war. The Royal Navy was faced with its two usual dilemmas, a worldwide commitment to defend the Empire against widely-differing potential opponents and a hostile treasury opposed to all attempts at increasing finances. Against Germany and Italy (the main European Axis partners) the threat came from hundreds of land-based bomber aircraft. Hence, although *Ark Royal* had been built without one, the need for armoured decks was by now considered essential. These were designed to keep out 500lb bombs, but, by the time the ships were completed, the Luftwaffe was using 1,000lb weapons. This protection necessarily limited the number of aircraft that could be embarked, which is why the British fleet carriers could only carry the same number of aircraft as the American light carriers of the *Independence* Class. The trade-off proved worse when faced with a Japanese enemy whose carrier fleet could employ hundreds of aircraft.

To the traditional British dilemmas were added two further crippling handicaps. The first was that in the period 1918 to 1938 (and in effect for even longer) all aircraft designs and allocations were in the hands of the Royal Air Force who had zero interest in Naval aviation. The quality and numbers of naval aircraft therefore deteriorated in those two decades and while it had led the way in maritime application of air power in 1918, twenty years later the Royal Navy lagged far behind in both numbers and quality. The Americans and Japanese thought very differently, both spending these years in improving quality and increasing their numerical superiority ship-for-ship, sacrificing protection for hitting power.

The three principal navies did share a common belief, and this was in the effectiveness of the dive-bomber. Since the first combat dive-bombing had taken place in 1917 by British pilots on the Western Front, the Western air forces had largely rejected it, although they tinkered with it from time to time. The navies, however, were a different matter. Here accuracy was the requirement. Re-invented by the US Marine Corps flyers in Haiti and Nicaragua, the US Navy adopted the dive -bomber wholeheartedly, as did the Japanese. The Royal Navy also believed in this weapon as the deciding factor in the any carrier-to carrier air duel. All three navies concluded that it was the landing of the *first* blow, and with the *maximum* number of aircraft, that would decide the outcome of such a contest. It must always be remembered that, although of course highly desirable, it was not deemed *essential* to sink the enemy carriers in the first blow; merely to put their flight decks out of action was sufficient. While torpedo bombers might put the ships down, a surprise diving attack, which was proved in numerous exercises to be impossible to prevent, would turn these hugely potent weapons into mere floating targets, powerless to either defend themselves or attack. The only way to achieve such an objective was by dive-bombing.

The Royal Navy's answer was the Blackburn Skua monoplane. When first conceived it was a reasonable enough answer but three factors reduced its potency. Firstly, although the Navy wanted a dive-bomber first, with some fighter potential out at sea as a secondary requirement, the RAF, who controlled all such matters, reversed this priority. They themselves had rejected dive-bombing and knew little or nothing of it, and cared even less. So the Skua turned out to be a good dive-bomber but mainly used as a fighter aircraft against land-based types, in which role it was a very poor fighter. Secondly, the builders were notoriously slow at producing aircraft, and those they did build were heavy and slow. The gestation period meant that, by the time it finally appeared, design had moved on. Finally, it was only delivered in penny packets, and frequently used against impossible targets (500lb bombs against heavily-armoured battlecruisers like *Scharnhorst* and *Gneisenau* were never going to do them much harm). Thus, the Royal Navy, from 1941 onward, lacked any proper dive-bomber.

The Japanese, by contrast, believed in dive-bombers and dive-bombing, had the Chinese combat experience from 1933 onward to hone their skills and fine-tune their development of this form of aerial attack, and had the almost unlimited finances to produce large numbers of such aircraft. Thus the Japanese Navy proceeded to advance both in expertise, application and refinement of tactics and machines. They went further than any other naval air force in developing a technique that, just prior to the outbreak of the Pacific War, combined several carriers (as many as six) in one united striking force. Their different carrier air groups operated together, each carrier supplying parts of the combined force with a common doctrine, with the resulting unprecedented numbers of aircraft it could concentrate against any one target. The war in China had also shown the Japanese the advantage of range and this they concentrated on. Throughout the entire war in the Pacific, Japanese naval aircraft would always outrange those of the US Navy. The *Kido Butai* was the ultimate use of carrier air power when it was first unleashed in 1941 and the Allies had no answer to it. At the tip of this great attack-orientated team was the dive-bomber. In 1941 the

Japanese had the Aichi D3A[10] crewed by highly-trained and motivated aircrew. It was manoeuvrable and strong, but had one great weakness, and that was in the payload it was able to deliver. The Val toted a 250lb bomb into combat at a time when the Royal Navy was finding a 500lb bomb inadequate and the US Navy was developing dive-bombers that could carry a 1,000lb bomb.[11]

The United States Navy was, in many ways, at the forefront of naval aviation, both in thinking, belief and promotion of dive-bombing as a technique. They produced whole squadrons of such aircraft motivated with a firm belief in the method, thoroughly trained, and had developed a whole tenet of application, although it differed from the Japanese methodology in many ways. They also believed in the 'Hit First' definition,[12] which later became the accepted doctrine. These flying sailors were firmly convinced of their own prowess and many American admirals were 'air-minded'; some were aviators themselves, others became flyers to better understand the potential of the new weapon. Pre-war exercises conducted by the Scouting Force (essentially *Lexington* and *Saratoga*) had shown that, contrary to Air Corps' belief and preaching, naval aircraft *could* successfully take on, and defeat, land-based aircraft, with surprise as a main factor. The Panama Canal and Pearl Harbor itself were both subjected to successful carrier raids long before the war.

How the US Navy differed in technique from the IJN was in application. The American carriers tended to operate independently, each having their own procedures. The Japanese could fly off, assemble and despatch 140-plus aircraft from their carriers all within thirty-minutes; the Americans could

---

10 Subsequently coded as 'Val' by the Allies.

11 The Allies had two further aces in the hole that were to prove decisive; they had radar for early warning, which the Japanese lacked up to and including the Midway battle; and they possessed (although did not always appreciate or reward) far superior Intelligence which often meant they knew the Japanese plans, aims and detailed dispositions before key battles, Midway again being a case in point.

12 Following the Fleet Problem XVIII, held in April 1937, Admiral Frederick Joseph Horne Jr and his team of aviation experts – John Henry Towers, Arthur William Radford, Donald Bradley Duncan – concluded that, far from being tied closely to the Battle Fleet, that 'once an enemy carrier is within striking distance of our fleet no security remains until it – its squadrons – or both, are destroyed'. (*Aviation In the Fleet Exercises 1911-39*. Office of the Deputy Chief of Naval Operations (Air). Administrative History Volume 16, pp. 157-9. Duncan, Admiral Donald B – *Oral Transcript*, 1969: New York. Columbia University, p.240; Reynolds, Clark G – *Admiral John H. Towers: The Struggle for Naval Air Supremacy*, 1991: Annapolis. Naval Institute Press, pp.271-2.

take twice as long to muster and mount such an attack and each carrier would find its own solution to the problem. The ideal both navies sought, in addition to the vital one of striking the first blow with their maximum strength, was a combination of all the facets of such a strike. Torpedo-bombers had to go in low and deliver their ordnance and were vulnerable in the approach, but dive-bombers could appear suddenly out of the blue and evade most fighter interception and AA fire. Both were hopeful that their fighter protection would cull their opponent's defending squadrons, although for both sides, and in particular the Americans initially, this hope tended to be rather illusory.[13]

In developing the dive-bomber the United States was fortunate in possessing a whole series of dedicated designers in the 1930s. A large factor in this concentration on dive bombing stemmed from the Taylor Board, named after its first President, Admiral Montgomery Meigs Taylor, set up in April 1927, which included William Veazie Pratt and William Adger Moffett, the 'father' of US naval aviation, which concluded that 'General Purpose' aircraft (which dominated Royal Navy thinking for many years, mainly due to cost restrictions) were a waste of money, even if they appeared cheaper in theory. One member of the board, Commander Newton White, was very clear, insisting that any General Purpose aircraft was 'an inefficient hybrid in which both types were ruined'.[14] Despite this some years were to pass before the separation of 'light' dive-bombers and 'heavy' dive-bombers was finally abandoned.

The biggest problem encountered in designing an all-round dive-bomber was the stress factor. Structural strength was paramount if converted fighter types were not to disintegrate in mid dive, a problem that was never fully resolved. The aircraft company of Curtiss was well-established, as was Martin, but both built a succession of biplane prototypes that were less than satisfactory in the late 1920s and early 1930s. The USMC mount, the Curtiss OC-1 Falcon, was modified from its original design and fitted with an air-cooled Wasp engine, becoming the XF8C, but the prototype crashed during testing. Curtiss then built a heavier, sturdier variant, the F8C-4. Martin came up with the XT5M-1 in October 1929 but encountered problems with the wings through to March 1930. Further modifications resulted in the

---

13 The much-hyped 'Thatch Weave' was more of a defensive tactic for the fighters themselves and did little or nothing to assist the bombers to penetrate enemy air space.

14 This was an almost an exact definition of the RAF's insistence of the Blackburn Skua's role, against naval requests, taken a decade later. The US Navy, by contrast, was lucky enough to control its own destiny with regard to the aircraft it required.

BM-1 which crashed during acceptance trials. Although adopted and used into service with the Navy, this aircraft, although one of the first real dive-bombers to carry an effective bomb load, incurred further accidents which told against her. The problem of the bomb striking the aircraft's undercarriage when released in a dive required the introduction of a displacing gear arrangement, a 'swing crutch' which held the bomb in a pair of pivoted arms and, when deployed, swung it down and out from the aircraft's trajectory. This invention, pioneered by Lieutenant Commander (later Vice Admiral) Arthur Clarke Miles of the Bureau of Aeronautics, Commander C.L. Schuyler and George A. Chadwick of the Bureau of Ordnance, was trialled in 1931 by Lieutenant Commander John Edwin Ostrander Jr, on the XT5M-1 and, once perfected, eliminated this particular problem and was copied by foreign dive-bomber constructors, not least the Junkers team in Germany that produced the Junkers Ju.87 'Stuka'.

Development of types resulted in limited production orders from a range of manufactures between 1935 and 1939, the Chance-Vought SBU-1 and Great Lakes BG-1, the Curtiss SBC-3, Northrop BT-1 and Chance-Vought SB2U-1, the Naval Aircraft SBN-2 and Curtiss SBC-4. Biplanes became monoplanes, fixed undercarriages gave way to retractable gear, each introducing some innovation before fading. Of note to our story was the Northrop design, the BT-1. A former Lockheed and Douglas Aircraft employee, Jack Knudsden Northrop set up his own company at Inglewood, California, in 1932, but this became a subsidiary of Douglas in 1939. The XBT-1 itself first flew on 19 August 1935 and was later ordered as the BT-1 in 1936, this dive-bomber featuring the perforated dive brake design, to help eliminate 'buffeting' while in the dive, and joined the Navy two years later but did not prove a great success. Redesigned by Edward Henry Heinemann, Douglas' new chief designer, as the XBT-2, this aircraft was more what the Navy really required.

Under an accelerated test programme Heinemann incorporated the perforated dive-brake flaps (made by drilling 3-inch (76mm) holes in the inner section which reduced the 'vortex' problems); incorporated fully-retractable, inward-folding landing-gear; increased the sizes of the tail and rudder; modified both centre and outer wing forms and adopted a new cockpit canopy which was fitted with the Aldis telescopic bombsight. The forward-firing armament was increased to two fixed .50-calibre machine guns and a flexible .30 calibre machine gun (which was later doubled) on a flexible mounting carried aft to be used by the radio operator. The bomb crutch was further modified and a new power plant, the 1,000hp Wright

R-1820-32 radial engine was installed along with two auxiliary 15-US-gallon fuel tanks. This gave a range of 860 miles (1,384km).[15]

Subsequent to Jack Northrop's departure, the XBT was re-designated as the XSBD[16] The Navy placed orders for 144 of the new SBD-1 on 8 April 1939. The Naming Committee also allocated her name, and so the Dauntless arrived officially. The first fifty-seven machines were allocated to the USMC (VMB-2 of MAG-11 at North Island, San Diego) as the SBD-1, while the Navy took delivery of eighty-seven of a further improved version, the SBD-2 which had increased range, 1,125 miles (1,810km) for carrier work, and had an auto-pilot fitted. They were embarked aboard *Lexington* (VB-2 and VS-2) and then *Enterprise* (VB-6 and VS-6). Even so this model was still regarded as a stop-gap and much larger dive-bombers were under development. However, following the fall of Poland, Norway, the Low Countries and France in the spring of 1940 to the lethal combination of dive-bomber and tank, the need was for aircraft now and further modifications of the Dauntless to fill the gap until the new types arrived resulted in the SBD-3.

In came self-sealing fuel tanks, armour protection for the aircrew, bulletproof windscreens and the improved Wright R-1820-52 engine; range was again extended to 1,345 miles (2,164km). The first of these aircraft arrived in the fleet on 18 March 1941. The Dauntless did not have long to wait before seeing action, but, when it came, it was both unexpected and sobering.

---

15 This is only an outline; for a more detailed history of the development of the Dauntless see Smith, Peter C., *Douglas SBD Dauntless*, The Crowood Press Ltd, Ramsbury, 1997.

16 SB being the new designation for all US Navy single-engine dive/scout bombers.

Chapter 2

Opening Rounds 1941-42

When Japan finally decided that she would go to war with the United States, United Kingdom and the Dutch in the Pacific, she was already over-committed militarily in mainland Asia, so it was acknowledged that the Japanese Navy would be the principal driver here. Although the Imperial Army was in the driving seat and relations between the two services were, at best, acrimonious, the overriding need to obtain oil, without which the Empire would fall anyway, and a safe perimeter of bases from which to protect its flow to the home islands, was paramount. The Army had originated the seemingly unsolvable war in China and seemed unable to find a way to end it, and had already been involved with vicious skirmishes with Soviet Russia to the north of Manchukuo, its vassal state. These persistent problems ensured that the bulk of the Army would be required there, but it was agreed that sufficient troops would still be spared for the conquests of British Malaya and Burma and Borneo, along with the naval bases of Singapore and Hong Kong, as well the oil-rich but poorly defended Dutch East Indies (the DEI). With Britain at full stretch after more than two years of war against both Germany and Italy, little was to be feared from the Royal Navy, but the case of the United States Pacific Fleet loomed large and the need to eliminate this powerful force at source led to the attack on its main base of Pearl Harbor at Hawaii.

Fusing their main carrier fleet into a unique air-sea attack force, the *Kido Butai*, with six large aircraft carriers and over 350 aircraft trained to operate as a single striking group, the Japanese opened the war on 7 December 1941, as they had done successfully in previous wars with China and Imperial Russia, with a stunning surprise attack. Only in one respect did this opening gambit fail them; and it was to be a fatal (for the Japanese) and lucky (for the United States) omission. But only just so, and the margin was a very narrow one. The three American aircraft carriers were absent when the attacks took place.

Two American carrier task forces were at sea on 7 December – Task Force 11 commanded by Rear Admiral John Henry Newton built around the carrier *Lexington*, with heavy cruisers *Astoria, Chicago* and *Portland* and five destroyers; and Task Force 8 under Vice Admiral William Frederick Halsey, with the carrier *Enterprise* at its heart along with the heavy cruisers *Chester, Northampton* and *Salt Lake City* with nine destroyers. Both US carriers had Dauntless embarked; VB-2, Lieutenant Commander Harold Donald Felt, with sixteen SBD-2s and VS-2, Lieutenant Commander Robert Ellington Dixon, with eighteen SBD2-3s aboard *Lexington*, and VB-6, commanded by Lieutenant Commander William Right Holingsworth, with eighteen SBD2/3s and VS-6, led by Lieutenant Halstead Lubeck Hopping, with a further eighteen SBD2/3s aboard *Enterprise*.[1] Admiral Husband Edward Kimmel, Commander-in-Chief, Pacific Fleet, (CinCPac) had advised Halsey of a warning from the Chief of Naval Operations (CNO) in Washington DC, Admiral Harold Rainsford Stark, on the imminence of war. Consequently Task Force 8 was in a high state of readiness, but Kemmel had, for some reason, neglected to mention Stark's ominous prediction to Newton who sailed later.[2]

That fateful morning *Lexington* was on her way to Midway Island with a cargo of eighteen Vought SB2U-3 Vindicator single-engine scout bombers of Marine Squadron VMSB-231 commanded by Major Clarence Joseph Chappell Jr. These had longer range than earlier models and were scheduled to be launched on 7 December when some four hundred miles south-east of Midway.[3]

The *Enterprise* was returning to Pearl after conducting a similar mission to Wake Island where they had delivered twelve Grumman F4F-3 Wildcat fighter aircraft from Major Paul Albert Putnam's Marine Fighting Squadron 211 (VMF-211) to Marine Air Group 21 (MAG-21).

---

1 *Saratoga* was at San Diego ending a refit and had not yet embarked her air group.
2 Maybe because Newton was only deputizing for Vice Admiral Wilson Brown, Jr, Commander, Scouting Force (ComScoFor) who was conducting training exercises in the vicinity of Johnston Island. Even so, the omission of any hint of what was possibly brewing out there was extraordinary.
3 After some fruitless dashing hither and thither by Newton's ships, VMSB-231 was returned by *Lexington* to Marine Corps Air Station Ewa on 13 December and there they found that all seven of the reserve Vindicators they had left there had been destroyed by enemy action in their absence. On 17 December the seventeen serviceable Vindicators flew from Hickham Field the 1,137-miles to Midway led by a Catalina PBY flying boat and all arrived safely.

THE DAUNTLESS IN BATTLE

At 0615, in a position some 215 miles due west of Oahu, Halsey had despatched two aerial scouting forces totalling nine pairs of SBDs ahead of his ships. First off was Commander *Enterprise* Air Group (CEAG), Lieutenant Commander Howard Leyland Young, carrying Lieutenant Commander Bromfield Bradford Nichol of Halsey's staff with a report on the Wake Island operation for personal delivery as Halsey refused to break radio silence. Young's Dauntless was followed in quick succession by his wingman Ensign Perry Lee Teaf and twelve other SBDs, from VS-6 and four from VB-6, who were to conduct a search pattern to the north and east covering an area 150 miles (240km) from the carrier which centred on Oahu and embraced the islands of Ka'ula and Ni'ihau as well. These searches were uneventful, the orders were to then carry on and land at the Ford Island Naval Air Station (NAS).

Table 1: *Enterprise* Morning Launch 0615, 7 December 1941			
Pilot	**Aircrew**	**Aircraft**	**Sector**
Commander Howard Leyland Young	Lieutenant Commander Bromfield Bradford Nichol	CEAG	085^0-095^0 (T)
Ensign Perry Lee Teaff	RM3c Edgar Phelan Jinks	6-S-2	
Lieutenant Commander Halsted Lubeck Hopping	RM1c Harold R. Thomas Jr	6-S-1	095^0-105^0(T)
Ensign John Henry Leon Vogt	RM3c Sidney Pierce	6-S-3	
Lieutenant Commander Clarence Earle Dickinson Jr	RM1c William Cicero Miller	6-S-4	105^0-115^0(T)
Ensign John Reginald McCarthy	RM3c Mitchell Cohn	6-S-9	
Lieutenant (J.G.) Hart Dale Hilton	RM2c Jack Leaming	6-S-7	115^0-125^0(T)
Ensign Edwin John Kroeger	RM2c Robert Chapman	6-B-5	
Ensign Carleton Thayer Fogg	RM3c Otto Lee Dennis	6-S-11	125^0-135^0(T)
Ensign Cleo John Dobson	RM3c William Thomas Hoss	6-S-8	

Lieutenant William Earle Gallaher	RM1c Thomas Edward Merritt	6-S-10	075^0-085^0 (T)
Ensign William Price West	RM3c Louis Dale Hansen	6-S-5	
Lieutenant (J.G.) Frank Anthony Patriarca	RM1c Joseph Ferdinand De Luca	6-S-16	065^0-075^0 (T)
Ensign Walter Michael Willis	Coxswain Frederick John Ducolon	6-S-15	
Ensign Edward Thorpe Deacon	RM3c Audrey Gerald Coselett	6-S-14	055^0-065^0 (T)
Ensign Wilbur Edison Roberts	AMM3c Edgard Richard Jones	6-B-9	
Ensign Manuel Gonzalez	RM3c Leonard Kozelek	6-B-3	045^0-055^0 (T)
Ensign Frederick Thomas Weber	Sea1c Lee Edward Keaney	6-B-12	

On their return to Hawaii many of these SBDs ran into the enemy. Taken totally by surprise, VB-6 lost Ensign Manuel Gonzalez and his radioman RM3c Leonard Kozelek, and also Ensign John Henry Leon Vogt Jr and RM3c Sidney Pierce. Gonzalez's poignant last radio message, 'Please don't shoot. Don't shoot. This is Six-Baker-Six, an American plane', said all there was to know about this tragedy. VS-6 also took losses, Ensign Walter Michael Willis with Coxswain (F) Frederick John Ducolon in his rear seat, both disappeared and were assumed killed, when they ran into Aichi D3A1 Vals making their way to their own outward rendezvous. Lieutenant Clarence Earl Dickinson Jr and Ensign John Reginald McCathy both had their aircraft shot down and, while both pilots survived, their two radiomen, RM3c William Cicero Miller and RM3c Mitchell Cohn, respectively, did not. Meanwhile American AA gunners were firing at anything that flew and their victims included some SBDs.

After this bloody and one-sided encounter, some Dauntless pilots went back out again despite the carnage. Japanese submarines had been stationed in a crescent to the south of Oahu in order to intercept any American heavy ships that managed to escape the air attack. At 0600 on 10 December, one of them, the *I-70* (Lieutenant Commander Sano Takao) was damaged sufficiently by a near miss from a VB-6 Dauntless, flown by Ensign Perry Lee Teaff. His attack took place 121 miles north-east of Cape Halava,

Molokai, and his 1,000lb bomb so damaged the submarine that she was unable to dive. She was still proceeding slowly on the surface with her single 13-mm AA machine-gun manned when a second SBD arrived on the scene.

Lieutenant Clarence Earle Dickinson of VS-6 was aloft again in a replacement SBD and with a personal score to settle for Bill Miller as well as himself. He flew a course which he estimated would 'cut the corner' to reach the best-speed option of his target which was last seen heading north-east.[4] His judgement was rewarded with a sighting from 800 feet (245m) of a submarine on the surface fifteen miles (24km) away, some 180 miles (290km) north of Ohau. It took Dickinson a good ten minutes to gain sufficient altitude to avoid any return fire and to be able to make a diving attack, but he kept his enemy in sight throughout and, just after 0600, commenced his attack dive from 5,000 feet (1,500m). He later recalled, 'By the time I was able to pull out of the dive, and turn so as to get my plane's tail out of the way of my eyes it was probably fifteen seconds after the bomb struck, it struck right beside the submarine, amidships.' When he returned to the scene of his attack he could see the four gunners floundering on the surface but where the submarine had been there was only oil and bubbles. Dickinson reported a 'probable' hit, but in fact he had killed her, the first proper Japanese submarine to be sunk in the Second World War and another 'first' for the Dauntless.[5]

Saratoga did eventually join the fleet from San Diego, but not for long because she was torpedoed by the submarine *I-6* (Lieutenant Commander Michimune Inaba) 420 miles south-west of Pearl Harbor on 11 January. Closing the stable door, several of her SBDs were launched and made attacks on real (or imaginary) submarines, without effect. Her aircraft were flown ashore while she went in for massive repairs which meant she was out of the war for six months.

Between 25 and 27 January 1942, the carriers *Enterprise* and *Yorktown* carried out 'revenge raids' against the Marshall and Gilbert Islands. At 0443 on 1 February *Enterprise* made the first two attacks. Commander Howard Leyland Young as CEAG, led the strike in his own Dauntless, and

---

4 Dickinson, Clarence Earle (USN), *The Flying Guns: Cockpit Record of a Naval Pilot Pearl Harbor through Midway,* Charles Scribner, New York, 1942.

5 Of course this claim excludes the Type 'A' *Kō-Hyōteki* 'mini' submarines, launched from their parent submarines, five of which attacked Pearl Harbor that day, *HA-16, HA-18, HA-19, HA-20* and *HA-22*. These were all lost, *HA-20* being sunk by the destroyer *Ward* and *HA-22* by the destroyer *Monaghan,* while *HA-18* and *HA-19* were scuttled before they could enter the harbour. *HA-16* apparently succeeded, and torpedoed the battleship *Oklahoma,* contributing to her loss, before likewise being scuttled.

his force included a total of thirty-seven SBDs from VB-6 and VS-6 against Kwajalein, Roi and Tarora in the Marshalls.

Aircraft	Pilot	Aircrew
Table 2: *Enterprise* SBD Attack on Marshall Islands, 1 February 1942		
VB-6 Division 1		
6-B-1	Lieutenant Commander William Right Hollingsworth	ACRM James Francis Murray
6-B-2	Lieutenant Harvey Peter Lanham	ARM2c Edward Joseph Garaudy
6-B-3	Lieutenant Lloyd Addison Smith	AMM2c Herman Hull Caruthers
6-B-7	Lieutenant James Wickersham McCauley	RM2c Harrold William Nelson Jr
6-B-8	Ensign Keith Haven Holcomb	AMM2c Lloyd E Welch
6-B-9	Lieutenant (j.g.) Wilbur Edison Roberts	AMM1c James H. Shea Jr
VB-6 Division 2		
6-B-10	Lieutenant Richard Halsey Best	RM2c Lee Thomas McHugh
6-B-11	Lieutenant (j.g.) Edwin John Kroeger	RM3c Achilles Antonius Georgiou
6-B-12	Lieutenant (j.g.) John James Van Buren	RM3c Allen James Brost
6-B-16	Lieutenant (j.g.) Leonard Joseph Check	ARM2c Stuart James Mason Jr
6-B-17	Lieutenant (j.g.) Edward Lee Anderson	ARM2c Parham Screeton Johnson
6-B-18	Ensign Delbert Wayne Halsey	AOM2c Arie Turner Alford
VB-6 Division 3		
6-B-4	Lieutenant John Devereux Blitch	AMM2c William Burt Steinman
6-B-5	Ensign Norman Francis Vandvier	Sea1c Lee Edward John Keaney
6-B-6	Ensign Anthony Frederic Schneider	RM3c Glenn Lester Holden
6-B-13	Lieutenant Joseph Robert Penland	ARM2c Harold French Heard

Aircraft	Pilot	Aircrew
6-B-14	Ensign Clifford Raymond Walters	AMM2c Wilbur Thomas Thompson
6-B-15	Ensign John Joseph Doherty	AOM3c William Evan Hunt
VS-6 Division 1		
6-S-1	Lieutenant Commander Halsted Lubeck Hopping	RM1c Harold R. Thomas
6-S-2	Lieutenant (j.g.) Perry Lee Teaff	RM3c Edgard Phelan Jinks
6-S-3	Lieutenant (j.g.) Benjamin Henry Troemel	RM3c William Hart Bergin
6-S-7	Lieutenant (j.g.) Hart Dale Hilton	RM2c Jack Leaming
6-S-8	Ensign Cleo John Dobson	RM3c Roy L. Hoss
6-S-9	Ensign Percy Wendell Forman	RM2c William Henry Stambaugh
VS-6 Division 2		
6-S-10	Lieutenant Wilmer Earl Gallaher	RM1c Thomas Edward Merritt
6-S-11	Lieutenant (j.g.) Carleron Thayer Fogg	RM3c Otis Lee Dennis
6-S-12	Ensign William Price West	AMM3c Milton Wayne Clark
6-S-16	Lieutenant Reginald Rutherford	RM3c Earl Edward Howell
6-S-17	Lieutenant (j.g.) Norman Jack Kleiss	RM3c John Warren Snowden
6-S-18	Ensign Earl Roe Donnell Jr	AMM1c Alton John Travis
VS-6 Division 3		
6-S-4	Lieutenant Clarence Earle Dickinson Jr	RM1c Joseph Ferdinand De Luca
6-S-5	Ensign Daniel Seid	AMM3c David Franklin Grogg
6-S-13	Lieutenant Frank Anthony Patriarca	RM1c Ferdinand Joseph Cupples
6-S-14	Lieutenant (j.g.) Edward Thorpe Deacon	RM3c Louis Dale Hansen
6-S-15	Ensign Reid Wentworth Stone	AM3c Erwin G. Bailey

The Dauntless climbed to 14,000 feet (4,300m) and headed west, stacked together in stepped-down Vs with the Vs themselves forming other Vs and echelons. The attack was scheduled to hit at 0658 before the enemy was awake, but in order to correctly identify the various targets the dive-bombers were forced to make a wide circle around the atoll while Young satisfied himself on that score. Thus, the Dauntless were met by a fully alert defence with AA fire and fighter aircraft scrambling off the airstrip.

The six SBDs of VS-6, led by Lieutenant Commander Halsted Hopping, attacked first, adopting a long, flat glide approach to the target; they were followed by six more led by Lieutenant Earl Gallaher and then a final six under Lieutenant Clarence Dickinson. All aircraft bombed the airfield itself from a general height of around 1,000 feet (300m) and pulled away, but Hopping's lead aircraft absorbed most of the flak and failed to pull out. His SBD struck the water and sank like a stone, Hopping and his gunner dying but having made history by dropping the first bomb on Japanese-held territory in the Second World War.

The rest of his section cratered the airstrip, levelled administration buildings and blew up an ammunition dump with a satisfactory explosion, all with just their wing bombs. Then VS-6 conducted a second, strafing, run over Roi, hitting a variety of ground targets, two hangars, a fuel depot and an estimated seven enemy aircraft on the airstrip itself, and three Japanese fighter aircraft were claimed as shot down in the air-to-air combats; but the Americans did not find anything sufficiently worthy on which to expend their 500lb (257 kg) bombs. Interception by defending fighters and fierce AA fire brought down another three SBDs, however.

In the interim, Young had scouted Kwajalein anchorage where he found some warships and transports which he deemed far more suitable objects for the heavier bombs. Accordingly, VB-6 was instructed to hit these ships forthwith, along with the surviving Dauntless of VS-6.

Commander William Right Hollingsworth led VB-6 *en echelon* attack with a full-blooded 70 degree dive attack and claimed three direct hits. The SBDs then returned to the carrier where they were hastily refuelled and re-armed, the accompanying F4F Wildcats having discovered forty twin-engine bombers at the airstrip on Taroa; Bill Hollingsworth was instructed to destroy as many of these as he could in this second strike. His initial wave consisted of seven VB-6 and two VS-6 dive bombers and this was followed by a second wave led by Lieutenant Richard Halsey Best with a further nine Dauntless.

The first strike hit Taroa in a dive attack which was met with little but light flak, but Best's men found both Japanese fighters, Mitsubishi A5M4 Claudes, low-winged monoplanes with fixed undercarriages, and also heavier AA fire, awaiting them on their run-in. One enemy fighter was claimed destroyed by Ed Kroeger's gunner Achilles Georgiou, and Perry Lee Teaff was jumped by a second, but escaped unharmed after a good plane-to-plane scrap; but a Claude nailed Ensign John Doherty's mount, the last of the line in, and both he and AOM3c William Hunt, were killed outright. The Japanese fighter pilots claimed five SBDs destroyed in total in total. Lieutenant Clarence Dickinson identified his target as a liner of the 17,000-ton *Yawata* class which had been converted to a seaplane tender with one mounted aft at the time of the attack.

Thus, for the loss of five SBDs, with their aircrews, they and the accompanying torpedo bombers had only managed to sink one small naval auxiliary craft; they had also caused some damage to the light cruiser *Katori*, the ancient minelayer *Tokiwa* and four auxiliaries, including the submarine depot ship *Yasukuni Maru* damaged by a bomb hit aft, and the submarine *I-23*, losing a 25mm AA gunner from the bomb splinters of this hit which also ignited her float plane avgas, and the oiler *Toa Maru*, none of which were sunk, plus the transport *Bordeaux Maru*, which was sunk with three dead. In reply, the Japanese counter-attacked with five twin-engine Mitsubishi G4M Betty bombers and scored fifteen near-misses off the *Enterprise's* port side. One of these attackers then attempted a suicide dive, having already been damaged by protecting Wildcats. A sharp turn frustrated this intention, and one SBD gunner, AMM2c Bruno Peter Gaido, manning the rear guns of the aftermost parked Dauntless, engaged the incoming bomber from there. The Betty's right wing-tip cut right through this SBD within a few feet of Gaido who was still blazing away and knocked the rest of the aircraft over to the extreme port after-edge of the flight deck, from which precarious position he continued to fire the twin.30s into the wreckage of the Betty as it drifted away. Halsey promoted him on the spot.

Meanwhile, on 1 February, the *Yorktown* air group, including five VS-5 Dauntless under Lieutenant Wallace Clark Short, Jr, the Executive Officer, who hit Mili, and VB-5, with nine SBDs, led by Lieutenant Commander William Oscar Burch, Jr., struck at Makin. Worthwhile targets were sparse, VB-5 for example was reduced to bombing freshwater tanks on Mili in lieu of anything else; and for this meagre return six aircraft were lost:

Table 3: *Yorktown* attack on Gilbert Islands and Mili, 1 February 1942		
VS-5 and VB-5 against Makin Island		
Aircraft	Pilot	Aircrew
5-S-1	Lieutenant Commander William Oscar Burch Jr	CRM Oliver Wendell Grew
5-S-5	Lieutenant Stockton Birney Strong	RM2c John F. Hurley
5-S-2	Ensign Thomas A. Reeves USNR	Pho2c John Van Pflaum

16

5-S-6	Lieutenant Turner Foster Caldwell Jr	RM2c Leon Hall
5-S-7	Lieutenant (j.g.) Frederic Lewis Faulkner	Sea2c Charles Joseph Bonness
5-S-8	Ensign William Edward Hall	RM3c Onni Emil Kustula
5-B-1	Lieutenant Roger Blake Woodhull	RM2c Albert Woodrow Garlow
5-B-2	Lieutenant (j.g.) Stanley Winfield Vejtasa	Sea1c Frank Baron Wood
5-B-5	Ensign Walton Anderson Austin	RM3c Woodrow Andrew Fontenot
VS-5 and VB-5 against Mili Island		
5-S-17	Lieutenant Wallace Clark Short Jr	RM1c Carl Edgar Russ
5-B-11	Lieutenant Charles Rollins Ware	RM2c Joseph Ellsworth Roll
5-B-7	Lieutenant (j.g.) Arthur Latimer Downing	RM2c Elmer C. Jones
5-B-10	Lieutenant (j.g.) Earl Vincent Johnson	Sea1c Edgar W. Adams
5-B-13	Ensign Hugh Wilbur Nicholson	RM3c James Hedger Cales

while Burch's men destroyed two Kawanishi H8K flying boats and a small auxiliary, *Nagata Maru*, which was beached. A severe storm saw one SBD, piloted by Ensign Thomas A. Reeves, fly into the sea; fortunately both he and Sea2c Lonnie Gooch were rescued by the destroyer *Walke*. As the weather worsened a second strike was abandoned.

On 31 January *Lexington* sailed from Pearl with Task Force 11 to cover two important troop convoys from the Panama Canal; then, on 17 February, she was instructed to launch air strikes against the Japanese base at Rabaul, New Britain. Located by Japanese reconnaissance aircraft while still three hundred miles (480km) ENE of their target, the American warships were subjected to a heavy air attack on 20 February and the raid was cancelled. After a brief foray into the Coral Sea between 27 February and 4 March, *Lexington* rendezvoused with *Yorktown* off the New Hebrides on 6 March.

During that same period *Enterprise*, with Task Force 8, sailed from Pearl on 14 February and ten days later launched an air raid at 0500 on the Japanese defences on Wake Island with a force which included twenty-seven Dauntless from which just a single aircraft was lost.

Table 4: VB-6 - Attack on Wake Island, 24 February 1942		
Aircraft	**Pilot**	**Aircrew**
GC	Commander Howard Leyland Young	CRM(PA) John Murray O'Brien
First Division		
6-B-1	Lieutenant Commander William Right Hollingsworth	ACRM (PA) James Francis Murray
6-B-2	Lieutenant Harvey Peter Lanham	ARM2c Edward Joseph Garaudy
6-B-3	Lieutenant Lloyd Addison Smith	AMM2c Hermann Hull Caruthers
6-B-7	Lieutenant James Wickershaw McCauley	ARM2c Parham Screeton Johnson
6-B-8	Lieutenant (j.g.) John James Van Buren	RM3c V-3 Achilles Antonios Georgiou
6-B-9	Ensign Arthur Leo Rausch	RM3c Gail Wayne Halterman
Second Division		
6-B-10	Lieutenant Richard Halsey Best	ARM1c Henry William Nelson Jr
6-B-11	Lieutenant (j.g.) Edward Lee Anderson	RM3c Jay William Jenkins
6-B-12	Ensign Wilbur Edison Roberts	AMM1c James H. Shea Jr
6-B-16	Lieutenant (j.g.) Leonard Joseph Check	ARM2c Stuart James Mason
6-B-17	Ensign Keith Haven Holcomb USNR	AMM2c Lloyd E. Welch
6-B-18	Ensign Thomas Wesley Ramsay	AMM3c Sherman Lee Duncan
Third Division		
6-B-4	Lieutenant John Devereux Blitch	AMM2c William Burt Steinman
6-B-5	Ensign Norman Francis Vandivier	Sea1c Lee Edward John Kearney
6-B-6	Ensign Tony Frederic Schneider	RM3c Glenn Lester Holden
6-B-13	Lieutenant Joseph Robert Penland	ARM2c Harold French Heard

| 6-B-14 | Ensign Clifford Raymond Walters | AMM2c Wilbur Thomas Thompson |
| 6-S-18 | Ensign Delbert Wayne Halsey | CRM (PA) ACM2 Airie Turner Alford |

Table 5: VS-6 - Attack on Wake Island, 24 February 1942		
Aircraft	**Pilot**	**Aircrew**
Division 1		
6-S-1	Lieutenant Wilmer Earl Gallaher	ARM1c Thomas Edward Merritt
6-S-2	Lieutenant (j.g.) Perry Lee Teaff	RM3c Edgard Phelan Jinks
6-S-3	Ensign William Edward Hall	AMM1c Bruno Peter Gaido
6-S-16	Lieutenant Charles Rollins Ware	ARM2c William Henry Stambaugh
6-S-7	Lieutenant (j.g.) Hart Dale Hilton	ARM2c Jack Leaming
6-S-8	Ensign Percy Wendell Forman	AMM1c John Edwin Winchester
Division 2		
6-S-10	Lieutenant Reginald Rutherford	RM3c Earl Edward Howell
6-S-11	Lieutenant (j.g.) Norman Jack Kleiss	RM3c John Warren Snowden
6-S-12	Ensign Robert Keith Campbell	AMM2c Milton Wayne Clark
Division 3		
6-S-4	Lieutenant Clarence Earle Dickinson Jr	RM1c Joseph Ferdinand DeLuca
6-S-5	Lieutenant (j.g.) John Norman West	RM3c Alfred Robert Stitzelberger
6-S-6	Ensign Alden Wilbur Hanson	AMM2c Floyd Delbert Adkins
6-S-13	Lieutenant Frank Anthony Patriarca	ARM1c Ferdinand Joseph Cupples
6-S-14	Lieutenant (J.G.) Edward Thorpe Deacon	RM3c Louis Dale Hansen

Aircraft	Pilot	Aircrew
6-S-19	Ensign Midford Austin Merrill	AOM2c Thurman Randolph Swindell
Photographic Division		
6-S-17	Ensign Cleo John Dobson	RM3c LeRoy Albert Hoss
6-S-9	Lieutenant (j.g.) Benjamin Henry Troemel	RM2c William Hart Bergin
6-S-15	Ensign Read Wenworth Stone	AM3c Erwin George Bailey

At 0650 launching began, but Sail 3, piloted by Lieutenant (J.G.) Perry Lee Teaff, with RM3c Edgar Phelan Jinks as his tail-gunner, crashed on take-off. The destroyer *Blue* rescued the pilot but although Phelan was heard he could not be located. Unfortunately, Teaff was blinded in one eye and eventually was invalided out of the service. The seventeen surviving SBDs of VS-6, including three of the Photographic Flight Section, and the eighteen of VB-6 under Lieutenant Commander William Right Hollingsworth had formed up with the torpedo planes and fighters and headed toward their targets. The VS-6 Dauntless gradually moved up to 18,000 feet (5,500m) before pushing over in succession to dive down on the ten oil-storage tanks that were their prime target. They met no opposition and claimed to have hit and destroyed seven of the tanks. They suffered further casualties, Ensign Percy Wendell Forman and AMM1c John Edwin Winchester, whose Sail-8 was shot down, but both survived to become PoWs.

Between 0750 and 0805 VB-6 carried out their attacks on the Japanese airstrip and the surrounding installations. Each Dauntless toted a single 500lb Mk 12 bomb with an instantaneous fuse and two 100lb Mk 4 underwing bombs with instantaneous fuses and they also strafed targets of opportunity with both forward and rear machine guns. One section under Lieutenant (j.g.) Loyd Addison Smith, made a glide attack on small craft off the pier at Peale Island, while Ensign Delbert Wayne Halsey vainly chased a big Kawanishi flying-boat, which left him standing. Three SBDs took machine-gun hits in return but there were no casualties.

Moving swiftly westward, another raid was launched by the SBDs of *Enterprise* against Marcus Island at 0449 on 4 March, with Young leading a force of fourteen VS-6 dive-bombers along with eighteen more from VB-6 under Lieutenant John Devereux Blitch. The assembling of the force in the pre-dawn darkness was now becoming routine and the aircrew termed this manoeuvre the 'Group Grope'.[6] Heavy cloud was encountered at between 4,000 and 8,000 feet (1,200 and 2,400m) and this made their ascent even more hazardous. Nonetheless, the strike was despatched and sighted Marcus at 0630 through a break in the cloud.

The initial dive attack was made from 16,000 feet (4,800m) and was completed by 0645; the targets were oil storage tanks and the radio station. Defensive flak was the heaviest yet encountered and several SBDs took hits; this vicious AA fire brought down the VS-6 of Lieutenant Dale Hilton who survived a water landing and was taken prisoner, along with the rear gunner, Jack Leaming. The remaining aircraft were safely recovered by 0845.

Yorktown sailed from Hawaii with Task Force 17 on 16 February 1942 to make a similar raid on Eniwetok Atoll in the Caroline Islands, but this sortie was abandoned, and she was diverted to join *Lexington*. This concentration was made to cover the transport of the Americal Division from Brisbane to Noumea Island, New Caledonia, and the two Task Forces, 11 centred on *Lexington* and 17 based around *Yorktown*, were concentrated on 10 March 1942, when they attacked Japanese landing forces in Papua, New Guinea. A total of seventy-nine SBDs from the two carriers' four squadrons took part, flying off at 0749 from a position in the Gulf of Papua and crossing the southern neck of New Guinea, then striking at Lae and Salamua where the Japanese troops were disembarking.

The CLAG, Commander William Bowen Ault in his own SBD-3, had the following Dauntless at his disposal – VB-2 led by Lieutenant Commander Weldon Lee Hamilton with twelve Dauntless; VS- 2 under Robert Ellington Dixon with eighteen Dauntless; VB-5 commanded by Lieutenant Commander Robert Gordon Armstrong, who had seventeen SBDs, and VS-5 led by William Oscar Burch Jr with a further thirteen machines.

In the bay offshore a large assembly of Japanese shipping was caught by surprise and the attacks commenced at 0930. Confirmed sinkings were limited to the armed merchant cruiser *Kongo Maru* and the troop transports *Yokohama Maru* and *Tenryu Maru* (hit and beached), plus damage to the light cruiser *Yubari,* the minelayer *Tsugaru,* destroyers *Asanagi* and *Yunagi,* a third transport and two auxiliary vessels. In return one *Lexington* Dauntless, piloted by Ensign Joseph Philip Johnson, failed to return.

---

6 Brazelton, David, *The Douglas SBD Dauntless, Aircraft Profile* No. 196, Profile Publications, Windsor, 1967.

THE DAUNTLESS IN BATTLE

Between 2 and 25 April, *Hornet* was engaged in the Doolittle raid on Japan and was accompanied by *Enterprise* for her protection. Embarked aboard was VB-3 of the *Saratoga* Air Group, taking the place of VS-6 which was training with a new consignment of SBDs ashore. Running into a Japanese patrol line on 18 April, *Enterprise*'s Dauntless destroyed two small vessels and damaged two more. The sixteen North American B-25 Mitchell twin-engine bombers were launched early because of this, and the two carriers withdrew before the Japanese could react.

Chapter 3

Battle of the Coral Sea, May 1942

At the end of April 1942, the two prongs of the Japanese progression towards their aim of cutting off Australia from direct American aid, codenamed Operation FS[1] were discussed. This plan originated at Imperial General Headquarters (IGHQ) and was largely the brainchild of Baron Sadatoshi Tomioka, an admiral in the Imperial Japanese Navy, and Chief of Staff of the IJN's operations section. The plan itself was a watered-down version of a much bolder scheme that had called for the invasion and occupation of Australia itself. One of the backers of this very ambitious concept was General Tomoyuki Yamashita, whose stunning seventy-day campaign in Malaya and Singapore had overwhelmed a three-and-a-half-division-strong and widely-dispersed British/Australian and Indian III Corps, and, in just seventy days and earned himself the soubriquet 'The Tiger of Malaya', as well as a fearsome reputation. Emboldened by what he had seen of the British Empire's lack of fighting spirit in this theatre he quite believed that even a continent the size of Australia could be taken without much ado, certain in his belief that the key cities would fall to his battle-hardened troops who had minimal opposition to contend with.

Talk was that Admiral Isokroku Yamamoto also looked favourably on this scenario, but that he envisaged it taking place *after* the capture of Midway Island and not prior to it, as Tomioka's plan called for. Yamamoto got his way, not only because he threatened to resign if he did not, but because powerful personages at Imperial Headquarters were totally opposed to such an idea, including Prime Minister and Army Minister Hideki Togo himself and General Hijame Sogiyama, Chief of the Army General Staff, both of whom vigorously opposed committing so many troops to what they considered an adventure. It is therefore apparent that there was never any serious likelihood of a Japanese invasion of Australia.

The alternative to invasion was blockade, hence Operation FS. The IJA's Seventeenth Army was to allocate sufficient troops to maintain garrisons

---

1 FS = Fiji and Samoa.

progressively at strategically placed islands on which airfields would be constructed down along the Solomon Islands via Tulagi and Guadalcanal, then on to Esperitu Santo in the New Hebrides and subsequently the New Hebrides. From those a trident of advances would take in New Caledonia, Fiji and Samoa, thus cutting off not only Australia but also New Zealand from the west coast of the USA. It was a bold concept, but one the Army felt would not require such a large commitment, although how the garrisons so remote from the homeland were to be kept supplied was left unresolved. The various advances were to be screened by the carrier aircraft of the *Kido Butai* under Admiral Chuichi Nagumo, the Eleventh Air Fleet under Vice Admiral Nishizo Tsukahara with land-based Navy bombers, and carried out by the Second Fleet under Admiral Nobutake Kondo. Invasion dates for the furthermost invasions were set at New Caledonia on 8 July, Fiji on 18 July and Samoa on 21 July.

Operation FS would, if successfully implemented, turn the Coral Sea into a Japanese lake, but to protect its south-west flank the southern coast and south-east tip of New Guinea would also require to be taken and occupied. Thus, the initial stages were deemed to be the occupation of Port Moresby on the southern coast of New Guinea and the simultaneous occupation of Tulagi in the Solomon Islands, the latter as a precursor for the further expansion south-east. The carrying out of these objectives became Operation MO and was to be achieved by 10 May. The Army came on board with this plan but only on the proviso that continuous air cover was provided for their troops in transit. The Navy agreed to this and allocated two of it precious fleet carriers and one small carrier to the task. It was hoped that the two former vessels, *Shōkaku* and *Zuikaku of* the 5th (and, most Japanese considered, the weakest having 20 per cent understrength formations totalling just 121 aircraft – thirty-seven fighters and seventy-two bombers - embarked between them) Carrier Division, along with two heavy cruisers and six destroyers under Vice Admiral Takeo Takagi, would be able to complete their parts in this scheme quickly, and without undue loss, and then rejoin Nagumo's command so that Operation MI, the Midway occupation, would find the *Kido Butai* at full strength. The smaller carrier, *Shōhō,* along with four heavy cruisers and a destroyer, under the command of Rear Admiral Artitomo Goto, would give closer cover to the landings at Tulagi and Gavutu Islands, then move south to cover the troopships around the tip of New Guinea via the Jomard Passage when the convoy entered waters dominated by Allied air power based in northern Australia.

Even in its original initiation Operation FS overreached available resources and Admiral Osami Nagano later confirmed that many target dates of the plan would have to be delayed by as much as two months due to the Midway and Aleutian Islands invasions taking precedence. Nonetheless, the first phase of the attack was initiated on 4 May as Operation MO when eleven troop transports, a supply ship and two oilers, with their escorting warships, a minelayer and three minesweepers, all under Rear Admiral Hiroaki Abe, sailed from Rabaul. Additional protection was given by the light cruiser *Yubari* and six destroyers commanded by Rear Admiral Sadamichi Kaijioka. The convoy was to pass through the Coral Sea, passing the ten-islet Louisiades Archipelago and then turn west along the southern coast of Papua to Port Moresby itself. Giving some limited air cover from a position to their north was a shielding force which comprised the light carrier *Shōhō*, escorted by four further heavy cruisers and one destroyer. If that seems like a small force for such an important convoy then it must be remembered that the Japanese, over-confidently, expected little or no opposition, least of all from the American Fleet.

All might have proceeded according to plan but for one thing. Japanese signals had been severely compromised, and the American were able to read some of enemy codes with a degree of certainty undreamed of in Tokyo through the *Magic* decryption system. On 9 April signals between the carrier *Kaga* and Vice Admiral Shigeyoshi Inoue of the South Sea Force indicated to the Americans that the big carrier might be moving to join his command and triggering alarm that Japan might well be moving to the south-east in strength very soon. Further signals were intercepted that made them believe that *Shōkaku* and *Zuikaku* would be joining *Kaga* and *Shōhō*[2]

Admiral Chester William Nimitz, Commander-in-Chief, Pacific Fleet at Pearl Harbor, and his staff, strongly suspected Port Moresby might be the target when they discussed these intercepts on 17 April, but another fortnight was to pass before Intelligence sources were finally able to confirm that this was indeed the case. Nimitz had four fleet carriers on hand, which should have been adequate for the task but, due to the planned air raid on Japan by the US Army's twin-engine North American B-24B Mitchell bombers, commanded by Lieutenant Colonel James Doolittle, two of these vessels were already committed elsewhere with Task Force 16, (*Hornet* to launch them and

---

2 Only *some* of the Japanese signals were intercepted so the fact that *Kaga* was *replaced*, rather than *reinforced*, by these two carriers in such a move, was missed. Likewise, the Americans totally mistranslated the identity of the *Shōhō*, consistently reporting her as a mythical carrier, *Ryōkaku*. Later they even added the small ferry carrier *Taiyo* to the list of Japanese forces, also totally without foundation.

Enterprise to protect her while she did so); only two, *Lexington* and *Yorktown*, remained to take on three (and possibly four or five by some calculations) Japanese carriers. Of course, the Americans were supremely confident in their own abilities (*Lexington's* crew had long boasted that they alone were worth four Japanese carriers!) and Nimitz decided to accept battle and put his plan to Fleet Admiral Ernest Joseph King during a conference held at San Francisco between 25 and 27 April. King duly approved and (despite some reservations on his lack of aviation knowledge) it was agreed that Rear Admiral Frank Jack Fletcher, commanding Task Force 17 in *Yorktown,* with three heavy cruisers and four destroyers, would take charge of the battle.[3] Fletcher was notified that he would be joined at Point *Buttercup* (16^0 S 161^045'E, some 250 miles west of Espiritio Santo) by Rear Admiral Aubrey Wray Fitch's Task Force 17.2, with *Lexington,* two heavy cruisers and five destroyers. A third force comprised Rear Admiral John Gregory Crace's Task Force 17.3 which consisted of two heavy cruisers, a light cruiser and two destroyers.[4]

On 3 May both combatants had completed their initial moves. *Shōhō's* aircraft covered the landings at Tulagi before heading to support the troop convoy as planned. However, Takagi's carriers were not in position 120 miles north of the Solomons to take over air cover, but were still attempting to offload nine Mitsubishi Zero fighters which he had as deck cargo and which were to fly off to Vunakanau on eastern New Britain on 2 May. Due to bad weather conditions this simple task ate up two precious days and was not finalized until the 4th. Fortunately for them, Fletcher's command was as desultory, both carriers being separated by 100 miles for much of the time and refuelling. Once word was received of the landings at Tulagi, Fletcher took *Yorktown* north and launched a lone attack with four separate sorties against the anchorage on the 4th, by which time most of the Japanese ships had disgorged their cargoes and left.

Yorktown's first attack was despatched at 0630 and consisted of fifteen SBD dive-bombers, thirteen SBD Scouts, both groups armed with 1,000lb bombs with impact fuses, along with twelve Douglas TBD Devastator torpedo-bombers. They attacked without any on-site direction because the

---

3 Both Nimitz and King expressed concern at Fletcher's 'possible lack of aggressiveness'. They concluded that 'Nothing could be done at the moment' to improve this but agreed that 'Fletcher's conduct of operations should be watched critically'. Potter, Elmer Belmont, *Nimitz,* Naval Institute Press, Annapolis, 1976.

4 These designations were not confirmed until 6 May – they being the original Fletcher force, Fitch's Task Force 11 and Crace's Task Force 44, reinforced by an additional destroyer, respectively.

air group commander remained back aboard the carrier. The second strike, by the same team, was launched around 1036 and attacked at 1210 when one of the torpedo bombers was lost. A third strike was mounted by Grumman F4F Wildcat fighters which strafed three Kawanishi H6K *Mavis* flying boats and lost two aircraft in so doing. The fourth and final strike was made by twenty-one SBDs (twelve scouts and nine dive-bombers) and they reported sinking four landing barges without loss. *Yorktown* then pulled out to rendezvous with Fitch's ships. Fletcher claimed to have destroyed two destroyers, a freighter, four patrol boats, to have beached a light cruiser and damaged a third destroyer, a freighter and a seaplane carrier. In reality, only one small transport and three minesweepers were hit, and all eventually sank, along with five seaplanes. The price paid for this meagre result was that the Japanese knew American carriers were in the area.

On their part the *Shōhō* and her destroyer escort *Sazanami* were sighted by an RAAF Mitchell off Bougainville. The pilot reported this pair as a carrier and two battleships, which prompted Fletcher to pull back two of his cruisers and accelerate his own withdrawal. By 5 March the Allied ships were concentrated some 320 miles south of Guadalcanal and again refuelling. Meanwhile *Shōkaku* and *Zuikaku* finally passed around the southern Solomon, rounded San Cristobal[5] and entered the Coral Sea on at midday, placing themselves on the northern flanks of Fletcher's force, which fielded 133 aircraft between them, of which 123 were operational, but neither side made contact that day. Indeed, for the next two days there was a sort of Mexican stand-off by both sides without either coming to grips.

Fletcher's force had, in fact, already been sighted by another Kawanishi *Mavis* flying boat from Rabaul on the mid-morning of 6 May, while the Americans were again undertaking one of their many refuelling operations, but fortunately the Japanese carriers failed to take in the aircraft's report although listening Allied operators did so. Nor did American reconnaissance sorties locate Takagi's force, although they came close to doing so. Things did not come to a head until the 7th when another Japanese aerial reconnaissance aircraft from Rabaul reported sighting an enemy carrier and cruiser early next day but, not for the last time in this confused encounter, it turned out to be a false identification and what had really been sighted was the oiler *Neosho* and her escorting destroyer *Sims* some 250 distant from Fletcher's ships. Thus the Japanese missed two separate opportunities to get in the first blows against the American carriers.

---

5 Currently known as Makira.

Fletcher despatched Crace's cruiser squadron to get between the enemy convoy and its objective while, at 0619 that morning, *Yorktown* began launching the first of many air searches with ten SBDs airborne to search a wide arc northward.

Japanese air searches included twelve Nakajima B5N *Kates* on a similar search to the south-west while amphibians were sent out from the various anchorages to the north to scout the waters their vulnerable troopship convoy was slowly plodding into. This time both sides made contact. Indeed, they could hardly have failed to do so after so much shadow-boxing earlier and the drawing together of the various sea and air formations.

At 0735 word came in from one of *Yorktown*'s scouts, Lieutenant Keith Edward Taylor, VB-5's executive officer, reporting two heavy cruisers north-west of Rossel, some 170 miles north-west of Fletcher. Then, forty minutes later, a second VS-5 Dauntless, flown by Lieutenant John Ludwig Nielsen, reported sighting two carriers, four cruisers and a destroyer screen bearing 325^0 from Task Force 17 at a distance of some 180 miles. This force was steering south-east toward Task Force 17 at between 18 to 20 knots.

Having been all set for such a sighting, the Americans, stationed to the south-east of the Louisiades, soon responded, *Lexington* launched her attack group at 0953 led by a three-plane section comprising the Air Group Commander (CLAG) William Bowen Ault with ARM1c William Thomas Butler as his rear-seat man, and two further SBDs, one each from VB-2 and VS-2, as his wingmen, these being Ensign Alva Alton Simmons with ARM3c Joseph George Teyshak and Ensign Arthur Joseph Schultz Jr with ARM3c Wayne Carson Colley respectively. The main Dauntless complement was fifteen SBD-2s from VB-2, each carrying a single 1,000lb bomb with a one-second fuse setting, and ten SBD-3s from VS-2, each armed with a single 500lb bomb with 1/3 second fuse setting and two 116lb underwing bombs, the same load as Ault's trio. Fuel tanks contained 250 gallons of 100 octane aviation fuel. The strike force could have been larger but two VB-2 and six VS-2 SBDs were retained for what was described as 'anti-torpedo defence'. The composition of the *Lexington* attack force was as below:

Table 6: Attack Organization of VB-2, 7 May 1942		
Aircraft	Pilot	Aircrew
B-1	Lieutenant-Commander Weldon Lee Hamilton	ACRM Gordon Chester Gardner
B-17	Ensign Clem Brandon Connally	RM3c Roy J. Haas

B-3	Ensign Frank Ronald McDonald	RM3c Charles Harold Owen Hamilton
B-4	Lieutenant Ralph Wynne Cousins	ARM1c James Riley Woods
B-6	Ensign Joseph Archer Riley	RM3c George Eldo Eiswald
B-7	Lieutenant Walter Franklin Henry	ARM1c Michael Maciolek
B-8	Lieutenant (j.g.) George Orr Wood	ARM2c Clifford Ernest Schindele
B-9	Ensign Jack Donald Wakeham USNR	RM3c James Warren Nelson
B-10	Lieutenant (j.g.) Harry Brinkley Bass	ARM2c Harold Sidney Nobis
B-11	Ensign Robert Pershing Williams	Sea1c Charles John Young
B-13	Lieutenant James Harold Newell	Sea1c Robert C. Hynson
B-14	Lieutenant (j.g.) Robert Boone Buchan	ARM2c Forest Glen Stanley
B-18	Ensign Russell Paul Lecklider	RM3c Otis Alan Bowling
B-16	Lieutenant (j.g.) John Gracie Sheridan	RM2c Arthur Silva Margarido
B-5	Lieutenant (j.g.) Paul Joseph Knapp	ARM2c Leonardo A. De Salvo
B-15	Ensign Thomas Jarred Ball	RM3c Leonard T. McAdams
B-2	Ensign John M. Clarke	ARM3c Ralph Hubert Horton Jr
B-12	Ensign Alva Alton Simmons	ARM3c Joseph George Teyshak

Table 7: Attack Organization of VS-2, 7 May 1942		
Aircraft	**Pilot**	**Aircrew**
S-1	Lieutenant Commander Robert Ellington Dixon	ARM1c Ferdinand John Sugar
S-2	Lieutenant (j.g.) Joseph Grant Smith	ARM3c Lawrence Sargent Craft
S-3	Ensign Richard Franklin Neely	ARM3c Ralph Arthur Gowling
S-13	Lieutenant Thomas Elbert Edwards Jr	ARM1c Clarence Haiman Garlow
S-12	Ensign John Arthur Leppla	ARM3c John Liska

Aircraft	Pilot	Aircrew
S-10	Lieutenant Edward Henry Allen	ARM3c Charles Wayne Rouser
S-9	Ensign Anthony Joseph Quigley	ARM3c Robert Earl Wheelhouse
S-8	Lieutenant (j.g.) William Edward Hall	ARM3c Doyle C. Philips
S-16	Lieutenant (j.g.) Chandler Waterman Swanson	ARM2c John Owen Edwards
S-17	Ensign Harry Wood	ARM3c Cyril Frederick Huvar Jr

The *Yorktown* attack force took departure between fifteen and twenty minutes later. Unlike Ault, Lieutenant Commander Oscar Pederson, *Yorktown*'s air group commander, was specifically ordered by Captain Elliott Buckmaster to remain aboard and conduct the air defence as Fighter Direction Officer, perhaps reflecting Fletcher's own concern for defence over attack. Thus, *Yorktown*'s striking force lacked an airborne co-ordinator once more. The organization was as follows:

Table 8: Attack Organization of VB-5, 7 May 1942	
Pilot	**Aircrew**
Lieutenant Wallace Clark Short Jr	ACRM John Warren Trott
Ensign John Neville Ammen Jr	RM3c Joseph Michael Lynch
Ensign John Windsor Rowley	ARM3c Desmond Christopher Musgrove
Lieutenant (j.g.) William Francis Christie	Sea2c Lynn Raymond Forshee
Ensign Leif Walther Larsen	Sea2c Wilburn Dayton Harp
Ensign Harry Alvin Frederickson	Sea1c John Michael Iacovazzi
Lieutenant John James Powers	ARM2c Everett Clyde Hill
Ensign Thomas Eugene Brown	Sea2c Robert John Hodgens

Table 9: Attack Organization of VS-5, 7 May 1942	
Pilot	**Aircrew**
Lieutenant Commander Oscar Burch Jr	ARM1c Willard Ellis Glidewell
Ensign John Harry Jorgenson	ARM2c Anthony William Brunetti
Lieutenant (j.g.) Hugh Wilbur Nicholson	RM3c Onni Emil Kustula

Lieutenant (j.g.) Stanley Winfield Vejtasa	Commander Walter Gabriel Schindler
Ensign Arthur Latimer Downing	RM2c Elmer C. Jones
Lieutenant (j.g.) Frederic Lewis Faulkner	RM2c Charles A. Jaeger
Lieutenant Turner Foster Caldwell Jr	ARM2c Leon Hall
Ensign Walton Anderson Austin	ARM2c Joseph Ellsworth Roll
Ensign Elmer Maul	RM3c Jack R. McLain
Lieutenant Stockton Birney Strong	RM2c John F. Hurley
Ensign Edward Blaine Kinzer	Sea1c Charles Joseph Bonness
Ensign Kendall Carl Campbell	RM3c Harold Joseph Wilger
Lieutenant Roger Blake Woodhull	RM2c Albert Woodrow Garlow
Ensign Samuel Jackson Underhill	RM3c Woodrow Andrew Fontenot
Ensign Walter Wesley Coolbaugh	Sea1c Lovelace Mark Broussard
Lieutenant (j.g.) Earl Vincent Johnson	ARM3c Franklin Delano Richesin
Ensign Lawrence Gilworth Traynor	ARM1c James Hedger Cales

The SBDs climbed to 18,000 feet and awaited the arrival of the torpedo bombers and fighters and did not take departure until 1013. It was not until a quarter-of-an-hour later that the SBD that had made the original sighting reports arrived back over the fleet. Initially Nielsen flew low over *Yorktown*'s flight deck and dropped a message which stated that he had sighted four light cruisers and two destroyers. There was some puzzlement as to whether these were additional to the carrier force he had radioed in and when he eventually landed back aboard the ship he was naturally questioned closely on the enemy carriers. He revealed that he had *not* sighted *any* carriers, only a pair of heavy cruisers and two destroyers; also, that was exactly what he had duly reported! According to the ship's on-loan Intelligence Officer, Lieutenant Commander Forrest Rosecrans Biard, the bemused pilot was hauled up the flag plot to face a less than happy Fletcher who was alleged to have accused him of losing the United States two carriers by his error. An investigation was immediately carried out and soon showed up the fact that Nielsen's coding machine had been misaligned. H.P. Willmott states unequivocally that '*Yorktown*'s pilot had misaligned the key and code in trying to make his sighting report …'.

This pilot error was compounded by a report received at 1021 from the unfortunate *Neosho* that the fuelling group was being bombed by three aircraft. By placing these two ships within maximum range of Japanese aircraft at Tulagi Fletcher was left in a dilemma of his own making as to whether the attackers were land-based aircraft from Tulagi or carrier-borne planes from Takagi's carriers.[6] Yet a further complication came when another scouting aircraft, flown by Lieutenant (j.g.) Henry Martin McDowell, was forced to turn back when only 165 miles into his north-east leg, leaving this vital sector unsearched.

The receipt of a signal time at 1022 from a USAAF patrol based in New Guinea brought some hope that something could be salvaged from the mistake. They reported a carrier and ten other escorts with ten transports close to the position of Nielsen's incorrect sighting. An *en clair* signal was sent out at 1053 ordering the strike forces to redirect their attacks against this force.

The Japanese in turn were in receipt of a sighting report from one of the band of twelve aircraft scouting an arc between 180 to 265 to a maximum distance of 250 miles. At 0722 this aircraft reported sighting the enemy fleet on a bearing of 182 at a distance of 163 miles from Takagi, which was amplified twenty-three minutes later by more detail which listed the American ships as one carrier, one cruiser and three destroyers. Between 0800 and 0815 *Shōkaku* and *Zuikaku* launched thirty-six Val dive bombers and twenty-four Nakajima B5N torpedo-bombers with an escort of eighteen Mitsubishi Zero-Sen fighters. Meantime another sighting report came in of an American oiler escorted by a heavy cruiser, allegedly twenty-five miles south-east of the previous sighting. Of course, both reports were mistaken, and both sightings referred to the same ships, this being the fleet oiler *Neosho* and her lone destroyer escort, *Sims,* patiently waiting the call to refuel Task Force 17 when required. These two unfortunates therefore became the totally false 'honeypot' that drew to them the seventy-eight strong Japanese strike force, with the inevitable result.

The SBDs of the American striking forces also attacked the secondary target and, lacking a strike co-ordinator, piled in remorselessly against the little *Shōhō*. *Shōhō*'s name (it translates as *Auspicious Phoenix*) belied her value. She was converted from the submarine support vessel *Tsurugizaki*, a transformation completed in January 1942 and, other than an aircraft-ferrying run to Truk, this was her first war mission. Perhaps a speedier equivalent of

---

6 The destroyer *Sims* was quickly sunk at 1148 with heavy casualties; there were only fourteen survivors; the oiler, resilient as these ships always seemed to be, was hard hit and left burning and powerless. She did not founder until the 11th and her survivors were rescued by the destroyers *Henley* and *Helm*.

American and British escort carriers, she was of 11,443 tons displacement but with a useful speed of twenty-eight knots. Her maximum aircraft capacity was thirty aircraft, but she only had embarked for this mission eight Mitsubishi A6M2 Zeke fighters, six Nakajima B5N2 Kate attack bombers and four Mitsubishi A5M4 Claude second-rate fighter aircraft. As for protection from the ordeal she was facing she had no armour whatsoever.

When sighted by the American aviators from the *Lexington* Group at 1040 to the north of Misima Island, to the west of the eastern extremity of New Guinea, the little Japanese ship had two Claudes and one Zero overhead as her combat air patrol and was frantically readying three further Zekes for take-off. The SBDs commenced their attack at 1100 as the Japanese fighters attempted to intercept and *Shōhō*'s captain, Izawa Ishinosuke, put his ship into a tight port turn as the first Dauntless dive-bombers hurtled down at his ship. As they descended, many SBD pilots once again experienced the 'fogging up' of their telescopic sights as they passed through the atmospheric layers.

Commander William Ault led his section of three in at 1110 from 10,000 feet to commence proceedings while the ten SBDs of VS-2 under Lieutenant Commander Robert Dixon positioned themselves to follow this trio down. VB-2, with their heavier bombs, circled to the east awaiting their turn. Ault himself claimed to have scored a direct hit with his 500lb bomb, but, in truth, he, like his two companions, missed entirely. Dixon's ten SBDs reduced altitude to 12,500 feet and attacked out of the sun. Late intervention by two Zekes was brushed aside with just slight damage to one SBD, that of Ensign Anthony Quigley, but *Shōhō* continued her turn until it became a full circle, and this negated Dixon's planned stern-to-bow attack leaving only her narrow beam as an aiming point. Again, VS-2 claimed three direct hits but scored none, the closest being over sixty-five-and-a-half feet away. Worse one Zero nailed Lieutenant Edward Henry Allen's Dauntless as it flattened out from the dive at 2,000 feet and shot it into the sea off the carrier's fantail. There were no survivors. They also damaged other dive-bombers but no more were lost. Ensign John Leppla endeavoured to drop his two small 116lb wing bombs in a second dive and claimed to have hit one of the screening heavy cruisers, but this proved equally inaccurate; no escort was as much as scratched. The first attacks petered out at 1117 having achieved nothing and *Shōhō* even had time to launch three more Zekes to take on the next wave.

A minute later, with Captain Ishinosuke Izawa repeated his circling manoeuvre as *Yorktown*'s attack group appeared in the distance and VB-2's fifteen SBDs prepared to take VS-2's place in the shooting gallery. The *Yorktown* men had twice been re-directed by Fletcher by plain language radio while en route and were pleased to finally have a target that they could see to go for. Before they arrived, VB-2's assault commenced at 1125 from 12,000 feet with bomb release around 2,500 feet and immediately Hamilton himself scored a direct hit with his thousand-pounder plumb central of the little carrier's flight deck. A Zeke made repeated attempts to shoot him down, following Hamilton's aircraft down all the way. This spectacular bullseye was followed within seconds by a second direct hit further along the deck from the first one. Hamilton's tail gunner, ACRM Gordon Chester Gardner, kept up a steady defensive fire and this fighter eventually sheared off in frustration. Meanwhile another VB-2 rear-seat man, ARM2c Forest Glen Stanley, from Lieutenant (j.g.) Robert Boone Buchan's aircraft, claimed to have destroyed another Zero. Five more direct hits were claimed by the returning VB-2 men, but these two were the only ones to hit the little carrier. Both bombs pierced into the body of the ship and started heavy fires in the main hangar where the fully-fuelled up Kates were being fitted with torpedoes. The smoke trail from this carnage was funnelled back over by her movement through the water and obscured her stern.

During the accompanying torpedo-bomber attack no fewer than five torpedo hits were made from nine claimed, and these devastating blows added to the inferno. But even before this crushing blow the twenty-five Dauntless of the *Yorktown* striking force, led by Lieutenant Commander William Oscar Burch of VS-5, were dropping down from their cruising altitude of 18,000 feet, ready to go into their attacks. Although intercepted by the three fresh defending fighters the seventeen SBDs of VS-2 commenced their dives at 1125. This time there was no high-speed evasive manoeuvre from the *Shōhō*, her engines were almost shot, and she just had to sit and take yet more punishment. It was like kicking a corpse. In the excitement of the moment one Dauntless pre-triggered his bomb, while another had his 1,000lb ordnance 'hang up' on him, but even so fifteen more bombs, of which nine were claimed as direct hits, were registered. Even this was not sufficient for the US airmen in full cry. Eight more SBDs, Lieutenant Commander Wallace Clark Short's VB-5, followed in at 1130, bombing through smoke and debris that covered the remnants of the *Shōhō*'s torn and riven hull, to claim yet a further six hits. The Japanese estimated that eleven of the fifteen claimed were actual hits. The actual final score was academic and another five torpedo hits from the Devastator torpedo-bombers was so overegging the omelette to the *n*th degree that it was futile. The four heavy cruisers, excellent targets, were relatively unmolested with only a single SBD, that of Ensign Walter Earl Brown Jr., taking one of them under assault.

BATTLE OF THE CORAL SEA, MAY 1942

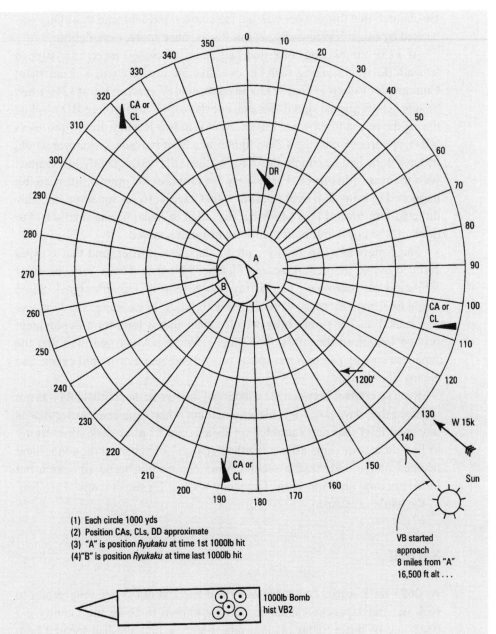

(1) Each circle 1000 yds
(2) Position CAs, CLs, DD approximate
(3) "A" is position *Ryukaku* at time 1st 1000lb hit
(4)"B" is position *Ryukaku* at time last 1000lb hit

VB started
approach
8 miles from "A"
16,500 ft alt . . .

1000lb Bomb
hist VB2

N.B. The *Shoho* was incorrectly identified as th
fictional *Ryukaku* throughout the battle.

dive bombing attack of VB-2 at the Battle of the Coral Sea.

He claimed that this cruiser was hit, rolled over and sank and this claim was backed by other *Yorktown* flyers, but it was, once more, pure fiction.

At 1135 the blazing hulk that had been the *Shōhō* mercifully slipped beneath the waves taking with her over five hundred crewmen.[7] Lieutenant Commander Robert Ellington Dixon confirmed this carrier kill at 1210 when he sent his oft-quoted signal 'Scratch one flat-top!' One further SBD was lost during the return flight when Ensign John Windsor Rowley, from *Yorktown*'s VB-5, apparently chasing a Zero fighter in a fit of bravado, (whatever would he have done had he caught this tiger by the tail!) consequently lost contact with the rest of his force. Fortunately for him and his gunner, his roaming happened to bring him over Admiral John Crace's cruiser squadron and they directed him toward Port Moresby. He failed to make it, and finally had to ditch off the coast, but both men were ultimately saved.

The Americans had finally nailed a Japanese carrier, and that is what counted at that moment. It spared Fletcher's blushes. There were scenes of jubilation on *Yorktown*'s Flag Bridge on receipt of Dixon's signal. Some might have thought these were tinged with relief. In exchange the Japanese had sunk Fletcher's only oiler which meant that a long-term deployment was no longer on the cards. One other positive achievement was that the Japanese convoy of troop transports was turned back north until events had cleared themselves.

Even so contact between the carriers of the two main combatants was not resumed that day, save for a bizarre incident when Japanese carrier planes launched later that day stumbled on Task Force 17 after dark while trying to find their own ships after a fruitless search.[8] Fletcher on the other hand decided not to undertake a second American carrier-borne air search but bided his time until morning. The scene was set for the climatic 'Part Two' of the battle on 8 April.

8 April

At 0625 on 8 April, *Lexington* launched her Dauntless scouting group to seek out the Japanese carrier force now known to be in the vicinity. At 0828 one of these SBDs made a report stating that she had located both

---

7   The escorting destroyer *Sazanamai* later managed to rescue just two hundred survivors, including her captain.

8   Lurid tales of Japanese carrier planes trying to land aboard US carriers are not verified and can be dismissed, but it did illustrate just how close the two forces were.

enemy carriers, along with four heavy cruisers and three destroyers but no position was given. Seven minutes later this scout reported that at 0820 two carriers, four cruisers and 'many' destroyers were in sight on a bearing of 006 at a distance of 120 miles, making fifteen knots. This was updated by *Lexington* herself at 0847 to 'Enemy bearing 028^0– 175 miles'.

Rear Admiral Fitch, as Commander Air, ordered the *Yorktown*'s attack a minute later. At the very last minute Fletcher had assigned the far more experienced naval aviator Fitch as Officer in Tactical Command (OITC) in order, he said, to facilitate signalling between the two carriers. Fitch was surprised by this late move, made after battle was joined and the first strikes of the day were still taking off, but it did allow him some welcome freedom of action in what was to be the first carrier-to-carrier battle of the war.[9]

Meanwhile, to the north of Fletcher's command, Rear Admiral Takeo Takagi's two carriers, with 121 aircraft, of which just 108 were operational, also lay poised to strike. Contact with the American carriers was confirmed and thus, at 0900 and 0908, both opponents' carriers commenced launching their strike forces. On the American side *Lexington* flew off nineteen Dauntless of VB-2 under Commander William Bowen Ault, along with three of VS-2's aircraft, all that remained aboard. Inexperience showed again for they were despatched with thirty-five gallons (160 litres) short of their precious maximum fuel load. *Yorktown* got away seven VS-5 dive bombers with another seventeen Dauntless of VB-5 soon after, all armed with 1,000lb bombs, and they set off to cover the estimated 175 miles (280km) between them and the two big Japanese carriers. They were homed onto the enemy at 0930 by Lieutenant Harley Rockey Dickson who had found the Japanese force again in the murk; he radioed his contact as 'Two CV, two DD bearing 000 degrees, 160 miles'.

As they closed with the enemy fleet, the *Lexington* air group began to lose cohesion: fighters lost bombers, some turned back, the dive-bombers lost the torpedo-bombers and started a box search to locate them, and the fuel shortage in the SBDs started to become a serious problem. Hamilton with VB-2 had reduced altitude down to 1,000 feet (300m) in his search but was unrewarded, and the whole squadron was forced to abort the mission, dumping their bombs in order to make it back safely to their carrier.

---

9 Fletcher himself had failed entry to flight training in 1928 and thereafter 'persistently denigrated naval aviation during cocktail chatter'. Admiral John Henry Towers, the Navy's senior naval aviator, once remarked of Fletcher's attitude in this respect that 'He doesn't know what he's talking about. It's no use discussing it'. Reynold, Clark Gilbert, *Admiral John H Towers: The Struggle for Naval Air Supremacy*, Naval Institute Press, Annapolis, 1991.

It was thus left to the indefatigable *Yorktown*'s group yet again to get in the first attack, and, at about 1050, they sighted both Japanese carriers operating approximately eight miles apart with their respective screening ships. *Zuikaku* opportunely found low cloud in which to conceal herself just in time, but her sister was not so fortunate. However, the dive-bombers had arrived over the target well before the slower Douglas TBD Devastators, and in order to make a concerted attack as per the book, Lieutenant Commander William Oscar Burch Jr Was obliged to keep his squadron circling for half an hour, waiting for the torpedo bombers to come up. Thus, all surprise was forfeited and *Shōkaku* was able to launch more defending Zero fighters. Not until 1100 did the VS-5 Dauntless attack go in from a height of 17,000 feet (5,000m) and, as they opened their dive flaps and commenced their dives, they were intercepted by the defending Zekes. In the resulting mêlée the dive bombers claimed to have shot down four of the defending fighters, while all seven SBDs themselves took hits, many in the fuel tanks – fortunately of the self-sealing type – while one SBD, flown by Ensign John Harry Jorgenson, with rear-seat man ARM2c Anthony William Brunetti, was splashed; luckily the crew survived to be rescued later.

Meanwhile the aircraft of VB-5 were caught out of position and had to go around once more before following them down, and the torpedo-bombers launched at too great a distance to be effective. Moreover, the problem with the fogging of the telescopic sight recurred and hampered the VS-5 aircraft, who achieved no hits whatsoever. Fortunately, the seventeen Dauntless of VB-5, led again by Lieutenant Wallace Clark Short Jr, made no mistakes, even though they were equally beset by Zeros, of which they claimed to have destroyed no fewer than five! The Americans made two direct hits, one on the port forward side and one to the starboard side of *Shōkaku*'s bridge, both of which penetrated her flight deck, wrecking it and starting huge fires in the aviation fuel stowage below. The fires were eventually brought under control and the carrier could land her aircraft, but could not launch fresh ones.

The SBDs lost two of VB-5's aircraft in this attack, one of them the brave Short who, true to his ideas, had held his dive down to below 300 feet (90m) before releasing, even though his aircraft had been hit and his gunner wounded; his aircraft failed to pull out and plunged straight into the sea alongside the Japanese carrier. Short was posthumously awarded the Medal of Honor. The other VB-5 Dauntless lost was 5-B-16, the mount of Ensign David Elliott Chaffee and his tail gunner, John Anthony Kasselman. Chaffee was wounded and Kasselman killed during the dive and their SBD punctured by cannon fire with her port wing gouged out, engine cowling shot away and part of the rudder missing, and one wing burnt off. The Dauntless spun in with no survivors.

Finally, at 1040, the remnants of the *Lexington* strike arrived. This was an inexperienced combat group, however, and only eleven torpedo planes launched, and all their torpedoes missed. Most of the dive-bombers had not even managed to locate the target, including all eleven of VB-2's Dauntless that had turned back; but four SBDs that did make dives claimed two direct hits; by Ault himself, who scored a hit at 1140 on the starboard flight deck just abaft the bridge island, and a second claimed by Ensign Harry Wood. Another Dauntless, that of Ensign John Davis Wingfield, had her bomb 'hang up' on her. In fact, only one aircraft scored any hit, and this was on *Shōkaku*'s after-starboard side of the flight deck; it was not fatal, but it completed the wrecking of her flight deck. Thus, as a combat carrier, she was out of the fight, and, although she was not terminally damaged and her casualties were comparatively light (109 killed and 114 wounded in varying degrees from a complement of over 1,660), once her fires were extinguished she was detached north, with two heavy cruisers and two destroyers as escorts, ultimately to be repaired in Japan. Forty-six of her aircraft complement managed to land aboard *Zuikaku* and were saved.

Inflicting this damage on the enemy had cost *Lexington* her Commander Air Group, badly damaged by Zeros during the withdrawal, with both Ault and his rear gunner, ARM1c William Thomas Butler, wounded. Commander Ault failed to join up with the division and became disorientated. Attempts to home him in were complicated by the fact that *Lexington* handed over to *Yorktown* after the former's damage. At around 1400 he enquired by radio if *Lexington*'s radar had him on screen, but they did not, and nor had *Yorktown*. Ault then told them he was flying course 110 degrees and was wounded in the both an arm and a leg. As his fuel drained away, Ault continued to talk to base in the hope that he could help them find him, asking at 1449 'Shall I circle? Do you want me to gain or lose altitude?' Lieutenant Commander Oscar Pederson aboard *Yorktown* replied 'You are not on the screen. Try to make the nearest land.' Ault could only point out the obvious, 'We would never make it,' to which Pederson answered 'You are on your own. Good luck'. His final communication was received by *Yorktown* at 1454, a poignant signal acknowledging his fate: 'OK, so long people. We got a 1000lb hit on the flat top.'[10]

Of the other three SBDs of the division, one of them was the gallant young Wingfield who had returned to the target alone to make a second attempt. He and his rear-seat man, ARM3c William Priere Davis, were never seen again and probably fell victim to the defending Zeros. The other victim was Harry Wood flying 2-S-5, who had to force-land offshore of

---

10   List of Despatches No. 32. USS *Yorktown*.

Rossel Island, the most eastern of the Louisiades Archipelago.[11] Both he and his rear-seat man, ARM3c Cyril Frederick Havar Jr, got ashore unharmed. Friendly natives helped them elude the Japanese as they spent four days crossing the island where they were later rescued. Just one Dauntless managed to get back safely aboard *Lexington*, that being 2-S-17 piloted by Ensign Marvin Milton Haschke with air gunner Sea2c Jack Lilley.

While the Americans were attacking the two Japanese carriers, with mixed fortunes, the Japanese flyers were, in their turn, assailing the two US carriers. *Shōkaku*'s Kawanishi Type 97 flying-boat scouts had carefully shadowed the American task force sending back a stream of sighting reports and remaining unmolested by defending American fighters in the process until the very last moments when one was destroyed in mid-air at 1015. The storm began to break over *Lexington* and *Yorktown* from 1055 onward when radar contacts on both US carriers reported an enemy squadron just sixty-eight miles from the American carriers where the enemy were met by not just Grumman F4F Wildcat fighters but by an extraordinary extra layer of defence, no less than twenty-three Dauntless being retained by the ultra-cautious Fletcher to fly defensive patrols, in a complete total reversal of their true role. The first tranche of the so-called 'anti-torpedo-plane patrol' had been flown off *Lexington* at 1012 due to a false alarm and consisted of six SBDs from VB-2 and four from VS-2 who were arranged thus:

Lexington VB-2		
Pilot	**Rear Seat Man**	**Position**
Lieutenant (j.g.) Robert Boone Buchan	ARM2c Forrest Glen Stanley	Port Quarter
Ensign Frank Ronald McDonald	RM3c Charles Harold Owen Hamilton	do
Ensign Arthur Joseph Behl Jr	ARM3c Joseph George Teyshak	do
Lieutenant (j.g.) Paul Joseph Knapp	ARM3c Leonard A. DeSalvo	Starboard Quarter
Ensign Robert Pershing Williams	Sea1c Charles John Young	do
Ensign John M. Clarke	ARM3c Ralph H. Horton	do

---

11 Also known as Yela Island.

Lexington VS-2		
Pilot	**Rear Seat Man**	**Position**
Lieutenant (j.g.) William Edward Hall	Sea1c John Arthur Moore	Port Bow
Ensign Robert Edward Smith	ARM3c Lanois Mardi Wheeler	do
Lieutenant Thomas Elbert Edwards	ARM1c Clarence Halman Garlow	Starboard Bow
Ensign Max Einar Eric Woyke	ARM3c Raymond Eugene Reames	do

Later *Lexington* got five more Dauntless away, who were assigned the following positions:

Lexington VS-2		
Pilot	**Rear Seat Man**	**Position**
Lieutenant (j.g.) Roy Orestus Hale Jr	ARM2c John Delmar Lackey	Port Bow
Ensign John Arthur Leppla	ARM3c John Liska	do
Lieutenant (j.g.) Chandler Waterman Swanson	ARM2c John Owen Edwards	Starboard Bow
Ensign Richard Franklin Neely	RM3c Ralph Arthur Gowling	do
Ensign Arthur Joseph Schultz Jr	ARM3c Wayne Carson Colley	Starboard Ahead

N.B. Schultz should have been paired with Lieutenant Hoyt Dobbs Mann and RM3c Leslie H Anderson but there was insufficient time to refuel their SBD before the attack.

Yorktown launched eight SBDs from VS-5, led by Lieutenant Birney Strong, which cruised at 1,500 feet, and were deployed thus:

Yorktown VS-5		
Pilot	**Rear Seat Man**	**Division**
Lieutenant Roger Blake Woodhull	RM2c Albert Woodrow Garlow	1
Ensign Edward Blaine Kinzer	Sea1c Charles Joseph Bonness	1

Yorktown VS-5		
Pilot	**Rear Seat Man**	**Division**
Lieutenant (j.g.) Stanley Winfield Vejtasa	ARM3c Frank Barton Wood	1
Ensign Samuel Jackson Underhill	RM3c Woodrow Andrew Fontenot	1
Lieutenant Stockton Birney Strong	RM2c John F. Hurley	2
Ensign Kendall Carl Campbell	ARM3c Leon Hall	2
Lieutenant (j.g.) Earl Vincent Johnson	ARM3c Franklin Delano Richesin	2
Ensign Walton Anderson Austin	ARM2c Joseph Ellsworth Roll	2

The idea of using the Dauntless thus was the brainchild of Captain Frederick Carl Sherman, *Lexington*'s captain, and had first been mooted back in December 1941 with the pinprick raids on Makin and Tarawa in the Gilbert Islands. The idea was for these SBDs to form a semi-circular supplementary low-level defensive screen some 2,000 feet up, some 6,000 feet out, to port and starboard off *Lexington*'s bow. The idea found little favour among the dive-bomber pilots themselves, who wanted to attack the enemy carriers, but Sherman had his way this day. The concept seems excessively cautious in retrospect but there was a chronic lack of fighter aircraft and, in a way, it was a tribute to the versatility of the Dauntless, more so perhaps a tribute to her manoeuvrability and agility.

However, maintaining their patrol, Woodhull's SBDs proved powerless to stop the Japanese torpedo-bombers which passed overhead some 3,000 feet (900m) higher and launched their missiles at a range of 2,000 yards (1,800m). The Dauntless of VS-5 were then pounced upon by the accompanying Zekes and two were shot down at once with two more following them in short order, the victims being Lieutenant (j.g.) Earl Vincent Johnson, Ensign Samuel Jackson Underhill, Ensign Edward Blain Kinzer and Ensign Kendall Carl Campbell. One of those sitting ducks, piloted by Lieutenant Stanley Winfield Vejtasa, bore a charmed life and claimed to have shot down three Zeros, while another SBD splashed a fourth.

In a similar manner *Lexington*'s anti-torpedo-patrol lost three Dauntless, 2-S-18 piloted by Lieutenant (j.g.) Roy Orestus Hale Jr, 2-S-16 piloted by Lieutenant (j.g.) Chandler Waterman Swanson and 2-B-13 piloted by Ensign Frank Ronald McDonald, which went in while attempting to land on the carrier's canted flight deck. In addition, Ensign Walton Anderson Austin's aircraft was damaged by Zero fire and crashed into the carrier's island while attempting to land. In return the SBDs claimed to have destroyed no fewer than eleven of the enemy.

We have seen how just one *Lexington* air crew, Ensign John Arthur Leppla of VS-2 with rear-seat man ARM2c John Liska, was credited with shooting down no fewer than four Japanese aircraft already in this battle, and he was to add three more Zeros to the tally, making a total of seven 'kills', four with the forward guns and three with the flexible .30 calibre weapon. The harsh reality was that the Japanese lost no Zeros whatsoever in this brief battle, making Sherman's experiment a really expensive exercise in futility at a high cost. Many of the Dauntless aircrews questioned the use of their aircraft in this manner at the time; they considered it a misuse, and one even went so far as to accuse Admirals Fletcher and Fitch of carrying out 'an act that bordered on defensive paranoia'.[12] Perhaps due to these highly exaggerated claims this was one tactic that was to be tried again in subsequent carrier clashes in 1942 when extreme caution continued to dictate American carrier warfare tactics.

The Dauntless of VS-2 were luckier, at least having a glancing chance of intercepting the incoming Japanese torpedo planes. Five Kates were claimed shot down by Lieutenant (j.g.) William Edward Hall, Ensign Arthur Joseph Schultz, Jr, John Arthur Leppla and Robert Edward Smith. The facts are that three Nakajima B5Ns were destroyed, a tally that included Lieutenant Yoshio Iwamura, leader of 2 *Chōtai* while another nailed a second as the enemy withdrew. However, there was nothing the Dauntless could do to stop their Japanese counterparts, the Aichi D3A Vals, as they tipped over into their dives to finish off what the torpedo-bombers had started, scoring two direct hits and many near misses on *Lexington*, which caused underwater damage. Later internal fires broke out and the huge carrier finally sank. *Yorktown* was also badly damaged and had to return to Pearl Harbor for emergency repairs. She was got ready for the next great battle, in contrast to the two Japanese carriers, neither of which could be got ready, *Shōkaku* due to her damage and *Zuikaku* due to the heavy casualties in her air group. The Port Moresby invasion convoy never did turn back south: instead an overland campaign was considered safer for the Japanese attack, and ultimately foundered in the mud and dense jungles of the Owen Stanley mountains. Strategically, therefore, the Battle of the Coral Sea led to the Allies thwarting the Japanese advance for the first time in the war.

---

12 See Buell, Commander Dr Harold Lloyd, *Dauntless Helldivers*, Random House, New York, 1992. Buell was a highly distinguished dive-bomber pilot who saw action in all five Pacific carrier-to-carrier battles.

Chapter 4

The Battle of Midway

There are many mysteries still surrounding the most famous American naval battle of the Second World War. Equally there are a great many myths, seemingly growing annually, attached to this famous victory. I have described this battle in depth before[1] but here a much-abbreviated account can only highlight the main parts of the SBD's crucial role and question some of the 'fashionable' but largely unsubstantiated allegations still being touted on certain aspects.

The main Japanese threat across the central Pacific, Operation MI, was aimed at the two small islands, Sand and Eastern, that formed the Midway atoll. A pre-war American flying-boat fuelling stop, these tiny scraps of land lay just across the International Date Line in the centre of that vast expanse of water and formed an extension of the Hawaiian Chain in the east stretching to Midway, with tiny Kure Island[2] a further fifty-five miles to the west beyond the Pearl and Hermes Reef. Midway itself could either serve the Americans as a forward outpost to Pearl Harbor, a base for scouting aircraft, a trip-wire for invasion or, alternatively, if it fell into Japanese hands, could perform a similar function for them. But the real purpose for Japanese interest in mid-1942 was not originally for what the two islets could *provide* but what its occupation would most likely *provoke,* and that was the response of what remained of the US Fleet in its defence, or, if it fell to them, its regaining. That was what Admiral Yamamoto *really* sought and his whole aim was the destruction of any American fleet, and, American aircraft carriers, into which the humiliation of the Doolittle Raid had stung him.[3]

---

1 Smith, Peter Charles Horstead, *Midway – Dauntless Victory: Fresh Perspectives on America's Seminal Naval Victory of World War II*, Pen & Sword Maritime, Barnsley, 2007.
2 Also known as Ocean Island, and now known as Kure Atoll.
3 This point is often overlooked in histories: the IJN didn't send almost all their main strength out just to take Midway, it was the US Pacific Fleet that was their objective, but this aspect, duly acknowledged by Nimitz and his team at the time as a possibility, has been lost in the passing of the years. Oddly, having poked the wasps' nest, the Japanese seemed surprised to have been stung!

Being forewarned by their brilliant Intelligence sources at Pearl[4] of just about all what was coming, the US forces were busy cramming into Midway every available aircraft and gun they could muster; however, the defenders would still not have had much of a chance should the whole weight of the Imperial Fleet ultimately descend upon them, as seemed possible.

The dockyard at Pearl Harbor had worked miracles and managed to patch up the badly-damaged *Yorktown* so that she could take her place in the battle line with her reconstituted air group. She again formed Task Force 17 under Rear Admiral Frank Fletcher, with two heavy cruisers, *Astoria* and *Portland*, and six destroyers. Aboard her was VB-3 with eighteen Dauntless led by Lieutenant Commander Maxwell Franklin Leslie, and VS-3, with nineteen SBDs, led by Lieutenant Wallace Clark Short Jr. On 21 May, on the instructions of Rear Admiral Leigh Noyes, who had succeeded Vice Admiral Aubrey Wray Fitch as Halsey's shore administrator in April, the *Saratoga* squadron was embarked as the quickest way to replenish the carrier's dive-bomber strength in the short time available as their parent carrier had not yet finished her own repairs. VS-5 was really the old VB-5, re-designated to avoid confusion and made up from a mix of ten veteran survivors of that outfit with an influx of eight relatively new and combat-fresh pilots.

Task Force 16, under Rear Admiral Raymond Ames Spruance, comprised the carriers *Enterprise* and *Hornet,* five heavy cruisers, *Minneapolis, New Orleans, Northampton, Pensacola* and *Vincennes,* one AA cruiser, *Atlanta,* and nine destroyers. The dive-bombing complement of these two carriers was high, with VB-6 led by Lieutenant Richard Halsey Best, and VS-6 led by Wilmer Earl Gallaher aboard *Enterprise,* each having nineteen SBD-3s on strength, and with *Hornet*'s CAG, Stanhope Cotton Ring, was VB-6 under Lieutenant Commander Robert Ruffin Johnson, with a mix of nineteen SBD-1, 2s and 3s, and VS-7 Led by Lieutenant Commander Walter Fred Rodee, with eighteen SBD-2s and 3s (reduced by a crash on 29 May to seventeen.) Due to the fact that *Hornet* had been used as the base ship for the North American B-24 Mitchells of James Harold Doolittle's USAAC raiding force against japan, the bulk of her aircrew were also woefully lacking in training.

Even with the aircraft based on Midway itself, this appeared to be a pitiful force to stand against the main strength of the Imperial Japanese Navy, now well on its way towards them, for the Japanese had sortied out in great

---

4 but *not* by those in Washington DC.

strength, fielding no fewer than eleven battleships, six aircraft carriers, ten heavy and seven light cruisers, fifty-two destroyers and many lesser warships. However, although a massive and awe-inspiring force, the Japanese armada was widely dispersed in small isolated groups separated from each other by hundreds of miles of ocean, and therefore totally unable to provide each other with support. Therefore, despite the persistent over-estimation of Japan's warships engaged in the combat, the Battle of Midway was principally fought between the four Japanese fleet carriers against three American fleet carriers, plus the USMC air group based on Midway and some USAAF four-engine Boeing B-17 Flying Fortress bombers which, although they subsequently loudly bragged that they had won the battle singlehanded, actually contributed absolutely nothing to the fight.

Prior to 21 May 1942, the date which signalled the commencement of the reconnaissance and alert phase of the Battle of Midway, the only meaningful aviation unit on Eastern Island was Marine Air Group 22 (MAG-22) commanded by Lieutenant General Ira Lafayette Kimes, of which the strike element consisted of VMSB-241 under Major Lofton Russell Henderson. Henderson originally had twenty-one Vought SB2U-3 Vindicators, of which only sixteen were operational. On 26 May the US Navy aircraft transport *Kitty Hawk* arrived at the atoll with twenty-two officers and thirty-five men along with nineteen SBD-2s under command, of which eighteen were ready. Of these pilots, on the eve of battle where they would be pitted against Japan's finest naval aviators, seventeen were 'fresh out of flight school'.[5] As there were only twenty-nine pilots on strength, one pilot from VMF-221 was assigned to fly with VMSB-241 and thus eighteen Dauntless and twelve Vindicators were scheduled for employment on the first day of the battle.

At 0525 on 4 June 1942 the Commanding Officer of the Naval Air Station (CO, NAS), Captain Cyril Thomas Simard, received a report from a PBY Catalina patrol plane from VP-23, piloted by Lieutenant (j.g.) Howard Parmele Ady, that enemy carriers had been sighted at 0515, bearing 320 degrees, distance 180 miles (290km), course 135 degrees, speed 25 knots. At 0555 the radar reported 'Many bogey aircraft 310 degrees, distance 93 miles (150km), Angels 11.' By 0557 all the Marine aircraft were airborne.

Rendezvous was completed at Point Affirm, on bearing 90 degrees, distance twenty miles (32km), at about 0630. By the time the first Japanese

5 See Marine Aircraft Group Twenty-Two, Second Marine Aircraft Wing, Midway Island T.H., *Report of the Battle of Midway,* dated June 30 1942. With preliminary phase from 22 May 1942. Dated 7 June 1942. (DoD DIR 5200.10. DARA, College Park, Maryland.

bombs started to fall on Eastern island at 0635, the Marine dive-bombers were well on their way to their destiny. The Dauntless section of the force was organized in two divisions of four (uneven) boxes, as follows:

Table 10: Midway USMC Dauntless Initial Attacks, 4 June		
Aircraft	Pilot	Aircrew
First Division		
1	Major Lofton Russell Henderson	Private Lee Walter Reininger
2	Captain Richard Eugene Fleming	Corporal Eugene T. Card
3	Top Sergeant Clyde Heath Stamps	Private Horace Backsley Thomas
4	Captain Elmer George Glidden Jr	Corporal Meade T. Johnson
5	Second Lieutenant Thomas John Gratzek	Sergeant Charles William Recke
6	First Lieutenant Daniel Tore Iverson Jr	Private Wallace Jordan Reid
7	Second Lieutenant Robert Judy Bear	Private Truell Larkin Sidebottom
8	Captain Armond Hector DeLalio	Corporal John A. Moore
9	Second Lieutenant Maurice Andrew Ward	Private Harry Morton Radford
10	Second Lieutenant Albert William Tweedy Jr	Sergeant Elza Lester Raymond
11	Second Lieutenant Bruno Paul Hagedorn	Private Joseph Thomas Piraneo
Second Division		
16	Captain Richard Lloyd Blain	Private Gordon Russell McFeely
17	Second Lieutenant Bruce Henry Ek	Private Raymond Ralph Brown
13	Second Lieutenant Jesse Douglas Rollow Jr	Private Reed Thomas Ramsey
19	Second Lieutenant Thomas Carlyle Moore Jr	Private Charles W. Huber
15	Second Lieutenant Harold Gilbert Schlendering	Private Edward Oliver Smith

At about 0705 the Japanese fleet was sighted, and Major Henderson started a wide let-down circle from 9,000 feet (2,700m) with the intention of commencing the final attack by glide-bombing because the pilots were not deemed to have sufficient expertise in dive bombing, from an altitude of 4,000 feet (1,200m). He radioed to his team 'Attack two enemy CV on port bow'. Almost as soon as this manoeuvre commenced, however, and while still at 8,000 feet (2,400m) the SBDs were intercepted by defending Zeke fighters and, in addition, violent AA fire was received from the many adjacent surface vessels within range. Eyewitness to this was Captain Elmer Glidden, leader of the second section, who recalled: 'The first [Zero fighter] attacks were directed at the squadron leader in an attempt to put him out of action. After two passes one of the enemy put several shots through the plane of Major Henderson and his plane started to burn.'[6]

Henderson was, in fact, attacked by several defending Zekes and his aircraft was soon well ablaze. It was obvious that he was badly injured and out of action, so Captain Glidden took over and committed the squadron to the attack. The Japanese fighter attacks were very heavy, so the SBDs dived to the protection of a heavy cloud layer at 2,000 feet (600m) over one of the enemy carriers, and from that point completed the attack, the Dauntless releasing their bombs at altitudes that varied from 400 to 600 feet (120 to 180m). Even at this low altitude, the Japanese fighter attacks were persistent throughout, and each SBD was engaged by one or more Zekes long after their bombs had been dropped. The anti-aircraft fire over the Japanese ships at this point was reported as being 'of tremendous volume'.[7]

Second Lieutenant Robert Judy Bear, USMC (V), gave this graphic account in his Official Report.[8]

> After alarm, my SBD, Squadron No.7, was the last plane to take off from the field – approximately one minute after leaving the field, my gunner, Pfc Sidebottom, reported island under attack. Joined up on Captain Glidden. On contact, Major Henderson took over lead, circled squadron and also letting down. Meanwhile, enemy fighters were zooming all over the place, gave one fighter a 50cal burst just before Captain

---

6 *Henderson, Major Lofton: A Memoir,* Office of US Marine Corps, Washington DC. 17 June 1949.

7 ibid.

8 Bear, Second Lieutenant Robert J. – *Confidential - Statement,* dated 7 June 1942. Marine Aircraft Group Two Forty-One; San Francisco California.

> Glidden took our section through a cloud. Made dive broadside
> on a carrier; firing 50cal and releasing bomb. Zoomed along
> water right by battleship; after several minutes pulled up into
> small clouds and lost two enemy fighters on tail. Came back
> to field via Kure.

The surviving Marine Dauntless claimed to have scored two direct hits and
two close misses on the targeted carrier and this ship was observed to be
burning, with a large column of smoke issuing from it, as they withdrew at
masthead height. The plain truth was that the carrier attacked, *Hiryō*, did not
receive a single hit, and, although there were five near-misses, no damage
at all was done to the target, although the rear gunners, spraying the huge
ship as they passed over her, killed four Japanese flak gunners at their posts.
The Vindicators followed the Dauntless in but fared no better. One thing
that the surviving SBD aircrew agreed upon unanimously was that 'Glide
bombing is more hazardous than dive bombing in the absence of our own
protecting fighters'.[9]

Major Henderson had thought every aspect of his mission through in
a totally professional manner, and had even supervised the arming of his
squadron's aircraft; he had 'the fuse vanes of all the bombs carried by his
squadron screwed down about seventy turns out of a possible ninety turns,
thus, this, regardless of the extra hazard entailed, assuring the arming of
the bombs from a very low release altitude.'[10] Even this care and attention
to detail could not prevent heavy losses, and eight of the sixteen SBDs
failed to return to base and, of those that did, six were shot full of holes
and unserviceable. One machine, that piloted by Lieutenant Daniel Tore
Iverson Jr, had taken a total of 259 machine-gun hits, but still managed to
stagger home, landing on one wheel, such was the sturdiness of the Douglas
dive-bomber. Iverson was luckier than most on this occasion, because a
bullet had torn off his throat microphone without even nicking him![11]

---

9 ibid.

10 ibid.

11 Lieutenant Iverson continued to ride his luck in a tour of duty at Guadalcanal where
he also survived being wounded, but nemesis finally caught up with him on 23 January
1944 back home in the States when he, by then a Major, was killed in a mid-air collision
at NAS Vero Beach, Indian River, Florida, with an aircraft piloted by a tyro, Ensign
John VanBuren Nalls Jr. They were practising dive bombing when Nalls luffed up
directly beneath Iverson's aircraft, who could not see him and there was a conflagration
from which neither man survived. See *Miami Herald*, 24 January 1944.

Back at the MAG, all serviceable aircraft were placed on the usual alert condition, but no further air raids were received. One false alarm was occasioned by the arrival of twelve SBDs from *Hornet,* led by Lieutenant Commander Ruffin Johnson, that were short of fuel, of which more later.

Back with the American carriers, Fletcher had launched ten SBDs from VS-5 under Lieutenant Wallace Clark Short Jr from *Yorktown* at 0421 to make a search to the north over a 180-degree arc, just in case two Japanese carriers were lurking there. With a distance limitation of only 100 miles (160km) out these scouts were hardly likely to flush them out, had there had been any, at such a short distance.[12]

Scouting aircraft from the accompanying cruisers could have done the job better, and without the risk of revealing the presence of American carriers had they been sighted by the enemy but this option was expressly forbidden.[13] Radar-equipped PBYs from Midway could also have done the job despite the pre-dawn darkness. Moreover, Spruance had been ordered by Fletcher to conform to his movements, and therefore all three US carriers were consequently drawn away from the optimum ambush area centred around 'Point Luck', simply because *Yorktown,* having launched these aircraft, was subsequently thereby committed to their safe recovery later. This aerial scouting force was not finally landed back aboard *Yorktown* until 0830 where it was struck down, having, in Captain

---

12 The *Kido Butai* had begun launching *their* first striking force at 0426 and, within nineteen minutes, had despatched their first aircraft at 0445, and at 240 miles from Midway. With such a superior reach, had there indeed been any Japanese carriers north of *Yorktown* they would have found her long before she found them. Knowing also the composition of Nagumo's expected force, and that it only included eleven destroyers, there was no way that many escorts could have meaningfully protected two widely-separated groups of carriers and their accompanying heavy ships. Former codebreaker Michael Smith wrote that 'Fletcher had shown himself prone to ignoring intelligence provided by the Radio Intelligence Unit based on board the *Yorktown* and appeared to have totally failed to understand the potential and capabilities of tactical signals intelligence'. Smith, Michael. *The Emperor's Codes: Bletchley Park's Role in Breaking Japan's Secret Ciphers*, Bantam Press, London, 2000.

13 Ralph Wilhelm, a Curtiss SOC Seagull pilot aboard heavy cruiser *Portland*, told me, 'All four our SOC aircraft were always in full operational mode. The other heavy cruiser, *Astoria*, was the same as *Portland*. I did not fly on Thursday 4 June. We pilots were told we would not fly until early on Friday 5 June. We resumed our air operations the following morning.' Ralph Wilhelm to the Author, 25 March 2009.

Elliott Buckmaster's careful words 'Returned with Negative Results'.[14] Meanwhile, much had occurred.

At 0534 *Enterprise* took in Ady's further 0530 sighting report of 'Enemy carriers' but it was not until 0607 that Fletcher finally released *Enterprise* and *Hornet,* which were still at that time still complying with his earlier orders, enabling this pair to proceed towards a suitable attack position, while he continued to make his way to the recovery area of the aircraft returning from their abortive search mission. However, this 'release' signal included the proviso only to attack the enemy, 'as soon as definitely located'. Spruance duly complied but was now left with at least two hours' hard steaming to get within range of Nagumo, then some 200 miles distant, and the chance to hit the enemy with every available aircraft from all three US carriers, quickly, thus achieving maximum impact, which had been the optimum desire of all pre-war carrier attack planning, was seemingly lost.

Further signals were received by Spruance as he cranked the speed up to 25 knots, but he now had a lot more ground to cover to get within striking distance. His initial plan was to close the gap between himself and the *Kido Butai* to within 100 miles (160km) in order not to extend his air groups, but this would have resulted in allowing the Japanese a period of warning in which to prepare themselves. The limiting factor, apart from the enforced positional one, was the Douglas BT1 Devastator torpedo-bombers and Grumman F4F Wildcat fighters' maximum range, which was far less than that of the SBD. Instead, it was finally decided to launch at an estimated maximum range at 0700 and to then continue to steam hard so that the returning planes of the strikes would still be able to make the round trip safely. The final launch position was from 31 38' North, 176 04' West at 0906 (Zone +10 time which equated to 0706 Zone + 12 Midway Local Time.)[15] with an *estimated* distance of 155 miles to cover on a bearing of 239-240 degrees. In actuality the *Kido Butai* was 175 miles distant at this point and the American methods of launch and forming-up meant that in some cases a further three-quarters of an hour was lost before some sections of the groups took departure.[16]

---

14 *Report* Captain E Buckmaster to Admiral Chester Nimitz, dated 18 June 1942. CV5/AL6-3, (CCR/10-oah).

15 Log Report of Navigator of the destroyer *Alwin.*

16 VB-6 from *Enterprise* launched at 0906 [0706] and departed at 0930 [0730]. *Action Report VB-6* dated 10 June 1942. Others took much longer to get organized and the last departure was not until 0806. All the American carriers operated differently in contrast to the Japanese whose carriers acted in conjunction with each other.

THE DAUNTLESS IN BATTLE

The planned attack force from the *Enterprise* was to have included CEAG, Lieutenant Commander Clarence Wade McClusky Jr, with two accompanying aircraft, plus thirty-two SBDs from VB-6 and VS-6. From *Hornet* it was intended to despatch CHAG, Commander Stanhope Cotton Ring, with one accompanying SBD, and thirty-three Dauntless from VB-8 and VS-8. Of these seventy *assigned* SBDs, however, several failed to launch and others did not take part in the actual assault for various reasons. *Yorktown*, having recovered her scouts, followed on behind and did not commence her launch sequence until two hours later than the rest of the force. At the time this appeared a recipe for disaster – however, things turned out rather differently.

It was therefore about one-and-a-quarter hours later, from 1015 (Zone + 10) until 1050, that *Yorktown* launched her attack force. Even then it was a truncated one and, in the end, only VB-6 under Lieutenant Commander Maxwell Franklin Leslie launched with seventeen SBDS. En route to the target, however, the electrically-operated bomb release malfunctioned when the bombs were armed, and four aircraft (Leslie, Isaman, Lane and Merrill) lost their bombs right at the start. The other thirteen pilots were warned and armed their bombs manually. The *Yorktown* group was now four aircraft short but further reductions to her SBD strength had, unknown to Leslie, already taken place.

Wallace Short's VS-5 group, which, in the already agreed plan, was to have taken part in this strike, was, at the very last moment, held back by Fletcher. So last minute was Fletcher's order to retain Short's men aboard that even while Leslie was leading VB-3's attack he was still radioing to Short with target allocations in the belief that Short's force was still in position behind him as planned. Leslie radioed Short at 1015 'How about you taking the one to the left and I'll take the one on the right? I'm going to make an attack.' The one on the left was apparently *Hiryō* and Leslie went for *Sōryō* but, thanks to the last-minute change of plan of which he was told nothing, *Hiryō* escaped any attention for Short was still sitting on *Yorktown's* flight deck. Short and his companions sat there for three hours in a dejected group before ten of them were finally despatched on another reconnaissance sortie, ironically to try and find *Hiryō*, which, had they gone as planned, they might have already sunk or put out of action *before* she attacked *Yorktown*. The remaining seven of Short's misused orphans were struck down in the carrier's hangar.

52

The final configuration of the various SBD formations was as follows:

Table 11: Midway - USS *Enterprise* SBD Squadrons, June 1942		
Aircraft	**Pilot**	**Aircrew**
CEAG	Lieutenant Commander Clarence Wade McClusky Jr	ARM1c Walter George Chochalousek
S-8	Ensign William Robinson Pittman	AMM2c Floyd Delbert Adkins
S-11	Ensign Richard Alonzo Jaccard,	RM3c Porter William Pixley
S-1	Lieutenant William Earl Gallaher (CO)	ACRM (AA) Thomas Edward Merritt
S-2	Ensign Reid Wentworth Stone	RM1c William Hart Bergin
S-3	Ensign John Quincy Roberts	AOM1c Thurman Randolph Swindell
S-7	Lieutenant (j.g.) Norman Jack Kleiss	ARM3c John Warren Snowden
S-9	Ensign Eldor Ernst Rodenburg ***	Sea2c Thomas James Bruce
S-18	Ensign James Campbell Dexter	RM3c Donald Lee Hoff
S-10	Lieutenant Clarence Earle Dickinson Jr (XO)	ARM1c Joseph Ferdinand DeLuca
S-15	Ensign John Reginald McCarthy	ARM2c Earl Edward Howell
S-12	Ensign Carl David Pfeiffer	ARM3c Frederick Charles Jeck
S-16	Lieutenant (j.g.) John Norman West	ARM2c Alfred Robert Stitzelbergere
S-17	Ensign Vernon Larsen Micheel	RM3c John Dewey Dance
S-14	Ensign John Cady Lough	RM2c Louis Dale Hansen
S-4	Lieutenant Charles Rollins Ware (FO)	ARM1c William Henry Stambaugh
S-5	Ensign Frank Woodrow O'Flaherty	AMM1c Bruno Peter Gaido
S-6	Ensign James Arnold Shelton	RM3c David Bruce Craig
S-13	Lieutenant Frank Anthony Patriarca +++	ACRM(AA) Jack Richard Badgley

Spare		
Aircraft	**Pilot**	**Aircrew**
	Ensign Clarence Earl Vammen Jr	AMM2c Milton Wayne Clarke
B-1	Lieutenant Richard Halsey Best (CO)	ACRM (PA) James Frances Murray
B-2	Lieutenant (j.g.) Edwin John Kroeger	RM3c Gail Wayne Halterman
B-3	Ensign Frederick Thomas Weber	AOM3c Ernest Lenard Hilbert
B-5	Lieutenant (j.g.) Wilbur Edison Roberts	AMM1c William Burr Steinman
B-6	Ensign Delbert Wayne Halsey	RM3c Jay William Jenkins
B-7	Lieutenant Joseph Robert Penland (FO)	ARM2c Harold French Heard
B-8	Ensign Anthony Frederick Schneider. %%%	ARM2c Glenn Lester Holden
B-9	Ensign Eugene Allen Greene	RM3c Samuel Andrew Muntean
B-11	Ensign Thomas Wesley Ramsay	ARM2c Sherman Lee Duncan
B-12	Ensign Lewis Alexander Hopkins	RM3c Edward Rutledge Anderson
B-13	Lieutenant (j.g.) John James Van Buren	ARM1c Harold William Nelson Jr
B-14	Ensign Norman Francis Vandivier	Sea1c Lee Edward John Keaney
B-15	Ensign George Hale Goldsmith	ARM3c James William Patterson Jr
B-16	Lieutenant (j.g.) Edward Lee Anderson	ARM2c Stuart James Mason Jr
B-18	Ensign Bertram Stetson Varian Jr	ARM3c Charles Robert Young
B-4	Lieutenant Lloyd Adison Smith @@@	AMM1c Herman Hull Caruthers
B-10	Lieutenant Harvey Peter Lanham @@@	ARM1c Edward Joseph Garaudy

B-17	Ensign Arthur Leo Rausch @@@	AOM2c Harold Llewellyn Jones
	Ensign Stephen Clement Hogan Jr	Sea1c Eugene K. Braun
	Ensign Harry Warren Liffner	AMM3c Milo Lavern Kimberlin
	Ensign Don Lelo Ely	Sea2c George Henry Arnold

*** Aborted the mission.
+++ Non-starter
%%% Ran out of fuel before sighting enemy and ditched
@@@ Not launched

Table 12: Midway - USS *Hornet* SBD Squadrons, June 1942		
Aircraft	**Pilot**	**Aircrew**
CHAG	Commander Stanhope Cotton Ring	ARM2c Arthur Middleton Parker
VS-8	Lieutenant Commander Walter Fred Rodee (CO)	ACRM (PA) John Lenzy Clanton
VS-8	Lieutenant William John Widhelm (XO)	ARM1c George David Stokely
VS-8	Lieutenant Raymond Davis (FO)	ARM1c Ralph Phillips
VS-8	Lieutenant Edgar Erwin Stebbins (EO)	ARM2c Ervin Ross Hillhouse
VS-8	Lieutenant Benjamin Eugene Moore Jr (PO)	ARM2c Richard Cusack McEwen
VS-8	Lieutenant Laurens Adin Whitney (MO)	ARM2c Angus D. Gilles
VS-8	Lieutenant Orman Griffith Sexton III (GO)	ARM2c William Lee Payne
VS-8	Lieutenant (j.g.) James McMillan Forbes	ARM3c Ronald Wintergarden Arenth
VS-8	Lieutenant (j.g.) Ralph Bernard Hovind	ARM3c Charles Benjamin Lufburrow
VS-8	Lieutenant (j.g.) Donald Kirkpatrick Jr	ARM2c Harmon Librand Brendle
VS-8	Lieutenant (j.g.) Albert Harold Wood	ARM2c Richard Thomas Woodson

Aircraft	Pilot	Aircrew
VS-8	Ensign Philip James Rusk (NO)	ARM3c John Louis Tereskerz
VS-8	Ensign Stanley Robert Holm	ARM2c John H. Honeycutt
VS-8	Ensign Benjamin Tappan Jr	ARM2c James H. Black Jr
VS-8	Ensign Paul Edmond Tepas	ARM3c Earnest Raymond Johnston
VS-8	Ensign Helmuth Ernest Hoerner	ARM3c Moley Johnson Boutwell
VS-8	Ensign William Edwin Woodman	ARM3c David Terry Manus
VS-8	Ensign Harold Hunter White	ARM2c Gerald A. McAfee
VS-8	Ensign Augustus Appleby Devoe Jr.	ARM3c John Stephen Urban
VB-8	Lieutenant Commander Robert Ruffin Johnson (CO)	ACRM Joseph Grady McCoy
VB-8	Ensign William Douglas Carter	ARM2c Oral Lester Moore
VB-8	Ensign Philip Farnsworth Grant	ARM2c Robert Hougo Rider
VB-8	Lieutenant James Everett Vose Jr (FO)	ARM2c Joseph Yewonishon
VB-8	Ensign Roy Phillip Gee	ARM1c Donald L. Canfield
VB-8	Ensign Joseph Wiley King	ARM3c Thomas M. Walsh
VB-8	Lieutenant (j.g.) Frederick Leeson Bates (EO)	ARM1c Clyde S. Montesen
VB-8	Ensign Artur Caldwell Cason Jr	ARM3c Alfred D. Wells
VB-8	Ensign Clayton Evan Fisher	ARM3c George Edward Ferguson
VB-8	Lieutenant Alfred Bland Tucker III (XO)	ARM1c Champ Terry Stuart
VB-8	Ensign Gus George Bebas	RM3c Alfred William Ringressy Jr.
VB-8	Ensign Donald Dee Adams	ARM2c John B. Broughton Jr
VB-8	Lieutenant John Joseph Lynch (MO)	ARM1c Wilbur L. Woods
VB-8	Lieutenant James Austin Riner Jr	ARM2c Floyd Dell Kilmer
VB-8	Ensign Troy Tilman Guillory	ARM2c Billy Rex Cottrell

VB-8	Ensign Kenneth Broughton White (GO)	ARM3c Leroy Quillen
VB-8	Ensign Thomas Junior Wood (PO)	ARM3c George Francis Martz
VB-8	Ensign Forrester Clinton Auman	ARM3c Samuel P. McLean
Spare		
	Lieutenant George Warren Ellenborg	ARM3c Barkley Vaughn Poorman
	Ensign Frank Earl Christofferson (NO)	ARM3c William H. Berthold
	Ensign Donald Thomas Griswald	ARM1c Kenneth Cecil Bunch
	Ensign James Clark Barrett	ARM1c Elmer Edwin Jackson
	Ensign Henry John Nickerson	ARM1c Clarence C. Kilney
	Ensign Robert Pershing Friez	Sea1c George Ladanyi Nickey Jr ^

^ Removed from flying status prior to battle.

Table 13: Midway - USS *Yorktown* SBD Squadrons, June 1942		
Aircraft	**Pilot**	**Aircrew**
CYAG	Lieutenant Commander Oscar Pederson	Did not fly the mission.
B-1	Lieutenant Commander Maxwell Franklin Leslie ^^	ARM1c Wilmer Earl Gallagher
B-2	Lieutenant (j.g.) Paul Algodte Holmberg (ADO)	AMM2c George Albert La Plant
B-3	Ensign Paul Wahl Schlegel	ARM3c Jack Alvan Shropshire
B-4	Ensign Robert Keith Campbell (GO)	AMM1c Horace Henry Craig
B-5	Ensign Aldon Wilbur Hansen	ARM3c Joseph Vernon Godfrey
B-6	Ensign Robert Haines Benson	ARM3c Frederick Paul Bergeron
B-7	Lieutenant (j.g.) Gordon Alvin Sherwood (EO)	ARM2c Harmon Donald Bennett
B-8	Ensign Roy Maurice Isaman	ARM3c Sidney Kay Weaver
B-9	Ensign Phillip Walker Cobb ^^	ARM2c Clarence Eugene Zimmershead

Aircraft	Pilot	Aircrew
B-10	Lieutenant Harold Sydney Bottomley Jr (FO)	AMM2c David Frederick Johnson
B-11	Ensign Charles Smith Lane	ARM2c Jack Charles Henning
B-12	Ensign John Clarence Butler	ARM3c David Donald Berg
B-13	Lieutenant DeWitt Wood Shumway (XO)	ARM1c Ray Edgar Coons
B-14	Ensign Robert Martin Elder	RM3c Leslie Alan Till
B-15	Ensign Bunyon Randolph Cooner	AOM2c Clifton Raymond Bassett
B-16	Lieutenant (j.g.) Osborne Beeman Wiseman (PO)	ARM3c Grant Ulysses Dawn
B-17	Ensign Milford Austin Merrill ^^	ARM3c Dallas Joseph Bergeron
Spares		
	Ensign Jack Rugen	AOM1c Charles C. Brassel
	Ensign Raymond Morrow Reynolds	ARM2c Charles Westbrook Albright
		ARM3c Duane John Chafee
		ARM3c Theodore Schevon
		AMM3c William Robert Anderson

^^ Faulty bomb-release switches, premature drops shortly after take off.

Table 14: Midway - Reserve Force held back by Fletcher aboard *Yorktown*, 4 June		
Aircraft	Pilot	Aircrew
S-1	Lieutenant Wallace Clark Short Jr (CO	ACRM (PA) John Warren Trott
S-2	Lieutenant Harlan Rockey Dickson	ARM2c Joseph Michael Lynch Jr
S-3	Ensign Carl Herman Horenburger	ARM3c Lynn Raymond Forshee
S-4	Lieutenant (j.g.) Nels Luther Alvin Berger	ACRM (PA) Otto Russell Phelps
S-5	Ensign Leif Walther Larsen	ARM3c John F. Gardner

S-6	Ensign John David Bridgers	ARM3c William Johnson
S-7	Lieutenant Samuel Adams	ARM1c Joseph John Karrol
S-8	Lieutenant (j.g.) David Render Berry	ARM2c Earnest Alewyn Clegg
S-9	Ensign John Neville Ammen Jr	ARM3c John Michael Iacovazzi
S-10	Lieutenant (j.g.) Charles Neal Conatser	ARM2c Henry P. McGowan Jr
S-11	Ensign Benjamin Gifford Preston	ARM1c Harold R. Cowden
S-12	Ensign Robert Douglas Gibson	ARM3c Wilburn Dayton Harp
S-13	Lieutenant (j.g.) William Francis Christie	ARM1c Alvin Arthur Sobel
S-14	Lieutenant (j.g.) Henry Martin McDowell	ARM2c Eugene Clay Strickland
S-15	Ensign Liston Rhodes Comer Jr	ARM3c Harold Joseph Wilger+
S-16	Lieutenant Johnn Ludwig Nielsen	ACRNM (PA) Walter Dean Straub
S-17	Lieutenant (j.g.) Raymond Phillip Kline	ARM3c Norbert Anthony Fives
S-18	Ensign Richard Frederick Wolfe	ARM3c Leon L. Getz
Spares		
	Ensign Gerald Sylvester Richey	ACRM(AA) Otto Russell Phelps
	Ensign Raymond Miligi Jr	AAM3c William Ripley Mohler
	Ensign Elmer Andrew Conzett	Sea1c Gerald E. Hollingsworth

+ On loan from VS-5.

This was not the only lack of cohesion, for many of the squadrons lost contact with one another and, instead of combined attacks, many units made their own way to the target and, if they were lucky, out again. The *Hornet* dive-bombers failed to make contact at all[17], and the *Enterprise* dive-bombers were also extremely fortunate in finding their targets. All were at the extreme

---

17 This has led to much wild speculation and even conspiracy theories beyond all imagining, all with very little actual verifiable and accountable truth attached to them, see Appendix One.

limits of their fuel resources and several never made it back for that reason. The three torpedo-bomber squadrons took horrendous losses for often the Japanese defending fighters tended to concentrate on them due to the slow speed, inability to take avoiding action while concentrating on their attacks and because they felt them the greater threat. Fortunately for the Americans, those Dauntless that *did* arrive over the Nagumo force, and had bombs to use, found their foe at the ideal moment for dive-bombing success.

As with everything to do with the Midway battle there is continuing claim and counter-claim as to whether the four Japanese carriers had their air groups up on the decks ready to go at the time the SBDs found them, or whether they were mostly struck down in the hangars where they were being re-armed. Those carriers which had despatched Nakajima B5N Kates to Midway in their level bombing configuration were to have been re-armed for a second strike, as Nagumo ignored Yamamoto's cautionary warning about being caught unawares by US carriers appearing unexpectedly on his flank. On receiving reports that that was exactly the case, Nagumo determined on unloading those that had been bombed-up and re-equipping them with torpedoes to use against the American carriers in a classical combined attack. Those carriers who had contributed only Aichi D3A2 dive-bombers to the Midway strike had been sent with HE (high explosive) bombs for use against land targets and might require re-arming with (AP) armour piercing bombs to tackle warships. Carrier Division Two's commanding officer, Rear Admiral Tamon Yamaguchi, aboard *Hiryō*, with the dive-bombing expert Takashige Egusa on his team, was eager to send his aircraft off with whatever they had as long as they went, but he was overruled.

What can be fairly certain is that considerable confusion and turmoil reigned in the *Kido Butai* as their time finally ran out. By good fortune McClusky had turned north at 0930 when he reached the end of his search, while Ring had turned south toward Midway to find the enemy. By a bizarre series of events, at 0955 McClusky sighted the Japanese destroyer *Arashi* steaming at high speed to catch up with the Nagumo force after making a submarine hunt, and this vessel unwittingly led VS-6 and VB-6 straight and unerringly to their elusive target. Almost simultaneously Short's attenuated Dauntless force arrived in the same area, so all the SBDs were able to make their attacks at roughly the same time, 1000, and swamped the Japanese combat air patrol.

The Dauntless attacked, not without some confusion in target allocation, the three visible Japanese carriers, *Akagi, Kaga* and *Sōryō*, (*Hiryō*, as we have seen, was not attacked and, added to the unexpected shortfall in *Yorktown's* contribution; she also had the temporary fortune to be out of station due to the complicated manoeuvres carried out during the various torpedo-bomber attacks). Which unit attacked which carrier is also still vehemently disputed, but the result is not. In total forty-six Dauntless commenced their attack dives on *Kido Butai* targets – although of course four of them did so without bombs aboard. Two of McClusky's VS-6 aircraft, one piloted by Ensign Eldor Rodenburg, had turned back earlier on in the mission with engine problems and Lieutenant Frank Anthony Patriarca would not start. In addition, Ensign Tony Frederick Schneider from VB-6 ran out of fuel and had to ditch in sight of the enemy fleet. Some thirty-eight bombs were aimed at the three visible carriers, nine resulting in direct hits. Not all the SBDs chose the carriers as their targets: Lieutenant Osborne Beeman Wiseman and Ensigns John Clarence Butler both attacked a battleship, thought to be *Haruna*, but failed to score a hit; and Ensign Robert Martin Elder and Bunyon Randolph Cooner attacked a destroyer on the screen, but again with no success.

Akagi was made the target for twenty of the Dauntless assaults, and was hit twice: one bomb struck the edge of the centre lift, penetrated down the lift-shaft and exploded among the many bombs and torpedoes which the ordnance crews had been in the process of changing around in those confined spaces. The second hit detonated on her port quarter aft amidst parked bombers, and their fuel tanks ignited, which in turn set off their bombs and torpedoes in a chain effect of explosions. Huge fires spread rapidly, and although some were quenched by the indefatigable efforts of her fire-fighting teams, others raged on and gradually spread along her deck, igniting further aircraft and causing widespread devastation to her bridge structure. These fires raged internally all day, gradually wiping out engine and boiler rooms and their staffs, and then spreading with renewed fury as magazines blew up. With 221 officers and men dead, the survivors eventually abandoned ship and she was finally sunk by torpedoes from the escorting destroyers at 0500 the next morning. Her captain, Captain Aoki Taijire, elected to go down with his ship but was ordered off by his superior and survived.

Kaga was taken under attack by nine SBDs, these achieving no fewer than four direct hits on her, despite her barrage and a hard turn to starboard. The first hit aft, to starboard, again right amidst her parked dive- and torpedo-bombers and killing most of their aircrew as they sat. The second bomb hit close by the forward lift, blowing all the windows out of her bridge and setting off explosions among the bombs and torpedoes. The third bomb also detonated forward on the flight deck just in front of her bridge among the aircraft standing there, scything down most of those on the bridge and killing her captain, Captain Okada Jisaku, instantly. The fourth hit in the exact centre of the flight deck and punched down into her innards before exploding in her hangar deck and causing huge fires there among her fighter aircraft. Again, despite heroic the efforts of her crew, the fires raged out of control with many of the pumps destroyed; by evening there remained no hope of saving her and, at 1925, the forward fuel tanks blew up with two enormous detonations and she sank, taking with her all her surviving aircraft and some 800 of her crew.

The *Sōryō* was attacked by thirteen SBDs which, without loss to themselves, hit her three times. The Dauntless had again caught her with a deck-load of aircraft, with others refuelling and re-arming on her hangar decks. The first bomb hit amidships, just forward of her centre aircraft elevator, penetrating down to the hangar deck before exploding; the resulting blast threw her forward lift right up out of its well and against the front of her bridge. The second direct hit was almost in the same position as the first, but to port, among her massed air strike on deck; again, fireballs of fuel, bombs and other ammunitions, combusted in one lethal blast.

The third bomb struck on the port side further back, close to her after lift, and likewise drove on down into the lower decks. Again, the explosion chain-reacted through the great vessel's innards, wrecking engines and steering. The first bomb had hit at 1025 and by 1040 she was dead in the water, fiercely ablaze from end to end, with 'Abandon Ship' being ordered five minutes later. She burnt all day with spasmodic explosions, and, at 1915, slid under the waves, her boilers exploding as she went down, taking with her the captain, Captain Yanaginoto Ryūsako, and 717 members of her crew and aircrew.

The fact that they had failed to stop the SBDs destroying their home carriers gave added spleen to the defending Japanese Zeros to make amends on the retiring dive-bombers while they could, and eighteen Dauntless were lost in this mission.

Five of *Hornet*'s VS-8 made it back to their carrier, including Ring himself who flew back alone, Ensign Clayton Evan Fisher, likewise, and three others, while most of the remainder made their way to Midway Island to refuel. Some did not make it, but most did and eventually rejoined their carrier. VB-3 escaped unscathed but had to witness the dive-bombing of *Hornet* by Japanese Vals, and were forced to land instead aboard *Enterprise*, where, unfortunately, there was now plenty of space for them.

This event made it apparent that there was still at least one Japanese carrier still afloat and indeed these attacks were mounted from the *Hiryō*. Accordingly, a second strike was launched by the Americans in order to eliminate this final threat from the air. Ten SBDs from VS-5 were finally unleashed to conduct a search on a 200-mile (320km) leg to the north-west, and, at 1445, one of these scouts, piloted by Lieutenant Samuel Adams, located the lone Japanese carrier 110 miles (177km) out, and reported her to be steering north at 15 knots in company with two battleships, *Haruna* and *Kirishima,* the heavy cruisers *Chikuma* and *Tone* and four destroyers.[18]

The plucky *Hiryō* had managed to get in a second strike at *Yorktown* in the interval, which further damaged her,[19] but now her time had come. Another striking force was sent off at 1530 under the command of Lieutenant William Earl Gallaher of VS-6, with six aircraft, and VB-6, led again by Lieutenant Richard Halsey Best. Even this force, with only eleven SBDs between them, was soon reduced to just ten, when one was forced to abort the mission. However, there were fourteen more Dauntless on their way from VB-3, led by Lieutenant DeWitte Wood Shumway, to make up the numbers. It deserves to be recorded that only one aircrew on this second attack had *not* flown and survived the morning attacks.

These two-dozen Dauntless climbed to 13,500 feet (4,100m) and headed out, and, at 1630 *Hornet* launched her own second-strike force, Lieutenant Edgar Erwin Stebbins heading up a sixteen-plane strike from VB-8.

Table 15: Midway – Second SBD strikes against *Hiryū*, 4 June 1942		
Enterprise		
Aircraft	**Pilot**	**Aircrew**
S-1	Lieutenant Wilmer Earl Gallaher	ACRM(AA) Thomas Edward Merritt
S-2	Ensign Reid Wentworth Stone	RM1c William Hart Bergin
S-11	Ensign Richard Alonzo Jaccard	RM3c Porter William Pixley
S-7	Lieutenant (j.g.) Norman Jack Kleiss	ARM3c John Warren Snowden
S-17	Ensign Vernon Larsen Micheel	RM3c John Dewey Dance
S-18*	Ensign James Campbell Dexter	RM3c Donald Lee Hoff

18 In fact the light cruiser *Nagara,* to which Nagumo had shifted his flag, was seemingly mistaken by Adams for a heavy cruiser, and there was a total of eleven other destroyers with the force.

19 According to one source, the best thing she could have done was fled; that would have saved *Yorktown* of course, which can explain its appeal to American students of the battle, but such a course was not a serious option for a Japanese commander.

THE DAUNTLESS IN BATTLE

Aircraft	Pilot	Aircrew
S-13*	Lieutenant (j.g.) John Norman West	ARM2c Albert Robert Stitzelberger
B-1	Lieutenant Richard Halsey Best	ACRM (PA) James Francis Murray
B-2	Lieutenant (j.g.) Edwin John Kroeger	RM3c Gail Wayne Halterman
B-3	Ensign Frederick Thomas Weber	AOM3c Ernest Lenard Hilbert
B-12	Ensign Stephen Clement Hogan Jr ++	Sea1c Eugene K. Braun
B-13	Lieutenant DeWitt Wood Shumway	ARM1c Ray Edgar Coons
B-15	Ensign Bunyon Randolph Cooner	AOM2c Clifton Raymond Bassett
B-3	Ensign Paul Wahl Schlegel	ARM3c Jack Alvan Shropshire
B-16	Lieutenant (j.g.) Osborne Beeman Wiseman	ARM3c Grant Ulysses Dawn
B-17	Ensign Milford Austin Merrill	ARM3c Dallas Joseph Bergeron
B-12	Ensign Stephen Clement Hogan Jr (VB-6)	Sea1c Eugene K. Braun
B-17	Lieutenant (j.g.) Gordon Alvin Sherwood	ARM2c Harman Donald Bennett
B-8	Ensign Roy Maurice Isaman	ARM3c Sidney Kay Weaver
B-9	Ensign Phillip Walker Cobb	ARM2c Clarence Eugene Zimmershead
B-10	Lieutenant Harold Sydney Bottomley Jr	AMM2c David Frederick Johnson
B-11	Ensign Charles Smith Lane	ARM2c Jack Charles Henning
B-12	Ensign John Clarence Butler	ARM3c David Donald Berg
B-4	Ensign Robert Keith Campbell	AMM1c Horace Henry Craig
B-5	Ensign Alden Wilbur Hanson	ARM3c Joseph Vernon Godfrey
B-6	Ensign Robert Haines Benson	ARM3c Frederick Paul Bergereon
Hornet		
VS-8	Lieutenant Edgard Erwin Stebbins	ARM2c Ervin R. Hillhouse
VS-8	Lieutenant Benjamin Eugene Moore Jr	ARM2c Richard Cusack McEwen

VS-8	Lieutenant Orman Griffith G Sexton III	ARM2c William L. Payne
VS-8	Lieutenant (j.g.) Albert Harold Wood	ARM2c Richard Thomas Woodson ^^
VS-8	Lieutenant (j.g.) Ivan Lee Swope	ARM2c Harmon L. Brendle
VS-8	Ensign Phillip James Rusk $$$	ARM2c John H. Honeycutt
VS-8	Helmuth Ernest Hoerner	ARM3c David T. Manus
VS-8	Ensign Harold White	ARM3c John Stephen Urban
VS-8	Ensign William E. Woodman	ARM2c Gerald A. McAffe
VB-8	Lieutenant (j.g.) Frederick Leeson Bates	ARM1c Clyde S. Montensen
VB-8	Ensign Henry John Nickerson	ARM1c Elmer Edwin Jackson
VB-8	Ensign Roy Philp Gee	ARM1c Donald L. Canfield
VB-8	Ensign Kenneth Broughton White	ARM3c Leroy Quillen
VB-8	Robert Pershing Friez	ARM1c Clarence Courtland Kilney
VB-8	Ensign James Clark Barrett	ARM3c William H. Berthold
VB-8	Ensign Clayton Evan Fisher	ARM3c George E. Ferguson

*Hangar Deck – Not launched.
++ Flew with VB-3
^^ Volunteered to replace ARM3c John Lewis Tereskerz who was unavailable to fly,
$$$ Aborted and recovered.

The *Enterprise* aircraft found their target at 1650 and found only six defending Zero fighters above her for protection. The exhausted surviving Japanese bomber crews were having a hasty meal before being despatched on yet a third strike. Climbing to 19,000 feet (5,800m) the dive-bombers circled *Hiryō* and Gallaher split his force, with the *Enterprise* group ordered to plummet down on the carrier, while the *Yorktown* flyers were assigned the battleships as targets although, in the event, many found the open flight deck of the Japanese flat-top irresistible, and all save two, Ensign Robert Keith Campbell and Robert Haines Benson, who dive-bombed the *Haruna* without success, concentrated almost exclusively on *Hiryō*.

The defending Zekes attacked the SBDs during the dive and most bravely pursued them down into their own flak.[20] They destroyed Ensign Frederick Thomas Weber's Dauntless and there were no survivors, and thus, combined with a hard turn by the carrier, this attack initially resulted in no hits being made, despite the apparent surprise achieved.

The Dauntless of VB-6, arrowing in behind VS-6, suffered from similar attention, losing the aircraft of Lieutenant (j.g.) Osbourne Beeman Wiseman and Ensign John Clarence Butler; however, they managed to score four direct hits in very quick succession on *Hiryō* which ripped open her flight deck, spelling the doom of the vessel. The first hit was directly on the forward lift, and again it was flung up against the ship's bridge structure. Then two more bombs landed amidships, while the last landed forward of the island structure again. As before, fires broke out and were freely stoked by detonating bombs and torpedoes being made ready for the next sortie. Her fate seemed to be assured, so much so that, when the *Hornet's* air group arrived on the scene at 1730, Lieutenant Stebbins directed their attacks at the alternative target of the battleship *Haruna*, but her heavy anti-aircraft barrage was sufficient to put them off aim and again the elderly lady emerged totally unscathed from this attack.

Aboard the stricken *Hiryō* there were no longer many aircraft aboard to further inflame the blaze as had happened with her compatriots, and none of the bombs that hit her had penetrated deeply enough initially to affect her engines, so she still proved capable of steaming at 30 knots, an incredible achievement. Hopes were high that she might yet be saved, but gradually the fires spread, the engine room staff were trapped and died, and the carrier began to list and sink. Finally, she was abandoned and torpedoed by one of her escorts, although she did not sink completely until the following morning. With her into the depth went 416 of her crew and all her surviving aircraft. Both Rear Admiral Tamon Yamaguchi and Captain Tomeo Kaku elected to die with their ship.[21]

---

20 These brave Japanese pilots were described in some Stateside accounts as German Messerschmitt Bf 109s, as if it were still not thought possible that Japanese flyers could fly or fight so well – Xenophobia taken to extremes! Later some American aircrew stated 'we were told to expect Messerschmitts, so that is what we reported' – never mind that the Bf 109 had an in-line engine and not a radial and presented a totally different profile to the Zero. See Bryan, Lieutenant Commander Joseph, USNR, and Reed, Philip, *Mission Beyond Darkness*, Duell, Sloan and Pearce, New York, 1945, among sources others peddling this myth.

21 Another myth is that because of this battle the elite personnel of the IJN's Aviation aircrew were destroyed. In fact, under 25 per cent of these key men died at Midway, most of them from *Hiryō*, but all four supporting maintenance teams suffered heavily.

Meanwhile, at 1700 back at Midway Island, Captain Simard received a report of enemy carriers on fire bearing 320 degrees, distance 180 miles (290km) and asked that VMSB deliver an attack. Major Benjamin White Norris, onto whom command had devolved, was consulted and he stated that he and his officers would prefer a night attack since the target would be illuminated by her own flames and since the Zero fighters would not then be active. This plan was duly approved. In an effort to get all possible Marine Corps aircraft armed and into the air the flight was delayed until 1905, at which time Norris, with five SB2Us and Captain Marshall Alvin Tyler, with six SBDs, took off for their objective.

Table 16: USMC Night Sortie – SBD Section, 4 June 1942	
Pilot	**Aircrew**
Captain Marshall Alvin Tyler	Sergeant Robert Ackelson Underwood
Second Lieutenant Robert Wesley Vaupell	Sergeant Carl T.M. Hickman
Captain Armond Hector DeLalio	Private Reed Thomas Ramsey
Captain Elmer George Glidden Jr	Private Arlow A. Johnson
Second Lieutenant Robert Judy Bear	Private Truell Larkin Sidebottom
First Lieutenant Daniel Tore Iverson Jr	Private Wallace Jordan Reid

The mission was a tragic failure. The night was pitch black, the target could not be found and only the six Dauntless returned on schedule at 2200 without having sighting their objective. Worse, Norris himself flew into the water on the return leg and he and his gunner were lost.

The destruction of four carriers was not the end of the Japanese casualties in this epic encounter. The 7th Cruiser Division, commanded by Vice Admiral Takeo Kurita, with four heavy cruisers *Kumano, Suzuya, Mikuma* and *Mogami,* escorted by a pair of destroyers, *Asashio* and *Arashio*, was en route to conduct a bombardment of the Midway defences when they were recalled. While reforming they caught a glimpse of an American submarine, the *Tambor*, and made a violent turn of the line to avoid any torpedoes that might have been fired at them. In doing so, the two rear cruisers collided and *Mogami* was heavily damaged, *Mikuma* less so. Nonetheless, they were only then some eighty miles (125km) from Midway when the two undamaged ships sped off and left the other two ships, along with the destroyers, to follow on as best they might. Clearly the two damaged ships were in grave danger once daylight came. As they struggled back to the west they were pounded by air strike after air strike which compounded their already extensive damage. Normally very tough targets, with high speed and heavy anti-aircraft defences, these two ships were reduced to easy target practice for the Dauntless flyers, both for the Marine flyers ashore and the US carriers.

At around 0525 on 5 June, orders were received from Captain Simard to attack two enemy vessels, invariably misreported as 'battleships', one already crippled, on a bearing of 268 degrees, distance 140 miles (225km). At 0700 therefore Captain Marshall Alvin Tyler, with his six available SBDs and Captain Richard Eugene Fleming with six Vindicators, all carrying 500lb (227lb) bombs, executed this mission.

Table 17: USMC SBD attack on Cruiser Force, 5 June 1942	
Pilot	Aircrew
Captain Marshall Alvin Tyler	Sergeant Robert Ackelson Underwood
Captain Armand Hector DeLalio	Private Reed Thomas Ramsey
Second Lieutenant Robert Wesley Vaupell	Sergeant Carl T.M. Hickman
Captain Elmer George Glidden Jr	Private Arlow A. Johnson
First Lieutenant Daniel Tore Iverson Jr	Private Wallace Jordan Reid
Second Lieutenant Robert Judy Bear	Private Truell Larkin Sidebottom

Tracking *Mogami* from, the fifty-mile (80km) long oil slick that she trailed behind her, the dive-bombers were quickly in sight of the Japanese force. Arriving over the target ships at 0805, they attacked. Captain Marshall Alvin Tyler, the third commanding officer of VMSB-241 in little over twenty-four hours, planned for the Dauntless to make a dive-bombing attack from 10,000 feet (3,000m) while the Vindicators glide-bombed from 4,000 feet (1,200m). The Dauntless group attacked first and both sections were met by heavy and accurate AA fire. They claimed to have bracketed the heavy cruiser with all six bombs and to have scored one direct hit, but this proved not to have been the case. The Vindicators attacked *Mikuma* and Captain Fleming's aircraft was instantly hit and crashed, burning, into the sea.[22]

---

22 It was claimed at the time that Fleming steered his doomed bomber right into *Mikuma*'s No. 4 gun turret and that the remains of the Vindicator were visible in photographs taken later. It has, however, been more recently verified by American eyewitness reports at the time, that Fleming's aircraft went into the sea, and that the debris seen atop that turret resulted from a later explosion when her torpedo-tubes carrying her so-called 'Long Lance' weapons detonated.

At 12 knots the little Japanese detachment struggled onward which gave further SBD attacks the chance to inflict yet more pain and injury in the hours that followed. At 1543 the US carriers launched a striking force tasked with finding and striking any of the Japanese carriers still afloat. *Enterprise* sent out thirty-two SBDs and *Hornet* contributed a further twenty-six Dauntless to this task. Not surprisingly, they found the ocean devoid of such targets and were returning to their carriers empty-handed when, at 1820, they sighted a solitary Japanese destroyer heading west. This proved to be *Tanikaze*, which had been despatched to ascertain whether *Hiryō* was still afloat or not and was returning from this dangerous mission.

This one small destroyer showed just what could be achieved in the face of overwhelming air attack. *Tanikaze* had already been attacked twice that day, each time by high altitude B-17s, and had dodged all seventy-nine bombs on her with ease, even damaging one of the big four-engine bombers so that it later crashed. Now she was the subject of the concentrated fury of fifty-eight dive-bombers. In theory she should have been totally overwhelmed. In practice her captain, Commander Motomi Katsumi, conned her through this mass assault with skill and aplomb. The only damage was the result of a near miss which put a splinter in her No.3 gun mounting, killing six of its occupants but, in return, her accurate gunnery brought down Lieutenant Samuel Adams' aircraft, which was lost with both crew members. The rather chastened Dauntless aircrew returned to their carriers claiming that the near miss was 'a possible hit' on a 'light cruiser', both assumptions being false.

The crippled heavy cruisers presented Spruance with a less elusive and agile and more worthwhile target (they were still being reported as 'battleships'), and so the American carriers moved westward overnight and launched eighteen scouts at 0502 on 6 June to make a 200-mile-range search to locate them. Two reports were received and then an *Enterprise* SBD, piloted by Ensign William Douglas Carter, transmitted a third sighting, at 0645, some 150 miles out from base. Carter's radio-operator, ARM2c John Arthur Moore, erroneously reported 'One CV' instead of 'One CB' (CB = Battle Cruiser or, in USN terms – 'Cruiser Big'), which caused a flap when it was received. Both *Hornet* and *Enterprise* were ordered to launch maximum available attacks, which they did in three waves, with strong fighter escort, in case this report was genuine.[23] Fletcher had scorned

---

23 This error was corrected by Carter in a 'message drop' on his returned to his carrier and naturally also further amplified verbally when he finally landed aboard. *Enterprise* notified *Hornet*, whose own air group was already on its way. This information was duly radioed to Ring telling him the target was probably not a carrier after all, but a battleship! Of course, it was neither, and this only served to confuse matters further!

the use of cruiser-based float-planes in his abortive search on the 4th, but Spruance had no such qualms on the 6th, and two Curtiss SOC Seagulls from the heavy cruiser *New Orleans* took up the watch on the enemy group, accurately guiding in the attack groups.

The first wave included twenty-six Dauntless, led by Commander Stanhope Cotton Ring, from *Hornet*, which set off at 0800. These SBDs included eleven VB-8 aircraft led by Lieutenant Commander Robert Ruffin Johnson and twelve from VS-8 under Lieutenant Commander Walter Fred Rodee. This squadron also incorporated two *Enterprise* 'strays', one from William Christie of VS-5 and the other from Ensign Clarence Vammen Jr, of VS-6, who were ordered to rejoin their carrier after the attack had been carried out.

Table 18		
Table 18: Midway - First SBD Strike from *Hornet*, 6 June		
Squadron	**Pilot**	**Aircrew**
CHAG	Commander Stanhope Cotton Ring	ARM2c Arthur Middleton Parker
VB-8 1st Section		
VB-8	Lieutenant William John Widhelm	ARM1c George David Stokely
VB-8	Ensign Donald Kirkpatrick	ARM2c Richard Thomas Woodson
VB-8	Ensign Donald Thomas Griswold * KIA	ARM1c Kenneth Cecil Bunch * KIA
VS-5	Lieutenant (j.g.) William Francis Christie	ARM1c Alvin Arthur Sobel
VB-8	Lieutenant (j.g.) Ralph Bernard Hovind	ARM3c Charles Benjamin Lufburrow
VB-8	Lieutenant (j.g.) Helmuth Ernest Hoerner	ARM3c David T. Manus
VB-8	Lieutenant (j.g.) Ivan Lee Swope	ARM2c Harmon L. Brendle
VB-8	Ensign Paul Edmond Tepas	ARM3c Moley J. Boutwell
VB-8 2nd Division		
VB-8	Lieutenant Edgard Erwin Stebbins	ARM2c Ervin R. Hillhouse
VB-8	Ensign Philip James Rusk	ARM2c John H. Honeycutt

VB-8	Ensign Benjamin Tappan Jr	ARM3c Earnest Raymond Johnston
VS-8	Lieutenant Benjamin Moore Jr	ARM2c Richard Cusack McEwen
VS-8	Ensign Stanley Robert Holm	ARM2c James H. Black Jr
VS-6	Ensign Clarence Earl Vammen Jr * KIA	AMM1c Milton Wayne Clark*

The second group included thirty-one Dauntless led by Lieutenant Wallace Clark Short from *Enterprise,* of which five were from VB-6, six from VS-5 and the rest from the *Enterprise's* own squadrons. They were to have included two of *Hornet's* orphans, Lieutenants James Everett Vose Jr and Laurens Adin Whitney of VB-8, but they were both forced to abort the mission. The rest were despatched at 1045.

Table 19: SBD Strike from *Enterprise*, 6 May 1942		
VS-5 Division		
6-S-7	Lieutenant Wallace Clark Short Jr (CO)	ACRM (PA) John Warren Trott
6-S-6	Lieutenant Harlan Rockey Dickson	ARM2c Joseph Michael Lynch Jr
6-S-9	Ensign Carl Herman Horenburger	ARM3c Lyn Raymond Forshee
6-S-10	Lieutenant John Ludwig Nielsen	ACRM (PA) Walter Dean Straub
6-S-11	Lieutenant (j.g.) Nels Luther Alvin Berger	ACRM (PA) Otis Albert Phelps
6-S-12	Lieutenant (j.g.) David Render Berry	ARM2c Earnest Alwyn Clegg
6-S-15	Ensign Benjamin Gifford Preston	ARMa1c Harold R. Cowden
VS-8	Lieutenant Laurens Adin Whitney	ARM2c Angus D. Gilles ++++ Aborted Mission
VB-6 Division		
6-B-1	Lieutenant Lloyd Addison Smith	AMM2c Herman Hull Caruthers
6-B-16	Lieutenant (j.g.) Edward Lee Anderson	ARM1c Walter George Chocalousek

6-B-2	Ensign Don Lelo Ely	AOM3c Harold Llewellyn Jones
6-B-10	Lieutenant Harvey Peter Lanham	ARM1c Edward Joseph Garaudy
6-B-17	Ensign Harold Warren Liffner	AMM3c Milo L. Kimberlin
VB-8	Lieutenant Everett Vose Jr	ARM2c Joseph Yewonishon +++ Aborted Mission
VS-6 Division		
6-S-16	Lieutenant Frank Anthony Patriarca (CO)	ACRM(PA) John Richard Badgley
6-S-2	Ensign Reid Wentworth Stone	RM1c William Hart Bergin
6-S-11	Ensign Richard Alonzo Jaccard	RM3c Porter William Pixley
6-S-7	Lieutenant (j.g.) Normal Jack Kleiss	ARM3c John Warren Snowden
6-S-17	Ensign Vernon Lansen Micheel	RM3c John Dewey Dance
6-S-18	Ensign James Campbell Dexter	RM3c Donald Laurence Hoff
6-S-9	Ensign Eldor Ernst Rodenburg	Sea2c Thomas James Bruce ++++ (Aborted Mission)
VB-3 1st Division		
3-B-3	Lieutenant DeWitt Wood Shumway (XO)	ARM1c Ray Edgar Coons
3-B-14	Ensign Robert Martin Elder	ARM3c Leslie Alan Till
3-B-6	Ensign Milford Austin Merrill	ARM3c Jack Alvan Shropshire
3-B-4	Ensign Robert Keith Campbell (GO)	ARM3c Frederick Paul Bergeron
3-B-5	Ensign Aldon Wilbur Hanson	ARM3c Joseph Vernon Godfrey
VB-3 2nd Division		
3-B-7	Lieutenant (j.g.) Gordon Alvin Sherwood (EO)	ARM2c Harmon Donald Bennett
3-B-8	Ensign Roy Maurice Isaman	ARM3c Sidney Kay Weaver
3-B-9	Ensign Bunyon Randolph Cooner	AMM3c Clarence Eugene Zimmershead
3-B-10	Lieutenant Harold Sydney Bottomley (FO)	AMM2c David Frederick Johnson
6-B-10	Ensign Charles Smith Lane	ARM3c Jack Charles Henning

The third wave incorporated twenty-four SBDs from *Hornet* and was sent away at 1330. During this first three-hour mission Commander Stanhope Ring aircraft's radioman AMM2c Arthur Middleton Parker had sent out sighting and attack reports, but none of these had been received aboard *Hornet*. Likewise, the various updates sent from *Hornet* to Ring were never received. Examination found that the aircraft's radio was faulty and, because of this, CHAG was unable to fly the second mission as there proved insufficient time to replace it. So, this second attack was led, instead, by Lieutenant Commander Walter Fred Rodee of VS-8 who acted in the role of temporary CHAG. The VS-8 team included two 'orphans' from VS-5, Lieutenants (j.g.) William Francis Christie and Henry Martin McDowell

Table 20: Second *Hornet* SBD strike, 6 May		
VS-8 1st Division		
Squadron	**Pilot**	**Aircrew**
VS-8	Lieutenant Commander Walter Fred Rodee (CO)	ACRM John Lenzy Clanton
VS-8	Ensign Paul Edmond Tepas	ARM3c Moley J. Boutwell
VS-8	Lieutenant Benjamin Moore Jr	ARM3c Richard Cusack McEwen
VS-5	Lieutenant (j.g.) William Francis Christie	ARM1c Alvin Arthur Sobel
VS-5	Lieutenant (j.g.) Henry Martin McDowell	ARM2c Eugene Clay Strickland
VS-8	Lieutenant (j.g.) James McMillan Forbes	ARM3c Ronald H. Arenth
VS-8 2nd Division		
VS-8	Lieutenant William John Widhelm	ARM1c George David Stokely
VS-8	Lieutenant (j.g.) Ralph Bernard Hovind	ARM3c Charles Benjamin Lufburrow
VS-8	Lieutenant (j.g.) Albert Harold Wood	ARM3c John Louis Tereskerz
VS-8	Ensign Hellmuth Ernest Hoerner	ARM3c David T. Manus
VS-8	Lieutenant Edgard Erwin Stebbins	ARM2c Ervin R. Hillhouse

Squadron	Pilot	Aircrew
VS-8	Ensign Harold White	ARM3c John Stephen Urban
VS-8	William E. Woodman	ARM2c Gerald S. McAffe
VB-8 1st Division		
VB-8	Lieutenant Alfred Bland Tucker III (XO)	ARM1c Champ T. Stuart
VB-8	Ensign Don Dee Adams	ARM2c John B. Broughton Jr
VB-8	Ensign Joseph Wiley King	ARM3c Thomas M. Walsh
VB-8	Lieutenant John Joseph Lynch (MO)	ARM1c Wilbur L. Woods
VB-8	Ensign Clayton Evan Fisher	ARM3c George E Ferguson
VB-8	Ensign Henry John Nickerson	ARM1c Elmer Edwin Jackson
VB-8 2nd Division		
VB-8	Lieutenant (j.g.) Frederick Leeson Bates (EO)	ARM1c Clyde S. Montensen
VB-8	Ensign James Clark Barrett	ARM3c William H. Berthold
VB-8	Ensign Gus George Bebas	RM3c Alfred W. Ringressy Jr
VB-8	Ensign Frank Earl Christofferson	ARM2c Barkley Vaughn Poorman
VB-8	Ensign Robert Pershing Friesz	ARM1c Clarence Courtland Kiley
VB-8	Ensign James Austin Riner Jr	ARM2c Floyd Dell Kilmer

These separate groups attacked the two cruisers at 0945, 1230 and 1445 respectively, their runs being well pressed home against strong flak. Both heavy cruisers were hit hard, *Mogami* taking two bombs in the first assault, including one direct hit on No. 5 turret which cremated its crew. In the second attack the same ship took two further hits, which started large fires, while the third attack annihilated the entire ninety-man team of one of her engine rooms, to add to more than 200 others who died. But she did not finally sink; she resolutely fought the fires and overcame the damage, and managed to win through to Truk anchorage, and was later fully repaired in Japan.

Her sister, *Mikuma,* was less fortunate. She was hit once in the first attack, although this caused only minor damage, but in the second attack no less than five direct hits were received, and fierce fires consumed her innards, wiping out her engine and boiler-room complement and bringing her to a halt. These blazes eventually reached a magazine at 1058 which duly exploded, and this blow proved terminal. Her captain ordered the ship to be abandoned, and while this was being done the third wave arrived at 1200 and hit the wallowing wreck two or three more times, causing carnage among those abandoning her. The two escorting destroyers were both hit and damaged, but not fatally so, but the loss of life among the *Mikuma* survivors crammed aboard, was high. Around 680 of *Mikuma*'s crew were estimated to have been killed in total, including Captain Shakao Sakiyama, who died of his wounds later. The destroyer *Arashio* was hit on the stern by Ensign Clayton Evan Fisher's bomb, which killed thirty-nine men and caused carnage among others of the cruiser survivors assembled there. However, she managed to control the damage and survived the ordeal.

For the SBDs this had become mere target practice and the only aircraft lost in these three sorties was to AA fire. A final sortie was launched by a pair of Dauntless from *Enterprise,* Lieutenants Edwin John Kroeger of VB-6 who had Fox Movietone News cameraman Alfred Dillemtash Brick in his rear seat, and Cleo John Dobson of VS-6, with Chief Photographer (PA) J.S. Mihalovitch as his cameraman, and they photographed the final moments of the doomed cruiser for posterity. *Yorktown,* along with the destroyer *Hamman* alongside, was finally torpedoed by the submarine *I-168* at 1331 on the 6th and was later abandoned. She did not finally sink until 0501 on the 7th. When she sank she took nine Dauntless of VS-5 to swell the total lost in this battle, but this was little enough when compared with the magnitude of their achievement. Their loss was immediately made good, because *Saratoga* finally arrived on station on 8 June with her own thirty-four strong complement of Dauntless ready to take her place should she be required. But by then Admiral Yamamoto had thrown in the towel and was withdrawing.

The Marine Corps flyers had also suffered heavily. In total MAG-22 lost eight SBDs shot down and five severely damaged.[24] It was reported

---

24 Sherrod, Robert, *History of Marine Corps Aviation in World War II*, Naval Institute Press, Annapolis, 1948.

after the battle that 'The SBD-2 airplanes, while being far superior to the SB2U-3 type, are deficient in performance to such a degree as to indicate that their only practical usefulness is for training purposes'.[25]

Whether this judgement was correct or not, the Dauntless would go on to perform many other valiant deeds in the hands of both Marine and Navy pilots. Viewed in hindsight, the Battle of Midway was the supreme justification of the dive-bombing ethos and the acme of performance for the Douglas SBD Dauntless. Midway won her the supreme accolades, but there was much yet for the SBDs to do.

Commander in Chief, Pacific Fleet *Report of Action 4-6 June 1942,* Serial 01849 of 28 June 1942, CVS/A16-3> 0F10/Ld, USS *Hornet.* Serial 0018. San Francisco, Calif., June 13, 1942.

From:	Commanding Officer.
To:	Commander-in-Chief, U.S. Pacific Fleet.
Via:	Commander Task Force SIXTEEN.
Enclosure:	(D) Report of Commanding Officer, VF-3.
	(E) Copy of reference (b) (paraphrased).
	(F) Squadron track charts.
	(H) Statement of Quillen, L. ARM3c, U.S. Navy.
	(I) Constructive Time analysis of events of June 4, 1942.

1. In accordance with CinCPac Operation Plan 29-42, the *Hornet* got underway from Pearl Harbor at 1130, May 28, 1942, recovering the Air Group at sea, at 1530 the same afternoon. One SBD would not start at EWA Field, and the pilot was flown to the ship in the rear seat of a TBD. This particular Pilot, Lieutenant W. J. Widhelm, U.S.N., was later credited with two direct 1000lb bomb hits on a battleship, or heavy cruiser, on June 6. An additional SBD, Ensign R.D. Milliman, U.S.N.R., pilot, was lost the following morning when it crashed about 15 miles from the ship while on intermediate air patrol, probably due to engine failure. No personnel were recovered. The Air Group then consisted of 27 VF, 35 VSB, and 15 VTB, which aircraft strength was maintained until contact was made with the enemy, except for temporary decommissioning for minor repairs.

---

25 Report - *Marine Aircraft Group Twenty-Two,* op. cit.

2. After passing through KAUAI Channel, course 296° T. was maintained until the afternoon of May 31, when course was changed to 290° T., and maintained until arrival at Point "Luck" on 1 June. On the night of May 30, a CinCPac intelligence report, giving an accurate estimate of the Japanese Midway force organization, was received. During May 31 two reports were received that Japanese bombers had been sighted northwest of Midway. At 1630, June 2, Task Force 17 was sighted. The two forces remained separated, but usually within visual contact. Task Force 16 remained in the vicinity of Point "Luck" until June 3. Word having been received that the enemy main body had been sighted bearing 261° T., 700 miles from Midway, course was set to the southwest.

3. It was at about this time that several despatches were sent to the Task Force Commander in high command ciphers. It is strongly recommended that carriers be issued a class 5 cryptographic allowance; these ships may well become separated during continuous air operations and the carrier commanding officers require all available information. The receipt of this information will obviate the necessity for a large part of the visual traffic so difficult to deliver by semaphore from the Task Force Commander to the carriers.

4. The first indication of the possible location of another enemy force was received at 0810, June 4, in CinCPAC 041807 which reported the sighting of a seaplane bearing 320° T., 100 miles from Midway. Two minutes later came a report of many planes in the same vicinity, and 14 minutes later another of 2 enemy CV on the same bearing, distance 180 miles. This ship was called to General Quarters, and remained in that condition until after dark.

5. At 0900 (all times given hereafter are zone plus 10) commenced launching the Air Group for attack; VSB loaded with 500lb. bombs, VTB with torpedoes and VF with M.G. ammunition only. The objective, enemy carriers, was calculated to be 155 miles distant, *bearing 239° T.*[26] from this Task Force; one division of 10 VF, Squadron Commander (Lieutenant Commander S.G. Mitchell, U.S.N.) in charge, was sent with 35 VSB and 15 VTB, to afford fighter protection. Deferred departure was used. A combat air patrol had been maintained since one half hour before sunrise. An unfortunate areological feature of the day's action was the fact that the wind was light (about 4 knots) and directly away from the enemy; every time the combat patrol was relieved, or a forced

---

26 My italics.

landing was recovered, our attack planes had a longer run back to the ship, and increased the distance between this force and the enemy. Between 1320 and 2100, launching and recovery operations were being conducted almost continuously on a generally easterly heading and at high speed. The VSB returned from the search in groups, Scouting 8 and Commander *Hornet* Air Group together. One section of Bombing 8 returned alone. Thirteen planes of Bombing 8 landed at Midway due to lack of gas; two of these ran out of gas and landed in the Lagoon at Midway. The remaining eleven were gassed, ordered to attack the enemy, and return to *Hornet* if possible. They were unable to locate the enemy and landed on board at 1727.

6. None of Scouting 8 or Bombing 8 made contact with the enemy on the above flight. After searching the prescribed bearing the Squadrons turned south to search in the direction of enemy advance. As it turned out, had they turned north, contact would probably have been made. This was due to the fact that when planes took off, they took course to intercept the enemy, at that time reported headed on course 140° T., speed 25 knots. About one hour after the planes had departed the enemy reversed his course and started his retirement. We did not break radio silence to report this to the planes. None of Fighting 8 which went with the attack group returned to the ship. They remained with the VSB until forced to head for Midway due to lack of gas. Five pilots have been rescued; without information as to point of rescue. They are assumed to have landed in the water on a line running 320° T. from Midway.

Chapter 5

Derailing the Tokyo Express

The Japanese onslaught had certainly been checked at the Coral Sea battle and given a very bloody nose at the Battle of Midway, but their probes down toward the northern coast of Australia continued, via the Solomon Island chain and New Guinea, and it was to prove a period of fierce eyeball-to-eyeball slugging at the tips of both these tentacles to stem once and for all the hitherto inexorable expansion of the Japanese 'Co-Prosperity Zone' as they grandly (and misleadingly) titled their areas of conquest. None of this came easily, however, and those who have written that the sinking of Vice Admiral Nagumo's four big carriers meant the end of hard fighting could not have been more in error. The scales had tipped back to the point of balance, but it was to take six months' hard fighting before they finally tipped in favour of the Allies. Many of the successes and the failure during this tough period of the Pacific war centred around the abilities, and limitations, of the Douglas Dauntless dive-bomber, in both in the expert hands of the Navy and in the indifferent hands of the Army Air Forces. The results could not have been starker in contrast.

In New Guinea it appeared that the turning back of the Port Moresby invasion fleet had only been a temporary reprieve. In order to attack that port overland, instead of via a direct seaborne assault, the Japanese sent another invasion convoy, consisting of three transports with 1,800 Japanese troops of Major General Tomitarō Horii's 'South Seas Detachment' embarked,[1] under Operation RI, from Rabaul on 20 July 1942. The troopships were protected by Rear Admiral Kôji Matsuyama's 18th Cruiser Squadron with two light cruisers, *Tenryō* and *Tatsuta,* the minelayer *Tsugaru* and three destroyers, *Asanagi, Yōzuki* and *Ukuzi.* The following day the Japanese disembarked the troops they had conveyed who stormed ashore at both Gona and Buna near Oro Bay, on Papua's north-eastern coast, the latter village possessing a vital

---

1 These troops were the advance force of some 4,500 men from Lieutenant General Harukichi Hyakutake's Seventeenth Army.

airstrip. The Japanese met little or no resistance ashore, although air attacks the next day sank one transport, *Ayatosan Maru,* after she had landed her troops, and these commenced advancing along the Kokoda Track[2] toward Kokoda itself, which also had an airstrip. The village was on a plateau close to the narrowest part of the Owen Stanley mountain range and from there they could press their advance on Port Moresby overland from the north. Kokada itself fell on the 28th/29th. The Japanese pressed on but were halted when some twenty-eight miles short of their goal.

On receipt of the news of the Japanese action the USAAF immediately recalled 8 Squadron's Banshee dive-bombers from Australia and they were thrown in in a desperate attempt to attack these ships. These A-24s had been declared 'unfit for combat' and their aircrew were to be retrained on the Douglas A-20 Havoc twin-engine bomber but, in view of the desperate situation, this plan was abruptly abandoned. Major Floyd William Rogers led eight A-24s to Port Moresby via Cooktown and they all arrived safely at the Seven-Mile airstrip, whereupon Rogers arranged for a flight of eight dive-bombers to strike the Japanese invasion fleet twenty miles north of Gona.[3] En route to the target one A-24, piloted by Lieutenant Finlay McGillivray, was forced to turn back with engine problems but the remaining seven pressed on. In addition, First Lieutenant Robert Edward Cassels' bomb dropped off as they approached Buna, but he remained unaware of the fact and efforts by his companions to advise him of the fact failed; he therefore made his attack 'like an Old Maid'.[4]

The A-24s were provided with an escort of twenty Bell P-39 Airacobra fighters, one ten-strong squadron acting as high cover, the other ten supposedly accompanying them, but they became separated and ultimately failed to protect their charges. Thus the Banshees were almost alone when intercepted by twenty-seven Mitsubishi A6M3 Zeros of the Tinian Group, 25th Air Fleet, commanded by Captain Masahisa Saitō,[5] as they began to tip over into their attack dives from *echelon* right formation at 10,000 feet. The weather was fine, with a light overcast and the result was a massacre.

In return for a single bomb hit on one of the cargo hatches of the transport *Kōtoku Maru,* which only damaged her,[6] five of the seven Banshees were

---

2   100km as the crows flies but nearer 160km in actuality from Buna.
3   3rd Bomb Group, Operations; 3rd Bomb Group War Diary, 8th Squadron Composite Diary, Maxwell AFB, op. cit.
4   John Hill Interview in *3rdstories.*
5   The Japanese recorded that the attack was made at 1445 by approximately ten SBD and four P39s.
6   Most of her personnel were saved but she could not discharge her cargo.

destroyed in combat, one was shot to pieces but managed to stagger back to Milne Bay and only a single survivor, piloted by Lieutenant Raymond Harrell Wilkins, returned to base.

Table 21: A-24 Banshee Attack at Buna, 29 July 1942			
Aircraft	**Pilot**	**Aircrew**	**Area**
FIRST SECTION			
41-15797	Major Floyd William Rogers	Corporal Robert Ernest Nichols	20 miles north of Buna
41-15	Second Lieutenant John Michael Hill	Sergeant Ralph Sam	Landed Gurney Hill
41-15	Lieutenant Raymond Harrell Wilkins	Sergeant Alan Clark	Survived
SECOND SECTION			
41-15819	Captain Virgil Alvin Schwab	Sergeant Philip Howell Childs	20 miles north of Buna
41-15766	Second Lieutenant Claude Lee Dean	Sergeant Allan W. LaRocque	Vicinity of Ambasi
41-15	First Lieutenant Joseph Crockett Parker	Sergeant Franklyn R. Hoppe	Vicinity of Ambasi
THIRD SECTION			
41-15798	First Lieutenant Robert E. Cassels	Sergeant Loree Le Boeuf	20 miles north of Buna
41-15	Second Lieutenant Finlay MacGillivray		Aborted the mission

It was a gallant, but forlorn effort. Hill's rear-gunner, a native Indian, Ralph Sam, was hit in the right and in the right thigh and could not operate his machine gun. He reputedly stood up and fired his .045 handgun with his left hand at the enemy in an act of defiance. Such bravery deserved a better fate. He was alive when Hill landed and taken to hospital where he appeared to recuperate and was shipped out to Australia but sadly died of gangrene on 2 August. Equally poignant was the fate of the others who survived the crash landings. Five in number, four being badly wounded,[7] they were joined by a group led by Lieutenant Arthur Auchter Smith of the 1st Papuan Infantry

---

7 Parker was wounded in the leg, Hoppe in the hand as were two others.

Battalion, and which comprised five Australian soldiers, five Papuan soldiers, the Anglican priest James Benson and two missionary women from Gona, Sister May Hayman and the Mission teacher, Mavis Parkinson. Smith radioed in the news they were safe but while on air the transmission was suddenly cut off. It transpired that the whole group had been betrayed to an enemy patrol by a group of hostile Orokaiva natives, led by former Constable Embogi whom the Japanese had dubbed 'King of Sangaria'. The surviving men in the group, with the exception of Benson who became separated and was eventually shipped to Rabaul, were murdered by their captors, while later the two women were respectively stabbed and bayoneted by Japanese soldiers at Popondetia.[8] Three of the Americans' bodies were found near Dobudura in March 1943; the other two, Cassels and Le Boeuf, were never found.

The remaining A-24s were once again declared unfit for use and, back at Charters Towers, training was re-concentrated on the A-20, a twin-engine medium bomber. However, not even the A-20 would have survived such an onslaught without any fighter protection, but it seems that those who did not understand the dive-bomber used this opportunity as an excuse to get rid of it. They were far from the only ones to adopt this attitude in the USAAF and the RAF. The direct hits that they had managed to achieve when all other types of Allied bombers had failed to score a solitary one were conveniently ignored.

A more realistic view of the Army Air Forces' 'anti-dive-bomber' bias was given to the author by Richard K. Smith:

> If the US had not gotten kicked into the war when it did, and 'Pearl Harbor' had been delayed for a year, the USAAC would have had some time to work up experience with the A-24s it had and were forthcoming, and by the end of 1942 dive-bombing would have become familiar. But as it was, I suspect that there was an overwhelming urgency to simply get on with what they were already well familiar (viz: level bombing from higher altitudes.[9]

Meantime the Dauntless focus shifted away to the end of the other arm of the Japanese advance, and here there was no doubt or reservation about its

---

8   See Grahamslow, Thomas – *Recollections*. Papua New Guinea Association of Australia, September 2015.

9   Richard Kenneth Smith to the Author 13 February 1988.

efficiency at the job in hand. Like the Army, the Marines had been given little time to train with the new Dauntless before being thrown into action, as we have witnessed at Midway. It had long been the aim of the Corps to build up its dive-bomber strength, and when, in June 1940, Congress had authorized 1,167 new aircraft for them, it was planned to re-equip with the SBD fully. Amphibious landing exercises conducted in 1941 in the Atlantic had concluded even then that at least eight dive-bomber squadrons was a minimum requirement for such a task. Identifying the need and voting the funds did not, however, provide the planes immediately, although by the time of the Japanese landings at Tulagi in the Solomons chain of islands fresh supplies were beginning to reach USMC units.

Since the three attacks by the *Yorktown* air group on 4 May, the Japanese had been unmolested at Guadalcanal and were able to go about their business of setting up a base there much as they pleased. Operation WATCHTOWER was mounted to evict them from the area before they could become firmly entrenched, especially as it was known that their construction battalion had been hewing a ground landing strip out of the virgin jungle close to Lunga Point in the centre of the northern coast of the much larger island of Guadalcanal across the narrow strip of water of the Indispensable Strait from Florida Island.

The 1st Marine Division was charged with the task of getting the Japanese out, and it was to be put ashore from fifteen attack transports under Rear Admiral Richmond Kelly Turner, protected by a cruiser and destroyer force under Rear Admiral Sir Victor Alexander James Crutchley VC KCB DSO RN. In addition, air support was to be provided by the three aircraft carrier task groups –*Enterprise,* with thirty-six Dauntless embarked; *Saratoga,* with thirty-seven aboard; and *Wasp* with thirty in total with her VS-71 and VS-72 squadrons. It was a clear challenge to the Japanese and showed the new-found strength of the US Navy was not to be husbanded defensively but risked aggressively. On 7 August 1942 the men of General Alexander Archer Vandegrift's 1st Marine Division waded ashore at Tulagi, Gavutu and Guadalcanal, covered by gunfire from the assembled warships and bombing from the SBDs.

Wasp contributed fifteen dive-bombers to the destruction of the embryo Japanese seaplane base, while from *Enterprise* Lieutenant Turner Foster Caldwell had nine of VS-5's Dauntless airborne armed with 1,000lb (450kg) bombs in the pre-light hours at 0540. The targets for these aircraft were the anti-aircraft guns and the radio station on Tulagi's south-western coast. Overall direction at Guadalcanal was by Commander Harold Donald Felt,

Saratoga's CAG, while Lieutenant Commander Maxwell Franklin Leslie of *Enterprise* performed the same function over Tulagi. A second wave went in at 0700, including eighteen SBDs from VB-6, also armed with 1,000-pounders.

The initial Japanese reaction did not manifest itself until after midday, when strong air attacks from fighter-escorted bombers winged down from Rabaul. First of the Dauntless groups to become involved were eight SBDs from VB-6 led by Lieutenant (j.g.) Carl Herman Horenburger, who were over Tulagi at an altitude of 8,000 feet (2,400m) when they were jumped by two Zekes. A brace of the dive-bombers took machine-gun hits but were not seriously damaged, while the concentrated fire from all the SBDs despatched one of the enemy fighters in reply. The eight SBDs of VS-5's second strike were also taken under attack by enemy fighters at this time and claimed to have destroyed one Zero without loss to themselves. All the Dauntless then carried out their attacks without further aerial hindrance. The average Dauntless aircraft flew about seven such missions during WATCHTOWER and enemy strongpoints were hit as and when required by the Marines ashore.

All well and good, but Vice Admiral Frank Jack Fletcher had already announced in a pre-invasion meeting that he did not intend staying long in the battle area and he was as good as his word, keeping his heavy ships some 120 miles (190km) to the north-east of the landings; moreover, he then pulled back to the south-east on the evening of 8 August leaving the Marines ashore, and Crutchley and Turner's surface forces to face Japanese retribution on their own. Consequently, scant early warning was received[10] when a powerful Japanese cruiser squadron under Rear Admiral Gunichi Mikawa penetrated down New Georgia Sound, later to be better known as 'The Slot', from Rabaul and won a stunning surface action. This defeat forced Turner's transports to pull out, leaving Vandegrift's men totally isolated.

Although the incomplete airstrip at Guadalcanal was taken easily, it was not in a fit state to receive aircraft and, until it was, the Marines had to rely on the carriers, and they had gone. Work was intensified and, by 19 August, the airstrip, named Henderson Field in memory of the Marine Corps aviator lost at Midway, was ready – and not before time, because the Japanese had reacted strongly and were sending in troop convoys and warships to wrest

---

10 An Australian Lockheed Hudson patrol aircraft had reported sighting the Japanese squadron at 0927 but her report, sent *en clair* while under attack, was not given credence or priority.

the strip back again. For the next six months a series of intense sea/air battles took place which saw the end of many a proud ship and many an aircraft; and in this life-or-death struggle, the Dauntless again proved itself supreme.

At the end of June 1942, the forward echelon of Marine Air Group 23, containing VMSB-231 (Captain Ruben Patrick Iden) and VMSB-232 (Captain Elmer Glidden), under command of Major Richard Charles Mangrum, were to have flown into Henderson from a carrier – even before the pilots of the Dauntless had been taught how to land on, or take off, from a flight deck! It was not until 20 August that twelve SBD-3s of VMSB-232 took off from the escort carrier *Long Island* and landed on the improved airfield. Like their Army dive-bomber colleagues in Java and New Guinea before them the Marine flyers soon discovered that the primitive conditions caused enormous difficulties in just getting their aircraft into operational order. At Henderson in the early days there had been no bomb hoists put ashore and the 500lb (227kg) weapons had to be manhandled up to the SBDs and there loaded by hand. The Marine flyers' aircraft were still fitted with the hard rubber wheels required for carrier landings and not the normal pneumatic tyres for ashore use and these hard tyres churned up the coral surface of the airstrip 'like a plough shear'.[11] An attempt by Air South Pacific Command at Noumea, New Caledonia, to use wooden wheels proved to be no solution to this problem either, and in the end the dive-bombers operated from a nearby meadow, known as the 'Cow Pasture', leaving the strip itself to the fighter aircraft. In the interim VMSB-231 continued to train hard at Espiritu Santo in readiness to reinforce their colleagues.

There now began a period of intense activity for the SBDs and a time of ordeal for their air and ground crews; just keeping the dive-bombers flying was a major achievement as, quite apart from the usual battle damage from enemy fighters, and from the bombing, shelling and AA fire, the hazards of landings, the frequency of the operational flights and the lack of spare parts, all added to the difficulties. However, despite everything, a striking force of Dauntless was always maintained, and while the Japanese ruled the waters around Guadalcanal by night, the SBDs dictated events up to a 200-mile (320km) distance from Henderson Field during daylight. Their principal job was hitting the Japanese troop convoys, nicknamed 'The Tokyo Express', as they came down The Slot from Rabaul, and in clearing up the remnants from the many naval surface battles that raged up and down 'Ironbottom

---

11   See Sherrod, Robert – *A History of Marine Corps Aviation in World War II*, Naval Institute Press, Annapolis, 1948.

Sound' during the night hours.[12] The codename originally allocated to Guadalcanal itself had been 'Cactus' and from this time the Marine and Navy flyers who operated on that death-begirded isle became known as 'The Cactus Air Force'.[13]

The Dauntless of VMSB-231 soon established a routine of two-plane patrols up the Solomons chain every day at dawn and dusk, and these were supplemented by the eyes of the Australian and British civilians who, pre-war, had run the plantations in the islands; they were known as 'Coastwatchers'. In lieu of radar, their radioed reports of Japanese shipping movements, especially of troop convoys, the soon to be named 'Tokyo Express', and of squadrons of bombarding warships as well as incoming Japanese air raids, often gave the Marine dive-bomber crews the essential edge in knowledge of enemy intent. The SBDs also flew frequent anti-shipping strikes, land strikes in support of the Marine infantry protecting the fragile perimeter, anti-submarine patrols and liaison missions.

On 25 August a Japanese convoy with 1,500 reinforcements of Colonel Kiyonao Ichiki's detachment of the 28th Infantry Regiment, on its way down from Rabaul was sighted at 0223 by a flying boat. This led to the carrier battle known as the Eastern Solomons (detailed in the next chapter); but one unexpected event was the diverting of part of *Enterprise*'s striking force, seven Dauntless from VS-5 and four from VB-6, to Henderson Field for what was assumed to be a temporary measure following the onset of darkness. These unexpected reinforcements to the Marines' SBD strength were as below:

Table 22: Guadalcanal - Flight 300 from *Enterprise*		
Pilot	**Aircrew**	**Squadron**
Lieutenant Turner Foster Caldwell Jr	ACRM Willard Ellis Glidewell	VS-5
Ensign Walter Wesley Coolbaugh	ARM1c Charles A. Jaeger	VS-5
Ensign Harold Lloyd Buell	ARM3c John Laughan Viillarreal	VS-5

---

12 So dubbed because of the large numbers of sunken vessels that littered the seabed.

13 This chapter is mainly based upon the combat reports of the various squadrons involved, DARA, College Park, Maryland, but see also Miller, Thomas Guy, *The Cactus Air Force*, Admiral Nimitz Foundation, New York, 1969, Sherrod op. cit., and White, Alexander S., *Dauntless Marine: Joseph Sailer Jr – Dive-Bombing Ace of Guadalcanal*. Pacifica Military History, Fairfax Station, Va., 1996.

Lieutenant Blake Woodhull	ARM1c Albert Woodrow Garlow	VS-5 *
Ensign Walter E Brown Jr	ARM2c Norbert Anthony Fives	VS-5
Ensign Jesse Theron Barker	RM3c Eugene James Monahan	VS-5
Ensign Elmer Andrew Gonzett	ARM1c James Hedger Cales	VS-5
Lieutenant (j.g.) Troy Tilman Guillory	ARM1c Stuart James Mason	VB-6
Ensign Harry Warren Liffner	ARM3c Eugene K. Braun	VB-6
Ensign Harold Camp Manford	ARM3c Homer Lloyd Joselyn	VB-6
Ensign Christian Fink	ARM3c Milo L. Kimberlin	VB-6

As part of Operation KA', five Japanese destroyers conducted a bombardment of Henderson Field to prevent its use, before joining up with the troop convoy[14] and Rear Admiral Raizō Tanaka's escorting force, the light cruiser *Jintsū* and three further destroyers, all of the 2nd Destroyer Squadron.

Lieutenant Colonel Richard Charles Mangrum, Captain Daniel Tore Iverson and Second Lieutenant Lawrence Baldinus flew the first Dauntless mission during the early hours of that morning, taking off at 0230 to harry the bombarding ships; they went unrewarded, however. Three further SBDs from Flight 300 left at 0400; the patrol was led by Lieutenant Roger Blake Woodhull, VS-5's executive officer, with Ensign Walter E. Brown Jr, but again they failed to inflict any meaningful damage on the enemy destroyers and Brown's aircraft was forced to ditch off Malaita Island through lack of fuel.[15]

The third strike mounted that day was by five Marine Dauntless, which arrived over the convoy at 0740. Thinking that these were friendly aircraft, the Japanese initially held their fire which allowed the SBDs to make unopposed dives. This force was led by Mangrum again, but infuriatingly his bomb 'hung up' on him. He was followed in by Second Lieutenants Henry William Hise, Leland Evan Thomas and Charles Bern McAllister, who scored three near

---

14 Three troop transports escorted by the auxiliaries *P1, P2, P34* and *P35*.

15 Brown and his gunner, ARM2c Norbert Anthony Fives, got ashore and were rescued by locals; they finally arrived back at Henderson Field two weeks later.

misses which exploded hard alongside one transport. The fifth dive-bomber down, however, piloted by Lieutenant Lawrence Baldinus, scored a direct hit on *Jintsū*, his bomb exploding plumb between her two forward guns turrets; as well as destroying her radio office, the resulting fire threatened to engulf her. Her forward magazines were flooded, and this prevented a worse explosion, but her bulkheads forward had been buckled and Tanaka was forced to transfer his flag to the destroyer *Kagero* while his crippled cruiser made her way back to Truk for repairs. Mangrum returned for a second attempt. He got a close miss on the *Boston Maru* which kept on going.

A second part of this attack deployed at 0807. This time it was by three Navy Dauntless, again led by Lieutenant Turner Foster Caldwell and again one aircraft, piloted by Ensign Christian Fink, scored a direct hit, hitting the transport *Kinryu Maru*, setting her on fire and causing her to be abandoned later. Ensign Jesse Theron Barker's aircraft missed and took slight damage from flak.

Yet a further mixed Navy/Marine striking force of nine SBDs was assembled and sortied out under Mangrum during that same afternoon but all they discovered was a solitary destroyer some 150 miles (240km) north-west of Guadalcanal. Six dive-bombers attacked her and claimed to have scored three near misses, one on the starboard side and two to port, and to have left the ship badly damaged, but there appears to be no confirmation of this in any Japanese record.[16]

Table 23: Guadalcanal - US Marine Corps Dauntless Personnel	
VMSB-231	
Pilot	**Aircrew**
Major Leo Ray Smith	Private Barry Justin Arnold
Captain Elmer George Glidden	Private First Class V.S. Byrd
Captain Ruben Patrick Iden	Private First Class T.A. Costello
Captain Bruce Prosser	Staff Sergeant C.T. Hickman
Second Lieutenant Robert Judy Bear	Sergeant M.T. Johnston
Second Lieutenant Homer Vernon Cook	Sergeant J.B. McDougall
Second Lieutenant Yale Weston Kaufman	Private First Class Reed Thomas Ramsay
Second Lieutenant Owen Dale Johnson	Private First Class Wallace Jordan Reid
Second Lieutenant Dale M. Leslie	Corporal D.L. Rhodes

16 Buell, Commander Harold Lloyd, *Dauntless Helldivers*, op. cit.

Second Lieutenant Glen Borah Loeffel	Corporal Robert Samuel Russell
Second Lieutenant Vernon Grant Rubincam	Sergeant Truell Larkin Sidebottom
Second Lieutenant Alan Milton Smith	Private First Class Hollis Everette Smith
Second Lieutenant Robert Wesley Vaupel	Private First Class J.B. Strange
Second Lieutenant James Wesley Weintraub	Private First Class F.W. Thiessen
Second Lieutenant John William Zuber	Private First Class Horace Backsley Thomas
Staff Sergeant Lytton Fenimore Blass	Private First Class Warren Harding Tubbs
Staff Sergeant W.W. Witherspoon	Private First Class D.M. Winters

VMSB-232	
Pilot	**Aircrew**
Lieutenant Colonel Richard Charles Mangrum	Corporal D.E. Byrd
Major Fletcher Locke Brown Jr	Private First Class E.L. Eades
First Lieutenant Daniel Tore Iverson Jr	Private F.L. Fraley
Captain Bruce Prosser	Private First Class A.S. Gilbert
Second Lieutenant Lawrence Baldinus	Corporal C.B. Hallyburton
Second Lieutenant Robert B. Fleener	Corporal J.K. Humphreys
Second Lieutenant Henry William Hise	Private L.P. Marcias
Second Lieutenant Charles Bern McAllister Jr	Private T.L. Mohan
Second Lieutenant Donald Eugene McCafferty	Corporal William Ray Proffit
Second Lieutenant Oliver Mitchell Jr	Corporal Robert Samuel Russell
Second Lieutenant Thomas Carlyle Moore Jr	Private First Class Frank Oliver Schackman
Second Lieutenant A.F. O'Keefe	Sergeant D.E. Sewell
Second Lieutenant Donald Vincent Rose	Sergeant J.N. Stanner
Second Lieutenant Leland Evan Thomas	

On 26 August, 390 soldiers from the Japanese transports were transferred to four destroyers at Shortland and two days later they sailed to join up with four more destroyers with yet more troops embarked from Borneo. The Japanese were soon to dub these high-speed reinforcement attempts as the 'Rat Patrol' because the destroyers scurried in and scurried out again. Before these two groups with their total of 790 soldiers of the 3rd Kure Special Landing Force aboard could unite they were found at 1700 by a pair of SBDs piloted by Ensigns Jesse Theron Barker and Harry Warren Liffner, some 125 miles (200km) north-west of Guadalcanal, just to the south-east of Santa Isabel island. This duo attacked, but without result; but their radioed sighting report resulted in the scrambling of a mixed Marine/Navy striking force totalling eleven SBDs.

Flight 300, led by Lieutenant Turner Foster Caldwell Jr, reached the ships soon after 1830, sunset, on 28 August. The Japanese ships had reversed course, steering north to evade detection before nightfall, when they would again have turned in toward Guadalcanal. They had left it too late, however, for it was still light enough for the Dauntless to make a split attack, with the Navy men, coming in from the east and the Marine Corps from the south-west.

The Japanese anti-aircraft fire was later described as 'lousy' in one report and 'tremendous' in another; whichever *is* true what is certain is that one of the Marine Dauntless, piloted by Second Lieutenant Oliver Mitchell Jr, with gunner Private Frank Oliver Schackman, was shot down with the loss of both aircrew. The other SBDs pressed home their attacks down to an altitude of 2,000 feet (600m) before releasing their ordnance. Ensign Harold Lloyd Buell saw his bomb explode almost amidships. 'She started exploding in her magazines and I saw a heavy red fire burst out of her,' he later recalled. His victim was the destroyer *Asagiri* and she blew up with the loss of 122 crew and embarked soldiers.[17]

Ensign Christian Fink scored a hit with a 1,000lb (550kg) bomb and severely damaged the destroyer *Shirakumo* in her engine room, and although her only casualties were two men wounded, she subsequently had to be towed back to the Shortlands Island by a sister ship and then on to Truk for repairs. Attacks by Marine pilots set fire to *Yugiri*, with a bomb that hit between her fore funnel and bridge, killing Captain Yamada Yuji, commander of Destroyer Division Twenty and thirty-one other crew members, and she also had to turn back in the same manner. The USMC

---

17 Buell, Harold Lloyd, *Dauntless Helldivers*, op. cit.

flyers also slightly damaged *Amagiri*. The other Japanese destroyer squadron failed to make contact and instead joined forces with yet a third squadron, and these successfully landed soldiers near Cape Taivu the following night.

Casualties and wear and tear had reduced VMSB-232 to just nine operational aircraft by this date, to which could be added the ten from Flight 300, whose 'short-term' stay was somewhat extended. Thus, every available aircraft had to be flown time and time again, and regular maintenance had to go by the board just to 'keep 'em flyin''. Meanwhile at sea Japanese submarines had first damaged the carrier *Saratoga* on 31 August and then sunk the carrier *Wasp* on 1 September. These two devastating torpedo attacks by the *I-26* and *I-19* respectively, reduced the US carrier fleet to just one, *Hornet*, as *Enterprise* was still under repair.

Because most of the Japanese troop reinforcement runs were, of necessity, nocturnal affairs, thanks to the Dauntless' tireless daylight activity, some night sorties were flown from Henderson Field, even though relatively few of the pilots had night-flying experience. As in most things the others had to learn 'on the hoof'. Known as 'Night Harassment Flights', these missions were rarely successful in inflicting damage but just served to add yet more strain on friend and foe alike in this grinding conflict. One such night sortie, of three hours' endurance, was carried out on the night of 29/30 August, but no contact was made. A similar sortie was conducted the following night, but this had more dramatic consequences. This mission was to search for an enemy destroyer squadron, reported earlier by Coastwatchers, and as part of this force Captain Fletcher Locke Brown of VMSB-232 led a two-plane patrol with a Navy SBD piloted by Ensign Elmer Andrew Conzett with ARM1c James Hedger Cales as his rear-seat man. When Conzett was wounded by an AA shell from the Japanese ships, Cales managed to fly the SBD back to Henderson Field from his rear-seat position, an outstanding achievement. It was a miraculous escape for both men, but it showed what could be done by steady nerves, a stout heart and a rugged airplane.[18]

In a similar mission, at 2100 on the night of 1 September, the SBDs were scrambled from Henderson while it was under destroyer bombardment, the Dauntless rolling down the bumpy airstrip with 5-inch (127mm) shells dropping all around them. One section of three Navy planes, piloted by Ensigns Jesse Theron Barker, Harold Lloyd Buell and Harold Camp Manford, was caught by an accurate salvo and Buell's plane was written

---

18 Cales, James Hedge, *Remembrances of Guadalcanal*, article in *The Hook*, Volume 18, August 1990.

off in a collision with the airstrip's solitary steamroller. The Dauntless disintegrated, the engine parted company and was mashed into a metal ball, the wheels broke off along with the struts, and the wings outboard of the centre-section panel also went their own ways. Fortunately, the 500lb bomb failed to detonate, and both Buell and his rear gunner, John Laughan Villarreal, managed to get out, albeit both injured.[19] Under the same deadly hail of shells another SBD, that of Second Lieutenant Thomas Carlyle Moore Jr, was also written off when his engine was knocked out and his Dauntless taken apart by the trees at the end of the runway. The Dauntless was a tough old bird, but there were limits!

The next Japanese move was to try and infiltrate troops ashore by moving them from island to island in small landing barges, which they hoped might escape detection. Fifteen of these were located off San Jorge Island on 4 September and were attacked by a sixteen-plane strike from Henderson. Nine Navy and seven Marine SBDs carried out low-level bombing and strafing attacks throughout the morning, claiming the destruction of several barges along with their soldiers. An identical mission was mounted on 5 September as the Japanese persisted, and again the Dauntless claimed to have sunk three landing craft and to have damaged many more with Japanese casualties estimated to number 700 officers and men. Following this disaster, the Japanese reverted to the 'Tokyo Express'.

The war of attrition between the Dauntless and the Japanese destroyers therefore was continued unrelentingly. On 30 August twelve SBDs of VMSB-231, led by Major Leo Ray Smith reached Henderson Field, and on 6 September six SBDs from *Saratoga*'s VS-3 with Lieutenant Robert Miller Milner and Lieutenant (j.g.) Alan Stetson Frank, flew in from Espiritu Santo. On 10 September the light cruiser *Yura* had been attacked by two Dauntless, piloted by Ensigns Jesse Theron Barker and Harold Lloyd Buell, who approached undetected at 14,000 feet (4,300m) before making their dives out of the sun, scoring near misses which left her unimpaired. Salvoes from her main armament of 5.5-inch (13.97cm) guns followed the two dive-bombers out as they withdrew at low level, but they escaped unscathed. Bad weather rendered subsequent SBD sorties ineffective and the Japanese were able to complete their mission.

The night of 12 September saw the bombardment of the airstrip by the light cruiser *Tenryō* and three destroyers, an attack planned to coincide with a Japanese land attack. The front line was only some 2,000 yards (1,800m)

---

19 Buell, Dauntless *Helldivers,* op. cit.

from the airfield and the 5.5-inch (13.97cm) shells that fell short of this hit the aircrew dug-outs and trenches where the Americans had taken shelter. One direct hit landed on the Marines shelter and two of VMSB-132's pilots were lost, Lieutenant Lawrence Baldinus who died later of his wounds, and Donald Vincent Rose, while Captain Daniel Tore Iverson Jr and Staff Sergeant Truell Larkin Sidebottom, were badly wounded. Another Marine Dauntless, piloted by Second Lieutenant Owen Dale Johnson, was lost with her crew when she was ambushed by a Japanese Nakajima A6M2-N 'Rufe' seaplane fighter while landing with wheels down and rear machine gun unshipped. The following day the Marines lost yet another SBD when Second Lieutenant Yale Weston Kaufman and his gunner, Private Barry Justin Arnold, were splashed, while their companion aircraft, flown by Second Lieutenant Arthur Francis O'Keefe, was also hit and the pilot wounded in the same attack. Some compensation for these losses was the arrival at Henderson of the residue of *Saratoga*'s VS-3, twelve Dauntless led by Lieutenant Commander Louis Joseph Kirn.

On a mission on 16 September a mixed force of twelve Navy and Marine Dauntless, led by Kirn, made a late afternoon strike on a Japanese force coming down The Slot at 140 miles (225km). Meeting heavy AA fire, three Navy planes claimed near misses on a cruiser, while a direct hit and three near misses were claimed on one of the destroyers. None of these claims was confirmed in post-war records, however. In reply flak nailed the Dauntless of Ensign Oran Newton Jr of VS-3 and his radioman, ARM3c Robert Sarrel Thornton. Two days later Lieutenant Leland Evan Thomas' aircraft fell victim to 'friendly fire' while returning to base at low level.

The newly-appointed commander of the Cactus Air Force, fifty-seven-year-old Marine Aviator Brigadier General Roy Stanley Geiger, arrived on the island on 3 September, and on the 22nd led from the front by commanding a Dauntless strike at Japanese positions at Kamimbo Bay on the north-western tip of Guadalcanal. More reinforcements from Noumea, New Caledonia, landed the next day, namely five SBDs from Marine Squadron VMSB-141, followed by a further twenty-one from the same unit on 5 October. Captain Ruben Patrick Iden, commanding VMSB-231, was drowned on 20 September when both his machine, and that of Second Lieutenant John W. Zuber, were forced to ditch in Lake Tegano, at Rennell Island. Radioman F.W. Thiessen survived the crash as did both the aircrew of the other SBD. On the 28th six Navy Dauntless also flew in from Espiritu Santo, their arrival making up for the departure of the survivors of Flight 300 to Noumea.

These newcomers were soon in action against Tanaka's flotillas. On 24 September the destroyers *Kawakaze* and *Umikaze* were slightly damaged by near misses from the dive-bombers from Henderson Field. In reply, VS-71 lost Lieutenant (j.g.) R. Herbert Hoover Perritte's aircraft which failed to return from a sortie on 2 October. The same mission located two Japanese seaplane tenders laden with tanks, heavy artillery and 728 officers and men of the 2nd Infantry Division, with a six-destroyer escort, heading down The Slot toward Tassafaronga from Rabaul.

An eight-plane Dauntless strike was made against this force, led by Lieutenant (j.g.) Alan Stetson Frank of VS-3, but one SBD was forced to abort, and heavy flak negated the dive attacks of the remainder. The Japanese force continued to Cape Esperance and commenced discharging their cargoes of men and equipment. A night strike by four SBDs from each of the four squadrons at Henderson was then instigated, led by Lieutenant Commander John Eldridge Jr of VS-71; only two aircraft reached the target area, however, and their attacks, delivered blind, failed. On 5 October, in co-ordination with the SBDs from *Hornet*, nine Dauntless attacked enemy ships south of the Shortlands Roadstead. Bad weather meant that no results were achieved by the carrier flyers, although both hits and near misses were claimed on two ships by the Henderson Field aviators. In fact, only near misses were achieved on the destroyers *Minegumo* and *Murasame*, which had to return to base, but the other four destroyers unloaded at Lunga Point without harm, despite a further night strike during which the Dauntless dropped flares for the first time.

Yet another Japanese force, comprising the light cruiser *Tatsuta* and nine destroyers, was attacked by VMSB-241 north of New Georgia. Lieutenant William R. Fuller was sure he had scored a direct hit on the cruiser and one of the destroyers was reported as being damaged. However, it has been known for a long time now from Japanese records that no damage at all was done in this attack and that no ships were even damaged.[20]

Between 9 and 11 October the battle of Cape Esperance was fought between two opposing cruiser and destroyer task forces, during which the Japanese heavy cruiser *Furutaka* was sunk. On the morning of 12 October two destroyers turned back to rescue survivors and picked up Captain Tsutau Araki and 514 officers and men. But they had tarried too long in their humanitarian work and the SBDs caught them north of Russell Island with a series of attacks from a total of seventy aircraft.

---

20 Dull, Paul Shirley, *A Battle History of the Imperial Japanese Navy*, Naval Institute Press, Annapolis, 1978, p.216.

First in were sixteen Dauntless from VS-71 under Lieutenant Commander John Eldridge, and they reported a succession of hits and near misses, but, only a single near miss was achieved against *Murakumo*, splinters from which penetrated one of her fuel tanks. A second wave drove in at 0800, with six SBDs from VS-3, VS-71 and VMSB-141 under the overall command of Lieutenant Commander Louis Joseph Kirn. Between them these scored at least three close misses, knocking out most of *Murakumo*'s armament and engines; she was then hit by an aerial torpedo from an accompanying Grumman TBM Avenger, and then by yet another bomb, all of which reduced her to a flaming wreck with twenty-two men dead. Finally, she had to be scuttled by *Shirayuki* who took aboard the survivors.

Her loss left the destroyer *Natsugumo* crammed with survivors from both the cruiser and her sister and she tried to escape northward; but a third striking force, led again by Eldridge, this time with ten mixed Dauntless, found her just before sunset. The SBDs claimed one direct hit amidships and two bombs close alongside which caused her boilers to explode. As the sun went down so did *Natsugumo* along with her captain and fifteen crewmen. The destroyer *Asagumo* later rescued 176 survivors.

By 13 October the American air strength at Henderson had risen to about ninety aircraft, half of them SBDs – but that strength was soon to be diminished in a dramatic manner. On the night of 13/14 October, the Japanese battleships *Kongo* and *Haruna* bombarded Henderson Field, firing 913 accurate rounds of 14-inch (350mm) time-fused incendiaries and APHE shell[21] and destroying forty-eight of the ninety aircraft; this left only seven SBDs operational and with little fuel to boot. Casualties among the dive-bomber squadrons' complement included Major Gordon Arnold Bell, his executive officer, Captain Robert Asa Abbot, and three flying officers from VMSB-141, Captain Edward Francis Miller and Second Lieutenants Jesse Earl Blum and Henry Francis Chaney Jr, all being killed, as was Lieutenant William Perry Kephart of VS-71.

Four Dauntless were made serviceable and were sent off to attack the inevitable Japanese troop convoy sighted the following afternoon, but they failed to score any hits, nor was another night sortie, led by Lieutenant Commander Louis Joseph Kirn, any more successful. On a more poignant note, Lieutenant Colonel Richard Charles Mangrum was evacuated from the island that day. He was the last of the twelve original Marine pilots, half of whom had died. On the battle front, the dive-bombers were given no time to recoup their losses; orders went out for eight SBDs of VB-6, under

---

21 APHE = Armour-Piercing High Explosive.

Lieutenant Commander Ray Davis – then in reserve at Espiritu Santo with nine spare aircraft after the *Enterprise* had gone to repair at Pearl Harbor – to fly to Guadalcanal immediately, for nine fighter pilots to take over the rest and join them. But before they were able to do so, the Japanese fleet took a hand once more.

The IJN repeated their shelling of Henderson on the night of 14/15 October, this time with the heavy cruisers *Chōkai* and *Kinugasa*, under Vice Admiral Gunichi Takama, along with destroyers *Amagiri* and *Mochazuki*, bombarding from 0149 to 0216 and inflicting yet more damage with 752 rounds of 8-inch (200mm) and numerous rounds of 5-inch (130mm) shells which reduced the number of flyable SBDs to just four.[22] These aircraft had only sufficient fuel remaining for one return mission, and two of them were wrecked attempting to mount a night sortie. Under cover of these bombardments another Tokyo Express was confidently run in at the same time. Only a single Dauntless finally got airborne, flown by Marine Pilot Lieutenant Robert Michael Patterson, who made a lone attack on the ships, claiming one hit.

By an incredible feat of improvisation enough SBDs were patched up and sufficient fuel salvaged from wrecked aircraft to send out another strike at 1000 the following day with twelve machines. This dozen reached the discharging transports at Tassafaronga, the SBDs diving from 9,000 feet (2,700m) and claiming hits and near misses. After refuelling once more, a shuttle service of sorties was kept up from Henderson and at 1140 a second dive-bomber assault went in, followed by twenty more aircraft at 1315. Between them, the Dauntless hit and damaged *Azumasan Maru* and *Sasago Maru* off Bunani, both vessels being subsequently beached and lost, while *Kyushu Maru*'s cargo of ammunition in her rear hold exploded; she also was beached, bombed again and subsequently lost off Ruaniu Creek. In addition, the destroyer *Samidare* was slightly damaged. The surviving transports were sent back at 2300.

On the night of 15/16 October, the heavy cruisers *Maya* and *Myōkō*, under Rear Admiral Sentarō Ōmari, bombarded Henderson Field once more, firing off 450 and 465 rounds of 8-inch (200mm) shells respectively, while three screening destroyers contributed more misery from their 5-inch (130mm) armaments. The Marine units lost William Robert Alston and Delbert Baylifa of VMSB-231 and Paul Horace Kerr and Joseph Anthony Tortora of VMSB-141. Thus, in two days, twenty-three Dauntless had been destroyed and thirteen damaged, and this reduced the operational SBDs to

---

22 Some sources state only three were usable.

ten again. However, seven replacements were hastily sent up from Efate, Vanuatu, arriving at Henderson in the middle of a dive-bombing raid by Japanese Navy Aichi D3A2 Vals. One of these scored a hit on the destroyer transport *McFarland,* killing twenty-seven of her crew and passengers; but the Marine SBDs survived. These continued to attack shore targets, losing one of the VMSB-141 aircraft to flak that day. On the 17th another Dauntless was lost, that of Lieutenant (j.g.) Charles Herman Mester of VS-71, who was shot down by Japanese A6M2-N 'Rufe' seaplane fighters off Santa Isabel Island, but her crew were rescued.

In response to these setbacks the Americans changed their commanders, with Vice Admiral William Frederick Halsey replacing Vice Admiral Robert Lee Ghormley, while the carrier *Enterprise* and the new battleship *Indiana* were rushed down from Pearl Harbor to replace the damaged carrier *Saratoga* and battleship *North Carolina.* Events were building up to a climax: the Japanese Army was preparing to make a final assault on Guadalcanal, so yet more reinforcements were being run in almost nightly. On 19 October, during a Tokyo Express run, the destroyer *Ayanami* was damaged by SBD attack. Between 22 and 27 October the carrier battle of Santa Cruz was fought, a Japanese victory[23] that resulted in the loss of the carrier *Hornet* and more damage to *Enterprise.* On the disputed island itself, an all-out Japanese land assault on Henderson Field between 24 and 25 October only just failed to overcome the Marines' defences.

Six VMSB-141 Dauntless were airborne early on 25 October and one of these sighted the two approaching Japanese attack units heading down The Slot. The largest of these groups consisted of the light cruiser *Yura,* with the destroyers *Akizuki, Harasume, Mursame* and *Yudachi,* under Rear Admiral Takama Tamotso, while a further four destroyers were also on their way to attack Tulagi. Over-confidence by the Japanese Army ashore – who were certain they had captured Henderson Field, but, in the event, had not – led the Japanese Navy to believe they had nothing to fear from the SBDs anymore. They were wrong and were soon disabused of the fact. While deep in the Indispensable Strait, the *Yura* group was taken under repeated dive-bombing attack.

Again, it was Lieutenant Commander John Eldrige who led the first assault, with five Dauntless from VS-71, just after 1300 that afternoon.

---

23 John Prados wrote 'By any reasonable measure the Battle of Santa Cruz marked a Japanese victory – and a strategic one. At its end the Imperial Navy possessed the only operational carrier force in the Pacific. The Japanese had sunk more ships and more combat tonnage, had more aircraft remaining, and were in physical possession of the battle zone.' Prados, Dr John, PhD, *Islands of Destiny: The Solomons Campaign and the Eclipse of the Rising Sun*, NAL Caliber, New York, 2012.

His initial diving attack was made and his 1,000lb bomb was released from the unusual height of 3,000 feet (900m), but despite this he scored a direct hit aft abaft the engine room, and this was followed by another hit nearby and several near misses. The culmination of the damage and shockwave effect of these bombs knocked out *Yura*'s engines and the small cruiser began to settle by the stern.

At 1415 three Marine SBDs attacked but missed, but at 1500 a three-plane attack by Lieutenant Commander Ray Davis of VB-6, registered a further two close misses, accelerating her leakages, while Davis himself near-missed the *Akizuki*. By 1700 Captain Sato Shiro was attempting to beach his command on Fara Island but Eldrige returned with four SBDs and near misses rekindled the fires aboard *Yura*. At 1830 it was realized her fate was sealed and *Harsume* and *Yudachi* took off survivors then torpedoed her. She broke in half and went down with 135 of her crew.

Although the island was still in dispute, the two Navy Dauntless squadrons, VB-6 and VS-71, were withdrawn, leaving Marine squadron VMSB-141, commanded by First Lieutenant Wrotham Starr Ashcroft, to continue the fight, along with new arrivals VMSB-132 under Major Joseph Sailer Jr. These two dive-bomber units were joined by a third on 12 November, this being VMSB-142 under Major Robert Hamilton Richard with ten SBDs, thus giving Henderson a total of thirty Dauntless on strength. In fact, the newcomers soon took losses, and in a mixed night harassment sortie on 2 November, three of the SBDs involved, flown by the indefatigable Eldridge and Marine pilots Lieutenant Wayne Roy Gentry and Melvin Rollie Newman, failed to return. Another loss was First Lieutenant Wrother Starr Ashcroft who was killed on 8 November.

The Japanese decided to run in yet more troops under cover of further bombardments, and the Americans threw in all available warships, regardless of the risks, in an effort to thwart them. On 7 November another Toyo Express was run and on the way in they were attacked by seven dive-bombers from Henderson Field led by Major Joseph Sailer Jr who reported hits on a 'cruiser' target, but in fact no cruiser was present, although both the destroyers *Naganami* and *Takanami* were damaged in this attack.

On the night of 12/13 November, the Japanese battleships *Hiei* and *Kirishima* bombarded Henderson Field while a further Tokyo Express transport run was taking place, but the squadron was intercepted by an American cruiser force and *Hiei* was left a floating wreck by dawn with her steering gear severely damaged and her boilers only operating at reduced capacity. Dive- and torpedo-bomber attacks against this crippled giant were almost continuous during the day, and as fast as the SBDs could be refuelled and re-armed they were sent out again in relays. A single aircraft opened the dive-bombing at first light but missed the huge target. Two scouting Dauntless followed with the same result and then the first full strike was made, led by Major Robert Hamilton Richard with five VMSB-141 machines.

They only had to fly for a quarter of an hour to find their target and commenced their dives at 0615; they claimed one 1,000lb (450kg) bomb on target and one near miss. At 1120 five further Marine Dauntless waded in, claiming three further direct hits. A third sortie was far less successful, however, for only Major Joseph Sailer Jr found *Hiei* in the dusk and poor weather condition, and he claimed a near miss on a destroyer. Of the remaining six Dauntless from both VMSB-132 and VMSB-141, two – piloted by Second Lieutenants William Jared Knapp and Amedeo Sandretto of the latter unit – failed to return.

In addition to these blows, the thirty-year-old *Hiei* was hit by at least six aerial torpedoes and, by 1800, was clearly doomed; her crew abandoned ship. An hour later she settled and sank off Savo Island with 450 of her complement going down with her.[24]

The loss of the battleship did not deter the Japanese from continuing with the all-out effort and, on the night of 13/14 November further shelling followed. Next day, at 0806, five of the Henderson Field SBDs, again led by Joseph Sailer Jr, attacked the cruisers, starting fires aboard *Maya*. Meanwhile, at 0850, two scouting Dauntless from *Enterprise* also located this squadron, then south of Rendova Island. They were searching for a reported Japanese carrier group, and, sighting warships they reported the cruisers as 'Two battleships, two cruisers, one possible converted carrier'.[25]

After making their sighting reports and amplification reports, the two VB-10 pilots, Lieutenants Robert Douglas Gibson and Ensign Richard McGill Buchanan, made dives on the enemy. Gibson's Dauntless took a 5-inch (130mm) shell through her fuselage on the way down, but the tough little bomber carried on, and both aircraft dropped their 500lb (227kg) bombs accurately from 2,000 feet (600m). The heavy cruiser *Kinugasa* was

---

24 The scandal of US torpedoes continued, and many were seen to run straight and true only to be observed to bounce off *Hiei*'s sides! Fact not fiction, see Roskill, Captain Stephen Wentworth, *The War at Sea,* Volume II, HMSO, London, 1957, p.236. *Hiei,* built as a battlecruiser with a British designer in 1912, had been demilitarized as a training ship like the Royal Navy's *Iron Duke* and the US Navy's *Utah,* but unlike these vessels, the Japanese brought her back into service as a fast battleship and she had been re-commissioned in 1940.

25 Stafford, Edward Peary, and Stillwell, Paul, *The Big 'E'; The Story of the USS Enterprise,* Random House, New York, 1962.

hit on a forward gun turret and holed by a near miss. Big fires swept her decks and she also began to list as water poured in through the gaps in her side plating.

A second pair of VB-10 SBDs, piloted by Ensign Paul Mathew Halloran and Russell August Hoogerwerf, attacked at 0836, commencing their approach dives out of the sun from 17,500 feet (5,300m) and entering the attack mode at 12,000 feet (3,600m). Halloran's aircraft was shot down during the attack and this crashing Dauntless hit the side of *Maya*, wiping out an AA gun position, two of her searchlights and a torpedo tube, and killing thirty-seven of her crew. Hoogerwerf thought they had scored a hit and near miss on their target.

Shortly after this event *Enterprise*'s Dauntless team arrived to carry on the assault. A seventeen-plane group – seven from VB-10 led by Lieutenant Commander James Alfred Thomas and ten from VS-10, each armed with a 1,000lb (450kg) bomb and led by Lieutenant Commander James Richard Lee – after making a fruitless search for the Japanese carrier to the north, finally happened on the cruiser force just after 1030. While VB-10 went for the damaged ships, VS-10 selected the light cruiser *Isuzu* for their target.

Next to be taken under assault was the already-damaged *Kinugasa*. Although no direct hits were taken by her at this time, the near misses were close enough for the concussion to shake up her engines and boilers badly and to open her old wounds once more. She drifted helplessly until her crew took to the water at 1122, and she sank some fifteen miles west of Rendova Island. *Chokai* was not hit, but was also near missed and holed, while strafing by the Dauntless caused damage to her upperworks. Several bombs close alongside *Isuzu* shook her up considerably and started numerous leaks, and finally she had to be taken in tow; however, she did manage to reach the Shortlands anchorage. The destroyer *Michishio* was also crippled by close misses and she too had to drag herself to safety in the Shortlands.

Another bombardment had been scheduled for that night: the battleship *Kirishima*, three heavy cruisers and a light cruiser plus destroyers under Admiral Nobutake Kondō, was to have conducted it to facilitate the landing of troops, but this force was ambushed on the night of the 14th/15th by the American battleships and another titanic night battle ensued which resulted in the Japanese capital ship being so badly damaged that she had to be scuttled. While the SBDs had no chance to help in *Kirishima*'s demise they found ample work by concentrating their main efforts on the troop transports. Having badly mauled the cruiser squadron, the SBDs from *Enterprise* landed at Henderson Field and their companions, still scouting for the reported Japanese flat-top, soon turned their attentions to the Tokyo Express which was proceeding south with an escort of eleven destroyers and with limited air cover provided by the small carrier *Hiyo*. This group was located off Santa Isabel Island by two SBDs piloted by Lieutenants (j.g.) Martin Doan Carmody and William Edward Johnson who, after sending their sighting reports, very courageously attacked at 1000 with their 500lb (227kg) bombs. Johnson's aircraft was shot down by defending fighters, both the pilot and his radioman, ARM3c Hugh Price Hughes being killed, but Carmody and his rear-seat man, ARM2c John Liska, survived, claiming that one direct hit and one near miss had been scored on two separate troopships.

This attack was soon followed by others, as SBD sorties were despatched from Henderson throughout that day. At 1250 the transports were attacked by nineteen Marine SBDs from both VMSB-132 under Joseph Sailer Jr and VMSB-141 under Robert Richard, while deep within The Slot. The first wave achieved some hits and close misses on the transport columns, twenty-four Dauntless hitting the convoy at 1430. The last section of this assault to attack, including *Enterprise* pilot Robert Douglas Gibson once again, along with Ensign Lenard Robinson and Marine Sergeant Albert Carl Beneke, each of their aircraft being armed with a 1,000lb bomb, survived attacks by A6M Zeke fighters on their way into the target. They commenced their attack dives from 6,000 feet (1,800m) and strafed on their way down, claiming two direct hits which, they maintained, broke their target ship in half.

Four further Dauntless attacked at 1530; then three Marine aircraft, led by Ensign John Frazier Richley of VS-10 followed, then nine SBDs, seven more Marine aircraft and then two Navy lieutenants, James Richard Lee and George Glenn Estes Jr., Finally, at 1715, another eight SBDs from *Enterprise*'s VS-10 joined in the slaughter when the convoy was still some sixty miles (100km) north-west of Savo Island. Their attacks were followed by a lone effort, Charles Boyd Irvine claiming a direct hit despite a mass of protecting fighters.

Eight dive-bombers from *Enterprise* reached the stricken remnants of the convoy at 1615, and from 16,000 feet (4,900m) they split into two groups: the larger, of five aircraft, piloted by Lieutenants (j.g.) Ralph Hays Goddard, Bruce Allan McGraw and Frank Russell West, and Ensigns Daniel Hartzell Frissell and Nelson Eugene Wiggins, attacked from the starboard of the convoy lanes, while three others, Lieutenant (j.g.) Martin Doan Carmody and Edward Edmundson, with Ensign Robert Edwards, hit from the port side. Once more the defending Zeros tried to intervene, but Edwards' gunner,

ARM2c Wayne Carson Colley, shot one down, while Edmundson's rear-seat man, ARM2c Raymond Eugene Reames, nailed another. Between them the dive-bombers claimed to have made seven direct hits on various ships.

As they departed, even more Dauntless appeared over the horizon, flying at a height of 12,00 feet (3,700m). These were seven aircraft from VB-10 at Henderson Field, led by Lieutenant Commander James Alfred Thomas, who headed up the first section, with Lieutenant Vivian Warren Welch (Executive Officer) leading up the second with Lieutenant (j.g.) Robert Douglas Gibson and Ensigns Jefferson Haney Carroum, Edwin J. Stevens and Jack Donald Wakeham. Again, the SBDs were fiercely attacked by defending Zekes and had to fight their way through to the target ships. Two slashed into Gibson's machine, badly damaging it, and he only escaped destruction by hitting the deck and flying low over the water, but his two companions, Stevens and Thomas, made good attacks, claiming hits with 1,000lb (450kg) bombs on an apparently hitherto undamaged *Maru*. Wakeham's aircraft was another victim of the Zeros, and his wingman, Robinson, only survived by good flying and better fortune, eventually to reach Henderson and count eighty-six holes in his trusty Dauntless.

In the other section the Zekes were equally aggressive and brought down Welch's aircraft, while Carroum was hit by flak and crash-landed on the water – he survived but his gunner, ARM3c Robert C. Hynson, later died while trying to get back to Guadalcanal. The SBDs of Gibson and Robinson were also shot full of holes but made it safely back to Henderson Field. Then the three Dauntless of Lieutenant Stockton Birney Strong, and Ensigns Howard Reason Burnett and John Henry Finrow attacked; again, many hits and near missed were reported. This trio was followed down by Lieutenant Commander James Richard Lee with five more Dauntless who claimed to have scored four near misses, while two others had their bombs 'hang up'.

The final sortie of this eventual day came from three Dauntless led by Lieutenant (j.g.) George Glenn Estes of VS-10, which took off from Henderson Field a quarter of an hour behind Thomas. They claimed at least one direct hit after an attack out of the darkening skies.

All these attacks had left the troop convoy in dire straits. In the first attack the *Canberra Maru* and *Nagara Maru* were both hit and sunk, while the *Sado Maru* was damaged and had to be sent back. In the second assault the *Brisbane Maru* was set on fire and later went down, while in the third attack the *Arizona Maru* and *Shinanogawa Maru* were both sunk. In the final attack *Nako Maru* was set on fire and later sank. While some destroyers were sent back to pick up the survivors from the water, Tanaka pressed on with the remaining four transports and these, *Kinugawa Maru, Yamatsuki Maru, Hirokawa Maru* and *Yamaura Maru*, beached themselves off Tassafaronga. They were there subjected to repeated attacks and were all subsequently destroyed on the 15th.

In inflicting this disaster on Tanaka's force, the Dauntless casualties received were not light. One unit, VB-10 under Lieutenant Commander John Thomas, lost three out of seven aircraft to defending fighter attacks and, of the surviving machines, two, those of Lieutenant (j.g.) Robert Douglas Gibson and Ensign Leonard Robinson, were so badly damaged as to be written off on return to Guadalcanal. The Marine Squadron, VMSB-141, was finally relieved on 19 November, having had nineteen pilots and fourteen rear-seat men killed out of the thirty-nine aircrew, with which it had commenced the campaign.

The fight for Guadalcanal was not yet quite over, and Tokyo Express runs still featured for the rest of the year in sufficient quantities to keep the Marine Dauntless busy. On 7 December a force of eleven destroyers was intercepted by the Dauntless team, and although it was claimed that five of them were damaged in the subsequent attacks, only the destroyer *Nowaki* took minor damage. But the price extracted was a heavy one, Major Joseph Sailer Jr of VMSB-132 sadly had his aircraft hit and he and his radioman were killed. The Marines' Dauntless struck again when, on 16 December, the destroyer *Kagero* was hit.

From the night of 1/2 January 1943 the Tokyo Express began to work in reverse and Tanaka began secretly withdrawing all Japanese troops from Guadalcanal. This time 'Tenacious' had ten destroyers for this mission, but during the first attacks the SBDs damaged *Suzukaze* with a near-miss 1,000lb bomb which disabled one of her engines, reducing her speed to a mere 10 knots, so she had to be sent back to Shortlands under the escort of one of her companions. She had to be towed first to Rabaul and then to Truk for repairs. The remainder completed their mission unscathed.

On the night of 14/15 January, nine Japanese destroyers undertook yet another run, Operation KE, landing 600 soldiers who were to form the rearguard while the existing troops were evacuated. Although this was done successfully, the flotilla was caught by a force of fifteen Marine SBDs on their way back to Rabaul. Their attacks slightly damaged *Arashio, Hamakaze, Tanikaze* and *Urakaze*, all of which, however, safely returned to Shortlands.

From time to time Navy Dauntless once again lent a hand, and one such mission was conducted by *Saratoga*'s air group on 23 January, which operated two dozen SBDs from VB-3 and VS-3 under Lieutenant Commander Harold Sydney Bottomely Jr, from Henderson Field on a twenty-four SBD strike against the new Japanese airfield being constructed at Vila on Kolombangara Island. They suffered no losses.

The Marines were back in action on 1 February and did receive casualties. They attacked a twenty-strong Japanese destroyer force off the cost of New Georgia. The Dauntless, under command of Major Ray Livingston Vroome of VMSB-234, lost three SBDs in this operation. Outstanding courage was displayed by one radioman, Sergeant Gilbert Henry Henze: when his pilot, Lieutenant Abram Hugh Moss, was fatally wounded by flak, Henze took over the rear-seat controls, instructed by Major Vroome who flew alongside. Unfortunately, the SBD ran out of fuel and the radio failed, so Henze put the machine into a dive and baled out; but the stabilizer hit him, amputating one leg below the knee. He managed to staunch the flow of blood before he hit the sea and blacked out. Found by natives, he was returned to Tulagi in relatively good condition, although tragically the deeper effects proved long-lasting. After hospital treatment in New Zealand, he wrote to his parents that he was looking forward to returning home to them in California. He almost made it but finally died on 6 April from acute yellow atrophy of the liver in the US Navy Hospital at Mare Island, Vallejo.

On 1/2 February another Tokyo Express evacuation was run, Operation FE, with one light cruiser and twenty destroyers from Rabaul to Cape Esperance. At 1820 on the evening of the 1st a strike by seventeen Dauntless hit this flotilla at sunset. Despite the advantage of surprise, only a single ship was damaged, the destroyer *Makinami*, flagship of Rear Admiral Shintarō Hashimoto, who had replaced Tanaka, and near misses flooded some of her engine compartments. She was towed back to Shortlands by the destroyer *Fumizuki,* then on to Truk via Rabaul for repairs. Another one of the flotilla, *Makigumo*, struck a mine off Cape Esperance and was badly damaged.[26] Hampered by attacks from six Dauntless on a night harassment sortie, they failed to hit her. Nevertheless, with the coming of daylight her fate was obvious and, after her crew had been taken off, she was sent to the bottom with a torpedo by her would-be rescuer. Further attacks on the rest of the force by Marine SBDs the following day were unsuccessful.

On the nights of 4/5 and 5/6 February, the light cruiser *Isuzu* and twenty-two destroyers proceeded to Guadalcanal to evacuate the second group of Seventeenth Army survivors. This force was also continually

---

26 *Not* torpedoed or bombed – see Dull, Paul S., *Battle History of the IJN,* op. cit.

attacked by contingents from Henderson Field, which included thirty-three SBDs. Again, estimations of damage, both at the time and since, were exaggerated. The destroyers *Maikaze* and *Shiranuhi* were badly damaged, the former having to be towed back to the Shortlands anchorage, but *Kuroshio* and *Hamakaze* received only light damage and were able to continue the mission. In return the Marines lost ten aircraft of all types.

The final evacuation run was made on the night of 7/8 February with eighteen Japanese destroyers: in the process *Isokaze* was damaged, losing ten of her crew, while *Hamakaze* was again slightly damaged in attacks made through rain squalls by fifteen Marine SBDs led by Captain Roscoe Maughan Nelson's newly-arrived VMSB-144. Altogether some 10,695 Japanese soldiers were taken off Guadalcanal by Hashimoto's destroyers without the loss of a single man, and it was not until 9 February that the Americans finally realized their opponents had departed. Finally, the major credit for both the stubborn defence of Henderson Field and its securing must rest partly with the Douglas Dauntless dive-bomber, whether flown by Navy or Marine aircrew.

Not surprisingly, the toll taken from the SBD units which served on Guadalcanal was severe, for example the Marine Corps dive-bomber squadrons lost no fewer than five of the commanding officers there, these being:

Name	Squadron	Date
Captain Ruben Patrick Iden	VMSB-231	20 September 1942
Major Gordon Arnold Bell	VMSB-141	14 October 1942
Lieutenant Wrotham Starr Ashcroft	VMSB-141	8 November 1942
Major Joseph Sailer Jr	VMSB-132	7 December 1942
Major William James O'Neil	VMSB-233	4 September 1943

Chapter 6

Two Carrier Duels

We have already seen how, on 23 August 1942, the Japanese were determined to run through a strong convoy in order to land the 1,500 troops of Major General Kiyotake Kawaguchi's detachment of 35 Infantry Brigade, brought in from Borneo to reinforce their hard-pressed garrison on Guadalcanal and to retake the vital airfield which the US Marines had dubbed Henderson. Termed Operation KA, this basic objective proved to be the kernel of another of Admiral Isoroku Yamamoto's elaborate and complex schemes to bring the remaining United States naval strength in the south-west Pacific to battle, and there to destroy them with cunning and ambush.

To protect this troop convoy, which comprised three transports and four patrol boats, no fewer than three IJN naval forces were involved. Rear Admiral Raizō Tanaka's close escort force, and the four heavy cruisers of Vice Admiral Gunichi Mikawa which were to bombard Henderson Field at night, we have already dealt with. In addition to these forces, however, there was also a detached carrier strike force built around the light carrier *Ryōjō* (Captain Katō Tadao) with the heavy cruiser *Tone*, flagship of Rear Admiral Chōichi Hara, and two destroyers, *Amatsukaze* and *Tokitsukaze*. This group was placed some 190 miles (300km) to the north-west of Guadalcanal, from where her small air group could both contribute to the attacks on the airfield itself and provide some limited air protection for the convoy.[1]

To achieve the destruction of the American carriers, should they intervene, the veteran Vice Admiral Chōichi Nagumo was on hand with his carrier strike force, although this now consisted solely of the sister carriers *Shōkaku* and *Zuikaku,* escorted by six destroyers. To give these ships some

---

1 At this time she had embarked just twenty-four Mitsubishi A6M Zero fighters and nine Nakajima B5N2 Attack bombers. Most historians have claimed that the presence of the *Ryōjō* was merely a token and that she was really to act as a lure or bait for the US carrier aircraft; however, while this might be the case, her role was certainly not defined thus in the Japanese plans.

powerful artillery protection from both air and sea attack was the Vanguard Force under Rear Admiral Hiroaki Abe with the fast battleships, the heavy cruisers, the light cruiser and destroyers. There was yet a further force, under Vice Admiral Nobutake Kondō, which comprised the seaplane carrier *Chitose* (whose aircraft were to be used for scouting leaving the carriers to attack) and four destroyers.[2] To these ships were added five heavy cruisers, *Atago, Haguro, Maya, Myōkō* and *Takao,* a light cruiser *Yura,* and five further destroyers. We can see here how the old Japanese ploy of dispersal of forces was continued despite the devastation received at Midway from such tactics.

Nor was this the final count of Imperial warships, for Admiral Isoroku Yamamoto was also out, his flag flying in the new battleship *Yamato* (armed with nine 18.1-inch (45.6cm) guns), the escort carrier *Taiyō* and two destroyers while yet further distant, and destined not to be involved in the battle, was the light cruiser *Junyō,* the battleship *Mutsu* and three more destroyers. So, once more, instead of concentrating his carriers and heavy ships, Yamamoto had them strewn all over the area north and east of the Solomon Islands. In all then, the Japanese sortied out with fifty-eight warships and a total of 177 carrier-based aircraft.

Before the fighting commenced the Americans, although out-numbered in ships – they had only thirty in total – vastly exceeded the Japanese carrier air strength, for the carriers *Enterprise, Saratoga* and *Wasp* had a total of 259 aircraft embarked. However, Vice Admiral Jack Fletcher squandered this advantage right at the beginning when he sent the *Wasp* with her eighty-three aircraft away to the south to refuel on 23 August. On the first day Fletcher still apparently believed that the bulk of the enemy warships remained at Truk and that he had ample time. He was very wrong, and this decision reduced the US Navy carrier aircraft to just 176 machines, almost identical to the Japanese number. The Americans on the field of battle were thus left with Task Force 11, built around *Saratoga*, with three heavy cruisers, *Australia, Minneapolis* and *New Orleans*, the light cruiser *Hobart* and five destroyers, and Task Force 16, built around the *Enterprise* with the new battleship *North Carolina*, the heavy cruiser *Portland,* the AA cruiser *Atlanta* and six destroyers. The Douglas Dauntless strength on the two remaining US carriers was with VB-5 and VS-5 and VB-3 and VS-3.

At dawn on 23 August the two American carriers were steering NNE some 150 miles (240km) east of Malaita Island, north-east of Guadalcanal,

---

2 *Chitose* carried fourteen Mitsubishi F1M2 'Pete' single-engine floatplanes and five Aichi E13A1 'Jake' single-engine floatplanes, plus four reserve aircraft, which could be launched from four catapults.

heading up the eastern side of the Solomons chain of islands on an apparent collision course with Yamamoto, and, as usual, both sides were flying dawn searches to locate the other. Unbeknown to Fletcher, the Japanese had prepared a submarine line across this obvious approach path, while a second line was patrolled to the west and a third formed another trip-wire to the east of Santa Cruz Island.[3]

Not surprisingly then, with so many submarines lurking in the vicinity, the first contacts that the SBDs had in this battle were with vessels and *not* the Japanese carriers. The initial sighting was made at 0725 by Lieutenant Turner Foster Caldwell Jr, and Ensign Harold Lloyd Buell of VS-5, who picked up the small conning tower and upper hull of a submarine running southward on the surface. They nudged over to make a low-level bombing run but lookouts aboard the boat spotted the Dauntless at the same time and she crash-dived. Caldwell's single 500lb (227kg) bomb appeared to hit abeam the conning tower on the starboard side, while Buell was unsighted and withheld his release hoping for a better shot.[4] In fact, this bomb, useful enough for most purposes against surface ships, was of little practical use when used against a submarine. Their pressurized hulls were extremely tough, and a direct hit with this size bomb would have been required to do any sort of permanent damage to them.[5]

Another such attack was carried out by two VS-5 SBDs, those piloted by Lieutenant Stockton Birney Strong, the squadron commanding officer, and Ensign John Frazier Richley. They were also on the 0645 search patrol covering the 345 to 045-degree arc north-east of Malaita when, at 0805, they, too, spotted a surfaced submarine. Their sighting was about eighty

3 Group 1 comprised the submarines *I-121, I-123* and *Ro-34*; Group 2 consisted of the submarines *I-11, I-174* and *I-175* while Group 3 was the submarines *I-9, I-15, I-17, I-19, I-26* and *I-31*.
4 Buell, Harold Lloyd, *Dauntless Helldivers,* op. cit.
5 Interestingly, the US Navy SBD aircrew were re-learning a lesson already proven by their counterparts in the Royal Navy two years earlier. Among the very first attacks made by Fleet Air Arm Blackburn Skua dive-bombers, operating from the carrier *Ark Royal* were operations against German U-boats. Off the Orkney Islands, north of Scotland, in the very first days of the Second World War, the Skuas had attacked U-boats at low level in the same way that the SBDs attacked the Japanese submarine, and with the same results. Even more humiliating was the fact that in such a low height attack, one Skua was blown into the sea by the explosion of her own bomb, and her aircrew were taken prisoner by the very U-boat they had been trying to sink. One Skua pilot told this author that bombing submarines with such a weapon was, 'about as useful as throwing a tin of marmalade at them!' [See- *Impact! – the dive bomber pilots speak.*] London and Annapolis: 1981. John Murray.

miles (125km) away from that of Caldwell's but clearly part of the same patrol line. Both Dauntless swung into a low-level approach from 1,000 feet (300m) altitude, but, once more, vigilant Japanese lookouts spotted them coming and the target immediately crash-dived. This time two 500lb (227kg) bombs detonated close enough to their (by now) submerged target to shake her up severely, and, in a flurry of foam and spray, she bucked to the surface once more as the two Dauntless circled. There was little more they could do about it as they had no more big bombs, but they could machine-gun her, and this they proceeded to do vigorously until she made a more controlled dive and escaped.[6]

The Americans launched a second air search at 1445 that same afternoon, to cover the arc 290-354 degrees up The Slot and to the west and north of Malaita. Two Dauntless of this VS-5 patrol, those of Ensigns George Glenn Estes Jr, and Elmer Maul, flushed out *I-121* and attacked her. Like the previous two sightings, the surfaced submarine was running south at 5 or 6 knots when she was seen at 1530. Yet again, although both pilots attacked immediately, the submarine was alert and crash-dived. As the waters closed over her both 500lb bombs detonated in the swirl of her departure, and they obviously were close enough astern to rupture at least one tank because, about ninety seconds later, oil was visible on the surface.[7] The sea was flat-calm, and the oil slick gradually spread, observed by both pilots as they orbited the scene. They could only tarry for a certain time before moving on, but, based on that slick, they claimed *I-121* as 'probably sunk'. However, as we have seen, she survived intact.

---

6   While a 1,000lb (450kg) bomb would have been much more effective, scouting squadrons rarely, if ever, carried them on reconnaissance missions where range was the important thing. For purely anti-submarine patrols (ASP) around the task forces the Dauntless could carry a single 325lb (147kg) – or, later, a 650lb (295kg) – depth-charge which, being designed for the job, was much more potent; but the priority at this time was to locate the Japanese carriers before they found you. Nonetheless, in stumbling into such a wasps' nest as Fletcher's ships had done, sighting continued at an abnormally high rate throughout the battle. Good attacks were made, and it was claimed that the SBDs had definitely sunk one submarine and severely damaged two or perhaps three others. The truth was more prosaic, and, no Japanese submarine was sunk by the SBDs in this battle, and only one, the first, *I-121*, (Lieutenant Commander Fujimori Yasuo) of the 7th Flotilla, was damaged after the battle was over when, on the 27th, she was surprised while recharging her batteries 175 miles to the south of San Cristobal Island by two SBDs from the returning *Wasp*. One bomb struck her in her empty mine compartment and she started leaking. Unable to dive, she continued to operate on the surface until she withdrew for repairs at Truk on 1 September.

7   Stafford, *The Big 'E'*. op. cit.

The Japanese troop convoy was located at 1000 that day, heading down The Slot, and at 1445 *Saratoga* launched a force led by Commander Harry Donald Felt; this included thirty-one Dauntless, their job to check out a sighting report received from a Consolidated PBY Catalina long-range flying boat which included a cryptic reference to 'a small carrier' (which was presumed to be *Ryōjō*).

The striking force duly reached the area of the reported sighting, finding low cloud and bad weather, but seeing nothing at all of either the convoy or any aircraft carrier. After casting about for a while at the extreme limit of their range, and with fuel failing, the whole force landed at Henderson Field to overnight there and did not return aboard *Saratoga* until 1130 on the 24th. Tanaka, realizing he had been seen, had meanwhile reversed course and this manoeuvre, plus the bad weather conditions, had thwarted Felt for the time being.

At 0600 on the 24th, Tanaka and the other Japanese groups reversed course once more and headed back south. At 0905 they were once more located by a PBY Catalina working from Ndeni[8] Island, and again the *Ryōjō* was reported, this time in a position some 265 miles (426km) from Fletcher's ships. At 1128 another report placed this carrier another thirty-five miles (56km) closer. Fletcher had meantime despatched twenty-three aircraft, including fifteen SBDs, at 0630 that day to cover a 200-mile (320km) arc either side of 200-degrees, at 250 miles (400km) range from his flagship. In return the US Task Force had, in its turn, been located by the Japanese, one of *Chitose*'s ubiquitous float-plane scouts sighting them at 1100 and so Nagumo knew what he was up against. The Americans had thus wasted a whole morning's warning, giving the Japanese ample time to prepare. A second search was readied and took off at 1240, but not finally making departure until 1315 with a further fifteen Dauntless, eight from VB-6 and seven from VS-5, to cover a sector from 290-degrees out to due east at 250 miles (400km) depth.

Still Fletcher stayed his hand, preferring to wait, and putting his faith in his own scouts and waiting for *Saratoga*'s strays to be refuelled and re-armed so that he could launch a full strike. Even a spate of further sightings failed to alter his careful approach, and it was not until 1345 that he finally despatched the *Saratoga* striking force, with Commander Felt once again flying his own Dauntless in command of a mixed group, which included twenty-nine dive-bombers, his own plus thirteen SBDs from VB-3 under Lieutenant Commander DeWitt Wood Shumway, and fifteen from VS-3 under Lieutenant Commander Louis Joseph Kirn.

---

8   Also known as Nendö or Santa Cruz Island.

Table 24: *Saratoga's* Strike Force 1340 24 August 1942		
Pilot	**Aircrew**	**Squadron**
Commander Harry Donald Felt	ARM1c Cletus Arthur Snyder	CSAG
Lieutenant Commander DeWitt Wood Shumway	ARM1c Ray Edward Coons	VB-3
Lieutenant (j.g.) Paul Algodte Holmberg	AMM2c George Albert Le Plant	VB-3
Lieutenant (j.g.) Robert Martin Elder	RM3c Leslie Alan Till	VB-3
Lieutenant (j.g.) Carl Herman Horenburger	ARM3c Lynn Ray Forshee	VB-3
Lieutenant Raymond Philip Kline	ARM1c Edward Joseph Garaudy	VB-3
Ensign Milford Austin Merrill	ARM3c Dallas Joseph Bergeron	VB-3
Lieutenant Harold Sydney Bottomley Jr	AMM2c David Frederick Johnson	VB-3
Lieutenant John Thompson Lowe Jr	ARM1c Gabriel A Sellers	VB-3
Lieutenant (j.g.) Robert Douglas Gibson	RM3c Edward Routledge Anderson	VB-3
Lieutenant (j.g.) Roy Maurice Isaman	ARM3c Sidney Kay Weaver	VB-3
Ensign William A. Behr	ARM3c James Q. Olive	VB-3
Lieutenant Gordon Alvin Sherwood	ARM2c Donald Harmon Bennett	VB-3
Lieutenant Commander Louis Joseph Kirn	ACRM Carl Edgar Russ	VS-3
Lieutenant (j.g.) Elwood Charles Mildahn	ARM2c Balford Allen Sumner	VS-3
Ensign Alfred Wright	ARM3c Melvin M. Bryson	VS-3
Lieutenant Frederick John Schroeder	ARM2c Alfred Wayne Dobson	VS-3
Ensign Richard Peter Balenti	ARM3c K. L. Johnson	VS-3
Lieutenant Robert Miller Milner	ARM2c Gerald J. Farrell	VS-3
Lieutenant(j.g.) William Earl Henry	ARM3c Willard Leon Wright	VS-3

111

Pilot	Aircrew	Squadron
Ensign Roger Curtis Crow	ARM3c Thomas H. Milner	VS-3
Lieutenant (j.g.) Alan Stetson Frank	ARM2c Darrell Howard Beaman	VS-3
Ensign Oran Newton Jr	ARM3c Robert Sarrel Thornton	VS-3
Lieutenant Ralph Weymouth	ARM3c Clyde Robert Simpson	VS-3
Ensign Francis James Sauer	ARM3c Robert Hansen	VS-3
Lieutenant Martin Paul McNair	ARM2c William Michael Rambur	VS-3
Ensign Jesse Theron Barker	RM3c Eugene James Monahan	VS-3
Ensign Allard Guy Russell	ARM3c Gordon Dolan Bradberry	VS-3

Shortly after they took their departure at 1440, another enemy carrier sighting was made, this one placing her sixty miles (100km) north of the first one, by a pair of Grumman Avenger TBMs piloted by Lieutenant Commander Charles Melbou Jett and Ensign Robert J. Bye. This duo made a high-level bombing run ten minutes later, but all their bombs missed astern of the carrier and failed to score any hits. Interestingly, because this attack was delivered from a high altitude, the Japanese reported it as attack by four-engine Boeing B-17 Fortresses instead of the single-engine Avengers!

Twenty minutes later this same group was located by the SBD team of Strong (in Sail-1) and Richey (in Sail-2), they sighting the heavy cruiser *Tone* and two destroyers at fifteen miles (24km) range (reporting them as two cruisers and a destroyer), and, shortly afterward, sighted *Ryōjō* also. Accordingly, Strong sent off a plain language report, but then returned to *Enterprise* to report in person as they had received no acknowledgement from the ship. At just about the same time, 1510, yet a third team located *Ryōjō*; this was Dauntless Sail-18, piloted by Ensign John Harold Jorgenson, and a TBM piloted by Ensign Harold Lee Bingaman. They, too, sent off (unacknowledged) sighting reports and attempted to evade the Japanese combat air patrol (CAP) to deliver their own attack, but were sighted and chased away. They also finally returned to *Enterprise* but had to ditch through lack of fuel; they survived, however.

The bigger picture was slowly emerging, and yet another part of the mosaic fell into place when, also at 1510, B-13 of VB-3, piloted by Lieutenant John Thompson Lowe, Jr, and B-5 flown by Ensign Robert Douglas Gibson, located Admiral Hiroaki Abe's Vanguard Force.

Douglas SBD Dauntless production line at El Segundo, 1943.

First Marine Corps Dauntless with VMB-1 in 1940.

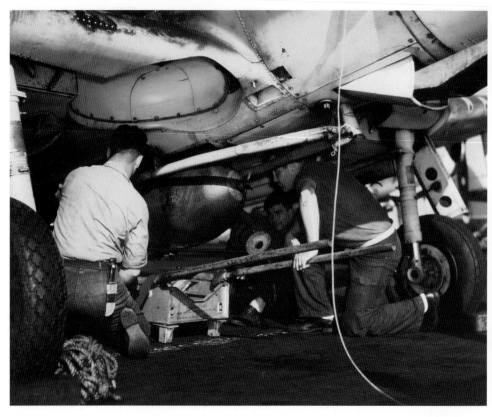

Above: Loading a 1,000lb bomb on the extending fork of an SBD. This device swung the bomb out and down to clear the propeller arc in a steep dive.

Left: VS-6 executing a classic 'peel-off' into the dive sequence, 17 October 1941.

The classic bomb release by a Dauntless.

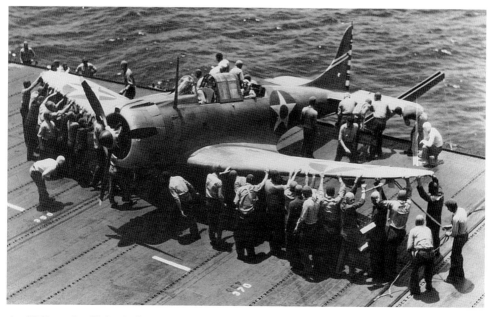

An SBD on the flight deck of USS *Enterprise* (CV-6) in spring 1942.

Above and below: SBDs awaiting take-off for the attack on Wake Island on 24 February 1942. Note the early tail markings.

Dauntless on the deck of *Lexington* (CV-2) in 1942.

Battle of Midway, 4 June 1942. A Dauntless lands aboard *Hornet* (CV-8).

Battle of Midway, 4 June 1942. A damaged SBD aboard *Yorktown* (CV-5).

An SBD from *Enterprise* (CV-6) seen over the carrier *Saratoga* (CV-3), 12 December 1942.

A formation of SBDs from Scouting Five.

A Dauntless from VMSB-232 on 29 August 1942 at Henderson Field, Guadalcanal.

A trio of SBDs from Marine Corps Squadron VMSB-236.

A formation of SBDs.

A Dauntless over Wake Island during the 5/6 October 1943 raids.

Overhead view of the Dauntless showing the cockpit layout and dive-brake configuration.

SBDs serving aboard the carrier *Essex* (CV-9).

A Dauntless from *Lexington* (CV-2) Air Group over the battleship *Washington* (BB-56), 12 November 1943.

No. 25 Squadron RNZAF SBD-4 at Espiritu Santo.

RNZAF Dauntless over Rabaul, one of their regular targets, 1944.

VB-10 from *Enterprise* (CV-6) in January 1944.

The attack on Truk, 11 February 1944.

SBD aircrew. Lieutenant Commander George Glacken, of VB-16, with his radio/gunner Leo Boulanger, seen over New Guinea during the attack on Palau, 30 March 1944.

Dauntless SBD-5s of VB-16 aboard the new *Lexington* (CV-16).

Left: A Dauntless from VMSB-231 in 1944.

Below: VB-10 in the spring of 1944.

SBD-5s, of VB-10 over *Enterprise* (CV-6) in 1944. The Battle of the Philippine Sea marked the final combat action at sea for the Dauntless.

Dauntless-5s from Composite Squadron VC-22, 'Hook down, Wheels down'.

Marine Corps SBDs from VMSB-231 at Majuro.

USMC Dauntless still at work in Central Luzon, Philippines, in 1945.

Left: A group of Dauntless from a Composite Squadron late in the war.

Below: A pair of Dauntless over the famous carrier Enterprise.

Felt's striking force had picked up Jorgenson's contact signal and had altered their direction to match the new co-ordinates, but, on arrival at that location, found that the target had moved on and was not in sight. Felt had therefore reverted to his original heading again, but it was not until 1606 that they finally homed in on the little *Ryōjō*, circling her at 14,000 feet (4,300m)

Unknown to Felt as he began to deploy his aircraft for the attack, far more important targets were in the offing, for while he was casting around for her, not aided in his quest by her convoluted movements, *Shōkakō* and *Zuikaku* had been finally sighted and reported. This important contact had been made at 1545 by VB-6's Lieutenant (j.g.) Raymond Davis, flying B-1, and Ensign Robert Carl Shaw in B-6. They had flown the 350-260-degree sector of the search and were at an altitude of 1,500 feet (450m) when they sighted two of the destroyers screening ahead of the carriers. As they pressed on and flew in over the screen, the two SBDs were rewarded with the sight of the huge yellow wooden deck of *Shōkakō* and, a little later, some five miles (8km) astern of her, *Zuikaku* hove into view, the most sought-after targets for the whole United States Navy!

The two big Japanese carriers had already launched their main strikes against Fletcher's ships, then some 200 miles (320km) distant, but *Shōkakō*, the closer vessel, was steaming hard at 28 knots, and had a deck-load of aircraft preparing for a second strike, with eight aircraft amidships and twelve more parked on her afterdeck.[9] Nor, apparently, had the two SBDs been sighted themselves, and so they were afforded the luxury of a fifteen-minute period of immunity during which time they were able to climb unhindered and up-sun to a height of 14,000 feet (4,300m). They broadcast their excited sighting reports as they climbed. Both Davis and Shaw then made their approach dives against *Shōkakō*, which had now finally seen them and was throwing up a belated AA barrage while turning hard to starboard, totally surprised. This manoeuvre was insufficient to deter either pilot and both made their attacks from 7,000 feet (2,100m), releasing their 500lb (227kg) bombs at 2,000 feet (600m). Both bombs near-missed off the carrier's starboard side aft, one detonating close enough for splinters to kill six of her crew, but her flight-deck and aircraft remained untouched. Both SBDs survived and made further sighting reports, then headed back home. It was 1600.

One mile (1.6km) away to the south-west and a quarter of an hour later, at 1615, Commander Felt, still in ignorance of the presence of the main Japanese carrier force, and with his own radio unable to receive messages,

---

9 Buell, *Dauntless Helldivers,* op. cit.

was circling the *Ryōjō* group at 14,000 feet (4,300m) and allocating targets to his striking force. He split his team, half being assigned the carrier as their target and half the heavy cruiser *Maya*.

The strike against the carrier was led in by VB-3's Lieutenant Commander Louis Joseph Kirn with his fifteen aircraft, and he took his flight to the north-west. Two further flights, each of three SBDs from VB-3, led by Lieutenant DeWitt Wood Shumway, meanwhile climbed to 16,000 feet (4,900m) and positioned themselves off the carrier's opposite quarter, thus splitting her defensive fire, while five Avenger torpedo planes went in at sea level. The remaining seven Dauntless, along with five more TBMS, made *Tone* their objective. Both dive-bomber formations began tipping over at 1620, as *Ryōjō* turned her bows into the wind in readiness for a far-too-late launch of her remaining seven Zeke fighter planes. The first ten SBDs released but none scored hits, only obtaining a few near-misses – the little flat-top appeared to bear a charmed life. As the other eleven Dauntless pulled out of their dives with the same negative results, Felt cancelled his original instruction and re-directed the *Tone* strike at *Ryōjō* instead.

This group comprised seven Dauntless from VB-3 led by Lieutenant Harold Sydney Bottomley Jr, and they had already commenced their approach dives against the heavy cruiser *Maya* when they received their new instructions but, despite this, most were able to abort and re-form. They followed Felt himself down, as the CSAG, frustrated at the lack of accuracy from his first waves, had made a singlehanded assault. Despite accurate flak fire which hit his aircraft, removing the mast of his already useless radio, and the attentions of defending fighters, Felt's effrontery was rewarded with a direct hit with his 500lb (227kg) bomb, amidships on the flight-deck. He witnessed the sight of thick black smoke gushing from the stricken carrier, which was continuing to circle at high speed.

Meanwhile the majority of Bottomley's team had climbed back to 15,000 feet (4,600m) and made a classic diverging attack on the carrier and, as befitted veterans of Midway, they made few errors, claiming no less than three hits and four close misses.[10] states that there were four to ten bomb hits; *Ryōjō's* Captain, Tadao Keno, was to testify that she avoided *all* the bombs except one near-miss, and that it was a solitary torpedo hit that sank her; Captain Tameichi Hara, Commanding Officer of one of the escorting destroyers, *Amatsukaze,* recorded that 'Two or three enemy bombs hit the ship

---

10 Accounts differ wildly on the number of hits scored by the SBDs on *Ryōjō.* Professor Samuel Eliot Morison, in *History of the United States Naval Operations in World War II, Volume V, The Struggle for Guadalcanal,* Boston: 1951. Little Brown & Co.

near the stern, piercing the flight deck ...' and that 'more bombs made direct hits ...'. See Hara, Tameichi, Saitō, Fred and Pineau, Captain Roger, *Japanese Destroyer Captain*. New York: 1961. Ballentine Books. More recently Anthony P. Tully states this confusion might be caused by the fact that two of the four 'attested' hits were on the extreme edge of the flight deck, which otherwise from photographs taken before she sank, show little evidence of damage but who attested the four hits is not specified.] *Maya* was attacked by the SBDs of Gibson and Lowe, but both missed and the heavy cruiser, adroitly handled by Captain Nabeshima Shunsaki, emerged totally unscathed; two Avengers from the accompanying VT-3 also launched torpedoes at her, but scored no hits.

The SBDs which attacked last faced the finally fully-alerted fighter defences in full cry and they were roughly handled, but although many were hit – Ensign William Anthony Behr, for example, survived the attentions of no fewer than five Zekes which peppered his aircraft but failed to down him – all got back safely to the Task Force. Lieutenant Frederick John Schroeder claimed to have shot down a Japanese Nakajima B5N 'Kate' attack bomber around this time, if true presumably on *Ryōjō*'s returning Guadalcanal strike.

Once again, the Dauntless was able to add to her claim to be a part-time fighter aircraft as well as a dive-bomber, because no fewer than three more Japanese aircraft were alleged to have been shot down by SBDs that day, all Aichi D3A 'Vals'. This was because, on returning to their home carriers, the returning strike found that the Japanese air attack was in full swing. Unable to land while this assault was in progress, some Dauntless took a hand in the defence. Both Lieutenants Robert Keith Campbell and William Earl Henry claimed kills and were joined by Lieutenant (j.g.) Howard Reason Burnett, returning to *Saratoga* from an inner air patrol (IAP) who nailed another. However, neither they, the CAP, nor the ship's gunners were able to save *Enterprise* from receiving heavy damage from the Japanese dive-bombers and she took three direct hits.[11] She was forced to retire and Fletcher, with only *Saratoga* operational against the two big Japanese carriers, retreated from the field of battle.

When the Japanese air attack had been plotted boring in on the American fleet, the carriers hastily scrambled away all available aircraft. From the *Saratoga* two SBDs, piloted by Lieutenant (j.g.) Robert Martin Elder with ARM2c Leslie Alan Till, and Ensign Robert Thornton Gordon respectively,

---

11 These occurred at 5.12. Hit one pierced No. 3 elevator and penetrated down 4.5ft; Hit 2 hit the flight-deck near the same spot and went down 18ft into the ship, exploding in VB-6's (empty) ready-room; Hit 3 hit the flight-deck close to elevator 2. Both these elevators were put out of action and only one remained useable. There was also a very close near-miss which warped the flight-deck and perforated her hull.

along with eight TBMs, were sent away at 1700, with orders to strike at Abe's Vanguard Force, now recognized as containing at least one battleship and five cruisers. *Enterprise* had managed to *get* away eleven Dauntless, all armed with 1,000lb (450kg) bombs, led by Lieutenant Turner Foster Caldwell, Jr, before she was hit, along with seven Avengers, and this force, Flight 300, was off the deck by around 1705.

Table 25: *Enterprise* Strike PM 24 August 1942		
Pilot	**Aircrew**	**Squadron**
Lieutenant Turner Foster Caldwell Jr	ACRM Willard Ellis Glidewell	VS-5
Ensign Walter Westley Coolbaugh	ARM1c Charles A. Jaeger	VS-5
Ensign Harold Lloyd Buell	ARM3c John Laughan Villarreal	VS-5
Lieutenant Roger Blake Woodhull	ARM1c Albert Woodrow Garlow	VS-5
Ensign Walter E. Brown Jr	ARM2c Norbert Anthony Fives	VS-5
Ensign Jesse Theron Barker	RM3c Eugene James Monahan	VS-5
Ensign Andrew Conzett	ARM1c James Hedger Cales	VS-5
Lieutenant (j.g.) Troy Tilman Guillory	ARM1c Stuart James Mason	VB-6
Ensign Harry Warren Liffner	ARM3c Eugene K. Braun	VB-6
Ensign Harold Camp Manford	ARM3c Homer Lloyd Joselyn	VB-6
Ensign Christian Fink	ARM3c Milo L Kimberlin	VB-6

After orbiting the Task Force for a while and seeing their home carrier hit and set on fire, Flight 300 received their mission orders to find and strike at the enemy carrier on her last reported bearing. This target was, of course, *Ryōjō,* which had already been dealt with, although they were not to know that.

The flight flew north-west following the CAG, Lieutenant Commander Maxwell Franklin Leslie's TBM. Gradually those two hours began to be eaten up with still neither sight nor sign of any enemy ships, let alone carriers. The sun set, and the fuel situation was giving grave cause for concern, especially to the shorter-ranged SBDs They reached the expected point of contact, found only calm but empty sea, and pushed on for a further fifty miles (80km), with the same negative result.

The Avenger flight had already jettisoned its torpedoes and headed back to the task force, and so, finally, Caldwell was left with no other option but to do likewise. It was already too late to return to *Enterprise*, even if she had been able to receive them, so eleven 1,000lb bombs were dropped into the wide Pacific, engine settings were carefully returned to lean fuel mix to give every precious mile of endurance, and course was set for Henderson Field. It was touch and go, but with the aid of a bright moon and good deal of beginners' luck, from 2020 onward, all eleven Dauntless bumped down safely on Guadalcanal and began their nomadic existence alongside their Marine Corps companions.

The *Saratoga* pair had better fortune, although they also failed to find their allocated targets. At 1740, after a forty-minute flight, what the two SBDs did come across was Vice Admiral Kondo's support force, main body, with *Chitose*, (Captain Furukawa Tamotsu) and the five big cruisers escorted by the light cruiser *Yura* and her six destroyers. Here was a target of sorts, and, climbing to 12,400 feet (3,800m) they tipped over into the diving attacks. Somehow, they identified *Chitose*, 11,023-ton seaplane carrier, armed with two twin 5-inch (12.7cm) guns and four catapults, as the 67,123-ton battleship *Musashi*!

The two SBDs faced a heavy flak barrage from the accompanying heavy cruisers as they made their dives out of the setting sun, but this failed to deter them from making odd runs, releasing at around 2,000 feet (600m). One shell ripped through the dive flaps of Gordon's aircraft, but both Dauntless got away and managed to land back aboard *Saratoga* that evening.

Both bombs were near-misses close alongside *Chitose's* port side, the concussion of which stove in her thin plating and caused some flooding in her port engine room, which was put out of action. Bomb splinters scythed inboard and set on fire some of her seaplanes. For a time, she looked to be in big trouble, taking on a 30-degree list but, eventually, her crew got the fires under control and the pumps working and, at 16 knots, she was towed by the destroyer *Minegumo* slowly back to Truk for temporary repairs.[12]

This attack marked the finale of the battle, named at the time the Battle of Stewart Islands.[13] The sacrifice of *Ryōjō* had been in vain. On the American side only two Dauntless had been lost, but on the other hand their bombing

---

12 *Chitose* eventually sailed back to Japan where she and her sister ship, *Chiyoda*, were both converted into light carriers. Both were later sunk off Cape Engano in October 1944, during the Battle of Leyte Gulf.

13 An atoll to the north-east of Malaita, now known as Sikaiana.

accuracy had taken a knock, with only four hits at the most scored from thirty-six bombs dropped in attacks. However, they were to more than make amends in the months that followed.

The result was claimed to be an American victory – whether it was so being very doubtful for it was Fletcher who withdrew even though *Wasp* was on her way to reinforce him. Morison later commented on this: 'every available carrier aircraft should have been used to protect tenuous lease on Guadalcanal. That was what they were there for.' He concluded, 'Fletcher won the battle to be sure; but only because the Japanese were more timid than he.' Lundstrom, as ever, exonerates Fletcher and blames poor communications. [Lundstrom, John B. – *Black Shoe Carrier Admiral,* op. cit.]

With the failure of Lieutenant General Harukichi Hyakutake's Seventeenth Army's all-out land effort to wrest back control of Henderson Field from the US Marines between 23 and 25 October, despite the pulverizing Japanese and cruiser bombardments of 14 October, Admiral Yamamoto was finally forced to seek a decision at sea once more. On the American side, the carrier *Saratoga* had been torpedoed and severely damaged by the *I-26* on 31 August and was out of action for three months, the carrier *Wasp* torpedoed and sunk on 14 September by the *I-19*. Frank Jack Fletcher soon departed and Vice Admiral William Frederick Halsey Jr had been appointed as ComSoPac (Commander South Pacific) and was determined not to yield an inch of Solomon Islands' territory: the stage was therefore set for the last great carrier duel of 1942.

On 11 October the Japanese fleet had begun moving out of Truk anchorage and heading south, once more divided in various complex forces, with the main change that the battleships were sent ahead of the carriers in the hope of luring all the US air attacks and leaving their own carriers, in the rear, free to strike at their opposite numbers. This led to the exchange known as the Battle of Santa Cruz which was fought between 22 and 27 October. Thus Admiral Hiroaki Abe led the way with his Vanguard Force, the battleships *Hiei* and *Kirishima*, three heavy cruisers, *Chikuma, Suzuya* and *Tone*, the light cruiser *Nagara* and seven destroyers, which, after marking time and waiting for a confirmation of success signal from the troops ashore that they had succeeded, by 25 October were some sixty miles (100km) south of Admiral Chōichi Nagumo's carrier strike force with the carriers *Shōkaku, Zuikaku* and *Zuihō*, the heavy cruiser *Kumano* and eight destroyers.

These Japanese carriers were on a course set to pass east of Malaita Island, in the same waters as the Eastern Solomons action had taken place. To the west of Nagumo was the Advance Force under Vice Admiral

Nobutake Kondō, with battleships *Haruna* and *Kongō*, heavy cruisers *Atago, Maya, Myōkō* and *Takao*, light cruiser *Isuzu* and her eight destroyers. Beyond these was the Air Group Force of Rear Admiral Kakuji Kakuta, with the light carrier *Junyō* and two destroyers.[14] In total then the Japanese sortied out with four battleships, two fleet and two light carriers, eight heavy and two light cruisers and twenty-five destroyers. In addition, twelve submarines again set up advance patrol lines.

One more the Americans were fully forewarned, and adopted the same battle tactics as before, with two carrier task groups, Task Force 16 under Rear Admiral Thomas Cassin Kinkaid, with the carrier *Enterprise*, battleship *South Dakota*, heavy cruiser *Portland*, and AA cruiser *San Juan* with seven destroyers. These had sailed from Pearl Harbor on 16 October and had rendezvoused with the other units below the New Hebrides on the 23rd. The other group was Task Force 17, built around the carrier *Hornet* under Rear Admiral George Dominic Murray, with two heavy cruisers, *Northampton* and *Pensacola,* two AA cruisers, *Juneau* and *San Diego*, and six destroyers. A third force, Task Force 64, under Rear Admiral Willis Augustus Lee, had the battleship *Washington*, one heavy cruiser, *San Francisco*, light cruiser *Helena*, AA cruiser *Atlanta* and six more destroyers. This gave the Americans a tally of two battleships, two carriers, four heavy, one light and three AA cruisers and nineteen destroyers. In the air the American carrier air groups fielded a total of forty-seven SBDs. In total air strength, as well as in ship numbers, the Japanese figure of 199 aircraft far outnumbered the US total of 136.

The Japanese Vanguard Force was located by a US Navy Consolidated PBY on the afternoon of 23 October and Yamamoto, who once more directed the battle at long range from aboard the battleship *Yamato* anchored at Truk, ordered his carrier forces to reverse course to the north, while his heavy ships continued south-east, therefore widening the gap between them and once again limiting mutual support. Thus, it was not until the 25th that these same US scouting aircraft also located the three Japanese carriers bringing up the rear. Shore-based air attacks, as usual, accomplished nothing, while *Junyō* sent her air striking force against Guadalcanal, bombing shore positions at Lunga Point. Neither of the two opposing *carrier*-based scout forces had managed to make contact on the 25th

At 0603 on the 25th, *Enterprise* launched eighteen SBDs, commanded by Lieutenant Commander James Richard Lee, in an attempt to locate the

---

14 The light carrier *Hiyō*, which had originally been part of this force, had been sent back to Truk with another destroyer when she had developed engine problems on 22 October.

Japanese carriers. A further six Dauntless followed them off *Enterprise's* flight-deck to carry out anti-submarine patrols (termed Inner Air Patrol or IAP) around the force while, at 0630, three other SBDs, piloted by Lieutenant William Inman Martin, Lieutenant (j.g.) John Henry Finrow (both VS-10) and Ensign Leonard Robinson (VB-10) were transferred to *Hornet* to make up her numbers. At this time the American ships were steering north-west and were closing the 220-mile (354km) gap between them and the oncoming enemy. The first search group searched in vain and, having made no contacts, returned and were recovered by *Enterprise* from 1008 onward. One returning Wildcat F4F fighter botched the landing aboard *Enterprise,* knocking overboard one Dauntless and trashing a further three SBDs on the deck. Suddenly the earlier generous transfer of Dauntless to the *Hornet* seemed like not such a good idea after all. When everything was finally untangled further sighting reports had come in at 1150 and Admiral Halsey, based ashore back at Nouméa, New Caledonia, immediately (and typically) signalled 'Attack – Repeat – Attack'.

Kinkaid opted to close the range before despatching his initial force and it was not until 1336 that Lee again led twelve VS-10 Dauntless on a second search-and-attack sortie with instructions to scout an arc 200 miles (320km) deep from west to north, but to return before nightfall if nothing was found. Lee's dozen was to be followed an hour later by a full attack strike force which included a further twelve Dauntless.

The scouting flight duly flew north to the limit of their range, but found the darkening seas empty. By the time these aircraft had returned to *Enterprise* the sun had set, and they were obliged to make a night landing, the first that many of the more junior pilots had ever undertaken. Not surprisingly, seven aircraft ditched, including three of the SBDs which had run out of fuel; fortunately their aircrew were rescued.

After Lee's dozen had droned off on their mission Lieutenant Commander James Alfred Thomas was scheduled to follow them with another twelve Dauntless, from VB-10. In the event, just five SBDs were launched in the second strike, due to the confusion on *Enterprise's* flight-deck.

Table 26: *Enterprise* Second Attack Force, 25 October 1042		
Pilot	**Aircrew**	**Unit**
Lieutenant Commander James Alfred Thomas	ARM3c Gordon Chester Gardner	VB-10
Ensign Dan Hartzell Frissell	ARM3c Charles Henry Otterstetter	VB-10

Ensign Paul Mathew Halloran	ARM3c Wilmer Earl Gallagher	VB-10
Lieutenant (j.g.) Robert Douglas Gibson	ARM3c Clifford Ermest Schindele	VB-10
Ensign Jefferson Haney Carroum	ARM3c Robert C. Hynson	VB-10

Lee's little group flew further than authorized, pushing out to 200 miles, which he (mistakenly) believed were Kinkaid's instructions, and then stretched that yet a further thirty miles, but still without any sighting. Meanwhile Lee's group, also without luck, had returned and had all been gathered back aboard *Enterprise* from 1902 onward.

Not so Thomas's flight. On reaching their furthest-out position, or new 'Point Option', they were thus already beyond the safety limit with regard to fuel and the plate-smooth sea remained disappointingly vacant. Their 1,000lb bombs were unceremoniously dumped into the sea and engines were re-set for maximum economy for the long, long trek homeward in the gathering dusk. They finally reached the Task Force at 1830 but, before they could drop down on the nearest friendly flight-deck, drained tanks finally ran out of Avgas and both Ensigns Frissell and Halloran, their Dauntless running on fumes alone, were forced to ditch. Fortunately, the two aircrews were rescued safely by the destroyers *Cushing* and *Porter* respectively. Thomas and Gibson barely got down but Carroum was not so fortunate, and, ignoring a wave-off because he had no fuel whatsoever, he missed the wires and thumped his mount into *Enterprise*'s island, knocking off one wing and his propeller chewing up the Dauntless of Gibson ahead of him, fortunately without fatalities. It had been both an abortive and an expensive mission. Thus, even before the battle was properly joined, the SBDs were taking heavy losses with nothing to show for them.

Both sides awaited the coming of light to locate and hit their opponents before they could be hit. In fact, early on 26 October, at 0650, a scouting seaplane from the heavy cruiser *Tone* finally sighted the US carriers and the three Japanese carriers launched their own strikes in two waves, followed by a third one of twenty-nine aircraft from *Junyō,* which tried to coordinate with her three sisters as best she could. On the American side, at 1150, a Catalina PBY from Espiritu Santo located the Abe force and also the Nagumo force. The latter had turned back south at 1800, but at 0400 the next day had reversed course yet again; however, the sighting report did not reach Kinkaid for some time.

As soon as it came in, Kinkaid launched two deck strikes; twelve SBDs commanded by Lieutenant Commander James Richard Lee began launching at 1336 on a 'Scout-and-Attack' mission. Thus the 26th brought about the action *both* sides sought, but *not* the results expected. Aboard *Enterprise* sixteen scouting SBDs were launched at 0619 with orders to cover an arc from 235 to 360 degrees.

Table 27: *Enterprise* First Scouting and Attack Force, 26October 1942		
Pilot	**Aircrew**	**Aircraft**
Lieutenant (j.g.) Thomas Wesley Ramsay	ARM2c Lawrence Sargent Craft	10-S-10
Lieutenant (j.g.) Joseph Bloch	ARM3c Henry Clay Blalock	10-S-6
Lieutenant Stockton Birney Strong	ARM1c Clarence Halman Garlow	10-S-13
Ensign Charles Boyd Irvine	ARM3c Elgie Pearl Williams	10-S-2
Lieutenant (j.g.) Martin Doan Carmody	ARM2c John Liska	10-S-7
Lieutenant (j.g.) Leslie James Ward	ARM3c Nicholas Baumgartner Jr	10-S-18
Lieutenant Commander James Richard Lee	ACRM Irby Andrews Sanders	10-S-1
Lieutenant (j.g.) William Edward Johnson	ARM3C Hugh Price Hughes Jr	10-S-8
Lieutenant (j.g.) Howard Reason Burnett	ARM3c Robert F. Wynn	10-S-4
Lieutenant (j.g.) Kenneth Raymond Miller	ARM2c David John Cawley	10-S-5
Lieutenant Vivian Warren Welch	ARM1c Harold Claude Ansley Jr	10-B-13
Lieutenant (j.g.) Bruce Allan McGraw	ARM3c Ralph H. Horton Jr	10-B-21
Lieutenant (j.g.) Harold Lloyd Buell	ARM3c George Eldo Eiswald	10-B-6
Ensign Russell A. Hoogerwerf	ARM2c Harold Sidney Nobis	10-B-11
Lieutenant (j.g.) J. Don Wakeham	ARM1c Forest Glen Stanley	10-B-1
Ensign Edward J. Stevens	ARM3c James Warren Nelson	10-B-12

This force was followed by the launching of an Inner patrol and also, at 0621, the transferring of various aircraft that had landed on the wrong carriers the night before, including three SBDs in each direction.

Two of *Enterprise*'s sixteen-plane scouting force, Lieutenant Vivian Warren Welch and Lieutenant (j.g.) Bruce Allan McGraw of VB-10, found the Vanguard Force at 0617 and made a sighting report, which they repeated a quarter of an hour later, but no Japanese carriers were mentioned. Not until 0650 did two more of the scouting group's SBDs – piloted by Lieutenant Commander James Richard Lee, CO of VS-10, and Ensign William Edward Johnson – sight Nagumo's ships. Lee's radioman, ACRM Irby Andrews Sanders, sent a sighting report of two carriers and accompanying vessels three times before the SBDs were chased away by the Zero CAP, and claimed to have shot down three of them before evading the rest in thick cloud.

These reports were picked up by two more Dauntless aircrews, and they surprised the enemy to make an unopposed, target-of-opportunity dive-bombing attack at 0720. This SBD duo, piloted by Lieutenant Stockton Birney Strong and Ensign Charles Boyd Irvine, with radiomen ARM1c Clarence Halman Garlow and ARM3c Elgie Pearl Williams respectively, left their own sector 100 miles (160km) away on their own initiative, and, at 14,000 feet (4,300m) unerringly zeroed in on the Japanese carriers and managed to get up-sun without being observed.

In the words of Irvine, they then 'split our wing flaps ... and pushed over into 80-degree dives, all the time expecting the fleet to start pitching up lead'.[15] To their continued surprise, however, nothing of the kind happened as they continued to bore in until they reached a bomb-release height of 1,500 feet (450m). Both their bombs left the crutches as the Dauntless hit the deck to escape from the inevitable Zekes which were now totally aroused, but far too late to influence events.[16] The rear gunners each claimed to have destroyed a Zero apiece in the stern chase that followed, and the Dauntless both took hits in return over a forty-five-mile (70km) battle before the fighters gave up. Both dive-bombers eventually made it back to *Enterprise,* as did all the other search teams.

Their daring had its just reward, for these two Dauntless obtained two perfect direct hits aft on *Zuihō,* one of which decimated her after anti-aircraft gun positions. The other went right through her flight-deck aft, and penetrated down into her hangar deck, leaving a fifty-feet-wide (15m) hole which meant that she could then no longer land her aircraft, although she

---

15 Buell, *Dauntless Helldivers,* op. cit.

16 According to a press interview with Eugene Burns, Lieutenant Strong recalled that there were 'about twenty planes parked on the forecastle (sic*).*' Burns, Eugene, *Then There Was One: The USS Enterprise and the First Year of War.* New York, 1944. Harcourt Brace & Company. But another account has it that 'There was just time to notice that both decks were empty', *The Big 'E',* op. cit.

remained manoeuvrable herself. She was thus still able to launch all her striking force before returning to Truk for temporary repairs. Another of the enterprising scout teams dive-bombed the heavy cruiser *Tone* at 0626, but without scoring any hits and they had no effect on her at all. The two US carriers had meanwhile despatched their own striking forces in three groups, totalling seventy-three aircraft. They were not very well co-ordinated and went off in three small waves, *Hornet* launching twenty-nine aircraft at 0730, *Enterprise* nineteen at 0800 and *Hornet* twenty-five more at 0810.

Meanwhile *Enterprise* also organized another IAP:

Table 28: *Enterprise* Second Inner Patrol, 26 October 1942		
Pilot	**Radioman**	**Unit**
Lieutenant Robert Conrad Frohlich	ARM3c Wayne Carson Colley	VS-10
Lieutenant (j.g.) Ralph Hays Goddard	ARM2c Charles Harold Owen Hamilton	VB-10
Lieutenant (j.g.) John L. Griffith	ARM3c Roy J. Haas	VB-10
Lieutenant (j.g.) Frank Russell West	ARM3c Leonard T. McAdams	VB-10
Ensign Leonard Lucier	ARM3C John Edgar Criswell	VS-10
Ensign Richard McGill Buchanan	ARM3c David Otto Herger	VB-10

The Japanese first air strike evaded the American CAP completely and, at 0910, commenced their dives. The Aichi D3A 'Vals' had to face a very heavy barrage, but in ten minutes they had overwhelmed *Hornet*'s defences, obtaining five bomb and two torpedo hits, while two further aircraft crash-dived into the ship where their payloads detonated, adding to the carnage. With 111 dead and many wounded, she was immobilized. Large fires were finally brought under control and she was taken in tow by the heavy cruiser *Northampton*.

The second main Japanese air strike arrived just after 1000 and this force located *Enterprise*, which had earlier hidden in a rain squall. A large number of aircraft concentrated on her and hit her twice, while also scoring a very near miss with bombs, killing forty-four of her crew and wounding seventy-five more, but no torpedoes struck home. Despite her damage she continued to operate her aircraft. Finally, at 1121, the *Junyō* air strike arrived and attacked the *Enterprise* group, but initially managed only a single hit and one near-miss on the carrier.

In reply, *Hornet*'s first strike found the burning *Zuihō* and *Shōkakō* at 0918. Fifteen SBDs from VB-8 and VS-8, led by Lieutenant Commander William John Widhelm, along with six TBF Avengers and eight Grumman F4F Wildcat fighters as escorts, arrived over the enemy ships.

Table 29: *Hornet* First Strike, 26 October 1942		
Pilot	**Radioman**	**Unit**
Lieutenant Commander William John Widhelm	ARM1c George David Stokely	VS-8
Lieutenant (j.g.) Ralph Bernard Hovind	ARM3c Charles Benjamin Lufborrow	VS-8
Lieutenant (j.g.) William E. Woodman	ARM3c David T. Manus	VS-8
Ensign Clayton Evan Fisher	ARM2c George E. Ferguson	VS-8
Lieutenant Benjamin Eugene Moore Jr	ARM2c Richard Cusack McEwen	VS-8
Lieutenant (j.g.) Donald Kirkpatrick Jr	ARM2c Harmon L. Brendle	VS-8
Lieutenant (j.g.) James McMillan Forbes	ARM3c Ronald H. Arenth	VS-8
Lieutenant (j.g.) George Glenn Estes Jr	ARM3c Jay Arthur Pugh	VS-8 *
Lieutenant (j.g.) Henry Nichols Ervin	ARM2c Lanois Mardi Wheeler	VS-8 *
Lieutenant (j.g.) John Frazier Richey	ARM2c Ralph Arthur Gowling	VS-8 *
Lieutenant James Everett Vose Jr	ARM2c Joseph Yewonishon	VB-8
Lieutenant (j.g.) William Douglas Carter	ARM2c Oral Lester Moore	VB-8
Lieutenant Frederick Bates Jr	ARM1c Clyde S. Montensen	VB-8
Lieutenant (j.g.) Kenneth Broughton White	ARM3c Leroy Quillen	VB-8
Lieutenant (j.g.) Philip Farnsworth Grant	ARM2c Floyd Dell Kilmer	VB-8
Lieutenant (j.g.) Roy Philip Gee	ARM1c Donald L. Canfield	VB-10
Lieutenant (j.g.) Forrester Clinton Auman	ARM3c Samuel P. McLean	VB-10

*Flying VB-10 aircraft.

They were hotly engaged by the CAP as they approached the target at 12,000 feet (3,600m) and the Zekes shot down up four of the SBDs, including Widheim's aircraft. He ditched in the water but both he and his radioman, ARM1c George David Stokely, survived and were rescued by a seaplane some days later. Another Dauntless staggered back to *Enterprise* with a wounded pilot, but the other two SBDs were lost without survivors.

As the remaining Dauntless tipped over into their attack dives, command of the dive-bombers devolved on to Lieutenant James Everett Vose Jr, and these eleven aircraft made a well-nigh perfect attack, scoring at least four, and probably six, direct hits with their 1,000lb (450kg) bombs on *Shōkakō*, two forward and four in the area of the after elevator, confirmed by Japanese photographs taken of the subsequent fire-fighting. These fires almost destroyed the ship and she was forced to withdraw from the battle. Many of her airborne aircraft found sanctuary aboard *Zuihō*.

Meanwhile the second wave had taken off from *Enterprise* and this group included three SBDs from VB-10 but piloted by VS-10's Lieutenants (j.g.) George Glenn Estes Jr, Henry Nichols Ervin and John Frazier Richey and they were armed with 1,000lb (450kg) bombs. These, along with the second *Hornet* strike, including seven SBDs, missed the Japanese carriers and, as their enemy had planned, dashed themselves against the heavy flak of Abe force's big ships. Ervin, Estes and Richey made their dives against the battleship *Kirishima* and claimed to have scored two direct hits, one on B turret and one starboard amidships, plus a near-miss off her starboard bow. Unfortunately for them Japanese records reveal that only slight damage was inflicted in these attacks which caused *Kirishima* little discomfort. All three SBDs returned to their carrier, again stating to have shot down at least one Zero fighter on the way back.

Table 30: *Hornet*'s Second Strike, 26 October 1942		
Pilot	**Radioman**	**Unit**
Lieutenant John Joseph Lynch	ARM3c James Riley Woods	VB-8
Lieutenant (j.g.) Joseph Wiley King	ARM3c Thomas M. Walsh	VB-8
Lieutenant (j.g.) Thomas Wood Jr	ARM3c George F. Martz	VB-8
Lieutenant Edgar Erwin Stebbins	ARM2c Ervin R. Hillhouse	VS-8
Lieutenant (j.g.) Philip James Rusk	ARM3c John Louis Tereskerz	VS-8
Lieutenant (j.g.) Albert Harold Wood	ARM2c Richard Thomas Woodson	VS-8
Lieutenant Raymond S. Davis	ARM1c Ralph Philips	VS-8
Lieutenant (j.g.) Benjamin Tappan Jr	ARM2c James H. Black Jr	VS-8

TWO CARRIER DUELS

Enterprise's Second Strikes, 26 October 1942		
Pilot	**Radioman**	**Unit**
Lieutenant (j.g.) George Glenn Estes Jr	ARM2c Ralph Arthur Gowling	VS-10
Lieutenant (j.g.) Henry Nichols Ervin	ARM3c Jay Burnett Pugh	VS-10
Lieutenant (j.g.) John Frazier Richey	ARM2c Lanois Mardi Wheeler	VS-10

Then the *Hornet*'s nine Dauntless, led by Lieutenant John Joseph Lynch, arrived over the Japanese force at 0915 and commenced their dives. The American pilots immediately scored two bomb hits on the heavy cruiser *Chikuma,* and these pierced her bridge from both the port and starboard sides, almost demolishing it and killing most of her bridge personnel. The splinters from three further near-misses very close alongside the same ship likewise perforated her hull and upper works and wiped out several AA gunnery crews. Then two more direct hits were made, one of which plunged through her deck and detonated in one of her engine rooms. The trio of VS-10 Dauntless, under Lieutenant (j.g.) George Glenn Estes Jr, having lost the turn made by their fighter and torpedo-bomber companions, now arrived and took up the cudgel – claiming two direct hits and a near miss. After all these claims it is sobering to record that Japanese records show that only three bombs actually hit this vessel; even so the Dauntless had seemingly crushed her, with 190 officers and men killed and 154 more wounded, including her commanding officer, Captain Keizo Komura, in this devastating assault. But those Japanese heavy cruisers were tough nuts to crack – and despite their accuracy, the SBDs still failed to sink her, and she was able to sail back to Truk at a speed of 23 knots, escorted by the destroyers *Tanikaze* and *Urakaze*, for temporary repairs. The rest of the American force kept up the barrage against other targets, but it lacked the concentration of effort shown to *Chikuma*, only registering near-misses on the heavy cruiser *Tone* and the destroyer *Teruzuki*.

On return the surviving SBDs found *Hornet* sinking and *Enterprise* very badly damaged. Nonetheless, while many were forced to ditch alongside various escorting cruisers and destroyers, *Enterprise* herself managed to land aboard thirteen SBDs at 1607, four of her own and nine orphans from *Hornet*.

After two escorting US destroyers, *Anderson* and *Mustin*, failed to sink the still-floating wreck of *Hornet* despite hitting her with three of the ten torpedoes they aimed at her and firing 430 5-inch (12.7cm) shells into her, they abandoned her when the advance guard of the Japanese surface force was sighted coming up. The Japanese had hoped to tow *Hornet* back as a trophy, but she was too far gone, and she was finally sent to the bottom by four torpedoes fired by the Japanese destroyers *Akigumo* and *Makigumo*. Not until 1800 did Abe and Kondo give up their hard stern-chase and retire to the north, frustrated. Meanwhile *Junyō* had joined *Zuikaku* which had retired through Indispensable Strait.

The Japanese had not lost any ships, but three carriers, a heavy cruiser and one destroyer had been damaged, *Shōkakō* and *Chikuma* very badly, and they had also lost ninety-seven aircraft, twenty-six of them to the anti-aircraft firepower of the battleship *South Dakota* alone.[17] The Dauntless also performed in the air defence role again and claimed to have destroyed at least seven of the enemy. The Americans lost eighty-one aircraft of all types, including thirty-one SBDS, and had the carrier *Hornet* (with 118 of her crew) and the destroyer *Porter* sunk, with *Enterprise, South Dakota, Portland, San Juan* and the destroyers *Morris* and *Smith* (fifty-seven dead), all damaged in varying degrees.

The results, like those of the Eastern Solomons battle earlier, would seem to indicate a Japanese tactical victory, albeit one which was very dearly bought – and the Japanese yet again failed to exploit their success to the fullest extent. In the end four Japanese carriers had not totally defeated two US carriers, and Guadalcanal would ultimately be lost, as would, eventually, the Empire.

---

17 Later the anti-aircraft gunners of *Enterprise* and *San Juan* claimed helping in the destruction of some of these.

Chapter 7

Kiwis at Bougainville 1944

By the spring of 1944 Allied dive-bomber squadrons were playing a major role in pushing back the great arc of Japanese conquests, known by them and to their unwilling new subjects as the 'South-East Asia Co-Prosperity Zone'. At the extreme west end of the battle line, on the Burmese-Indian border, it was the British and Indian Vengeance squadrons who had first held the line and then started the much-delayed and resource-starved advance to re-conquest.[1] In the southern centre it had been the Australian Vengeance Wing which had held up the standard first planted by their brothers in makeshift Commonwealth Wirraway squadrons in Papua and New Guinea. At the south-eastern end of this southern front, in the long Solomon Islands chain, steady progress was also being made toward the reduction of the Japanese main base at Rabaul and in this it was the Douglas SBD Dauntless squadrons of the United States Navy and Marine Corps which predominated from Tulagi and Guadalcanal onward. But even here the Commonwealth air forces were playing their part, and a vital part, in maintaining the dive-bomber pressure. It was during the next great step forward up the bitterly contested island route that one unique, but almost forgotten, Allied dive-bomber unit found its finest hours.

No. 25 Dive-Bomber Squadron had, as its first and only Commanding Officer, Theodore Jasper MacLean de Lange CBE DFC RNZAF, later Air Commodore, and he told me that the formation 'was the only squadron of its kind in the RNZAF'. But if it was special, its actual achievements during its short but eventful combat lifespan were second-to-none in that service.

As part of the original planned offensive against Rabaul, New Britain, it was envisaged that the Allies would methodically advance in two prongs, one under the auspices of the US Navy pushing up through the northern Solomon Islands while the other, as part of General Douglas MacArthur's

---

1   See Smith, Peter C., *Vengeance in Battle*, Pen & Sword, Barnsley, 2019.

ELKTON planned return to the Philippines, pushing along the northern coast of New Guinea to Wewak and the Admiralty Islands. MacArthur had called for at least 1,800 aircraft to support the twenty-one army divisions he needed to achieve this objective. As part of the South Pacific prong of this grandiose offensive, the US Navy, USAAF, USMC and RNZAF would all play their parts. Later it was decided merely to neutralize and by-pass Rabaul itself, but to do this, air bases would still need to be established within range of the many Japanese airfields in the vicinity of the town and its two very active volcanoes.

The job of landing and securing a toehold on Bougainville was given to 1st Marine Amphibious Corps commanded by General Alexander Archer Vandegrift USMC and was codenamed Operation CHERRYBLOSSOM.

On 1 November 1943 the US Marines put their reinforced 3rd Division, commanded by Major General Allen Hal Tornage, ashore at Empress Augusta Bay, halfway up the west coast of Bougainville, the largest island of the Solomons group, which was garrisoned by a large Japanese force of around 36,800 soldiers from the 6th and 17th Divisions, IJA, plus some navy personnel. The Japanese commander, Lieutenant General Masatake Kanda, had expected the attack to be made around Buin in the south of the island and thus the marines were able to establish their bridgehead easily, but their toehold remained small and precarious. This was, however, suitable enough for their purpose, which was to construct fighter airfields in the Cape Torokina area in order to support their bombing offensive in neutralizing Rabaul. For a short period, there was an uneasy stalemate, with the bulk of the island still in Japanese hands and counter-attack being organized by the largely still intact Japanese 6th Division.

Back in New Zealand the RNZAF had by 31 July 1943, taken delivery of nine SBD-3 dive-bombers on extended loan from the US Marine Corps Air Group 14 (MAG-14),[2] . which, by July 1943, was itself already based at the newly-constructed top secret airfield of Seagrove, at Clarks Beach, near Manukau Habour on the North Island, which had been hastily built to defend Auckland. They had recently been rested there after serving in hard combat with the Cactus Air Force on Guadalcanal and in the adjacent naval battles around 'The Slot'.[3]

---

2 RNZAF Memorandum No. 129, dated 26 July 1943.

3 This arrangement was purely on 'local arrangements' with the Commander, Air South Pacific (COMAIRSOPAC), Admiral Aubrey Wray Fitch USN and had nothing whatsoever to do with Lend-Lease.

As part of the original arrangement the RNZAF was to have been equipped with no less than 120 SBD Dauntless dive-bombers (or new Army A-24s direct from the production line in Tulsa, Oklahoma, at the rate of ten per month). These would equip four RNZAF dive-bomber units, Nos 25, (by September), 26, (by October), 27 (by December) and 28 Squadrons, ready to deploy by February 1944. which were to be fully trained in US Navy tactics, procedures and equipment in order to operate seamlessly into one integrated Allied system. As the bulk of the crew were to be found from personnel already flying totally obsolete RAF biplane types like the Hawker Hind and Vickers Vincent, such assimilation was not expected to be easy.

No. 26 Squadron was to have been based on Norfolk Island but this was later cancelled as the Allies moved over from a defensive to an offensive strategy that saw them steadily 'island-hop' towards the main Japanese base at Rabaul. However, this proved academic because the promised deliveries from Tulsa failed to materialise and RNZAF squadrons' readiness dates kept slipping back. As an interim measure, a number of surplus USMC SBDs at Espiritu Santo were suggested as short-term alternatives.

In January Admiral Fitch, with full agreement of the RNZAF and New Zealand Government, cancelled all SBD (A-24) and TBF Squadrons and transferred their crews to other units. This was later amended to allow No. 25 Squadron to carry out a single operational tour of duty in the Northern Solomons prior to their withdrawal. Political considerations further complicated matters, with that highly Anglophobic Fleet Admiral Ernest Joseph King back in Washington DC railing against any 'British' involvement in the re-conquest of Australian and New Zealand mandated areas of the Pacific Ocean, in what he considered 'his' bailiwick. The more reasonable Fitch suggested that the Kiwis share US Navy and Marine Corps facilities and be lent some of the battle-weary SBDs (and later SBD-4s) languishing at Espiritu Santo after hard combat, to train with as an interim measure.[4]

These aircraft were assigned serial numbers NZ5001 to NZ5009 respectively, replacing temporary serials NZ205 to NZ222 respectively, and were used to form the first of the planned RNZAF dive-bomber squadrons in order for New Zealand to contribute to the air contingent of the ELKTON plan. The unit concerned was 25 Squadron, RNZAF, which had been formed at Seagrove on 31 July 1943 with, initially, twelve and,

---

4 Duxbury, David – *No. 25 Dive Bomber Squadron: A Brief Administrative History,* 31 August 2016 version.

subsequently, eighteen crews. The squadron was originally due to move over to Waipapakauri, an RNZAF station to the north of Kaitaia, the following month and there be brought up to full strength later. This plan was never implemented and proved to be a curse because the unit remained in limbo and was regarded for most of the difficult forming-up period, and indeed beyond that, as merely a detached flight. Thus, none of the essentials, from office furniture to supplies, were easily available. Despite such inauspicious beginnings the squadron, thrown back on its own resources and fortitude to a far greater extent than usual, applied itself with dedication which led to a fierce pride in its own independence and established a reputation for self-reliance which was soon to stand it in very good stead.

The first nine aircraft were signed for, on behalf of the squadron, by a flight sergeant from the large RNZAF Whenuapai base, near Auckland. An Equipment Officer, Flying Officer Bruce Leo Barker, was posted from Onerahi, in the same location, on 11 August, and obtained some additional supplies from those airfields. Maintenance was a nightmare problem, for obviously the US Marines did not wish to part with their best aircraft. Although 1 Repair Depot at Hamilton supplied back up, and the Marines themselves generously chipped in with vital spares by cannibalizing some of their other 'flyable duds' before they soon departed, all routine maintenance was carried out by No. 25 Maintenance Unit at Seagrove airfield, north of Auckland Harbour but, even so, it took a week to bring even a single Dauntless up to a flyable condition. Even with an all-out effort, fewer than three or four aircraft could be kept in the air initially which seriously curtailed the strenuous efforts being made to get the squadron's training programme underway, despite the allocation of US Marine Corps Master Sergeant Edward W. Carmichael, USMC, as an instructor.[5] All these aircraft were ferried to New Zealand from Espiritu Santo via Norfolk Island by USMC aircrew.

A further four SBDs were acquired to help the squadron over some of this difficult situation, but those were in little better shape than the others and, in September, further urgings brought forth yet a further five, giving the squadron a total paper strength of eighteen. (NZ5019 to NZ5027) respectively) but on 13 September one of the original aircraft, NZ211,

5 *Edward W. Carmichael interviewed by Natalie Foosekis*, Oral History OH 368. pp. 13-14, 2007: Fullerton CA. El Toro Air Station/California State University. Carmichael was later assigned to No. 30 Squadron. He was made an honorary lifetime member of the Royal New Zealand Air Force Association for his nine month's work there before he was recalled to Efate.

piloted by 32-year old Pilot Officer William David McJannet, with Sergeant Douglas Martin James Cairns as rear-gunner, stalled and spun into the ground in a gully at Waiuku and burst into flames with no survivors. The reinforcements, once made flyable, enabled a limited start to be made on familiarization flights and conversion training of the assigned pilots, most of whom came from existing army co-operation squadrons and anti-aircraft flights. A start was also made on introducing the Wireless Operators/Gunners to the Dauntless, most of those aircrew being fresh from training courses in Canada. The various programmes gained momentum and were finally complete by 6 January 1944 when the squadron flew its full complement of seventeen aircraft over Auckland, prior to embarkation. This event was notable for being one of the largest assemblies of RNZAF aircraft seen up to that date.

Meanwhile, on 7 December 1943, the squadron's servicing unit was embarked aboard the 11,030-ton US transport *Octans (*AF-26) and sailed off to establish a forward base at Pallikulo Bay, Espiritu Santo, the northernmost island of the New Hebrides group. The squadron itself followed, the aircrew being air ferried by No. 40 Squadron in Douglas C-47 Skytrain and Lockheed Model C-60 Lodestar transport aircraft and arriving at that base on 30 January 1944 when flying training was immediately re-commenced. Between 7 and 13 January 1944 day and night flying practice, dive-bombing, and gunnery and beam practice were all conducted from Espiritu Santo. The original aircraft had by then been replaced and left behind at Seagrove in readiness to train the next planned squadron, No. 26, COMAIRSOPAC had already arranged that another group of twenty-seven SBD-4s allocated RNZAF serials NZ5015 to NZ5045, be prepared for the squadron at Paillikulo Bay airfield.

Yet further training and 'tropicalization' of the SBDs was carried out through into February by the squadron itself. By 6 February they had clocked up 40 hours 30 minutes of non-operational flying, but this training programme soon intensified and resulted in the squadron's second loss when, on 11 February, NZ5037, piloted by Flying Officer Alexander Moore, of Dunedin, with Flight Sergeant John Keith Munro of Tahuna, Morrinsville, in the back seat, failed to return from a beam-flying practice flight. They had taken off at 1345 for the one-hour flight but failed to return and no trace was found of them or their aircraft despite extensive searches.[6]

---

6   It was not until 1987 that the wreck was discovered in jungle, salvaged and returned to
    New Zealand by No. 3 Squadron, plus a C-130 Hercules.

Before moving into the combat zone, however, 25 Squadron was re-equipped yet again, receiving twenty-three new SBD-5s (assigned serials NZ5046 to NZ5068 respectively) on 11 February. The squadron commander had made very clear to those in authority that the existing SBD-4s had been in no better condition that the original SBD-3s and were not considered suitable aircraft to take into full combat duty. He was duly heeded this time but, even so, ultimately the squadron had to commence operations with fourteen new and four reconditioned aircraft. The aim was to have the squadron ready for battle by the end of February in order to be established at Piva, one of the new airstrips hastily constructed on Bougainville and known as Piva North bomber airfield. Yet further weeks flying time was still required to familiarize themselves with their new mounts, but that was all that the war permitted.

During the week 14 to 19 January the weekly flying time of 169 hours 10 minutes was up by dive-bombing practices and beam approaches, including combined operations with 30 Squadron's Grumman TBF Avengers and US Marne Air Groups 11, 12 and 21. One mass dive-bombing attack by all 102 aircraft took place against Cook Reef, to the south of the group, and other target areas included Sail Rock. Much valuable experience in methods of attack, rendezvous form up and break up and the like was gained at this time. Another 203 hours 50 minutes flying time was attained the following week and further exercises were conducted with MAGs 11 and 12, while 49 hours 15 minutes of practice flying was carried out between 28 February and 5 March. From 6 March until the squadron departed for Bougainville, transiting via Henderson Field on Guadalcanal, only a final 12 hours 15 minutes was achieved. No. 25 Squadron departed from Pallikulo in two groups of nine aircraft apiece. During the two-stage ferry flight, these SBDs were equipped with steel drop tanks, mounted on the underwing bomb carriers. These tanks were not normally used by land-based SBDs. Unfortunately, on landing at Henderson Field, one SBD (NZ5055), piloted by Flying Officer Bruce Graham, was written off in a hard landing.

The news from Bougainville was not good. Piva airstrip was being steadily shelled by artillery which the Japanese had moved up as they concentrated their attack ever closer around the restricted beachhead perimeter. It was rumoured that extra enemy aircraft had been flown into the Rabaul airstrips from the Japanese main fleet and the Allies' position was apparently becoming perilous in the extreme. However, the Japanese were, in actuality, pulling out most of their aircraft from Rabaul to Truk and this mass exodus, with extra flight activity, was misinterpreted by Allied observers. The actual area in Allied hands at Torokina at the beginning of March extended for about four miles along the coast of Empress Augusta Bay, and then ran inland from the beach to form a rough semicircle with a maximum depth of just three miles from the sea. The American 'Seebee' construction teams had quickly established three airstrips there, the original Torokina fighter strip, parallel with the beach, and a fighter and a bomber strip at Piva, respectively known as Piva Uncle and Piva Yoke, the latter being No. 25 Squadron's destination; this was located about two miles inland.

In late February US Intelligence had intercepted a code message to the Japanese commander in the south-west Pacific ordering an attack on the perimeter on 7 March. The Japanese plan was to launch a three-pronged attack under Major General Shun Iwasa, and Colonels Toyhorei Muda and Isashi Magata respectively, to drive the Allies back to the beaches where a naval attack would, they believed, complete their destruction. Right on cue, at 0600 on the morning of 8 March, the Japanese began an artillery bombardment and continued with intensive shelling for the rest of the month. Lieutenant General Kanda launched the bulk of the remaining 6th Division into the assault in three columns and for a time they came perilously close to achieving their objectives. Into this cauldron moved the servicing unit of No. 25 Squadron, their arrival coinciding with the Japanese shelling of the perimeter. Almost immediately the men had to be organized into defensive infantry platoons and allocated positions in the third line of defence in case the enemy should break through. In between those alarms they tried to prepare the strip for the SBDs to arrive with the enemy only a few hundred yards away from them. Much of the success of No. 25 Squadron's subsequent operations owed much to these men.

As their own report stated:

> The Squadron arrived at Bougainville when the activities around the perimeter were at their peak. The continuous shelling, particularly at night, and the noise of the return fire from our own guns prevented adequate sleep and rest. The shelling of the camp area and revetments while warming up and taxiing out for take-off was another mental hazard.

When the aircrew themselves arrived with their new aircraft all was ready. The squadron lost no time in getting their first sortie underway. Landing at Piva at noon on 23 March, they carried out their first operation at 0530 the following morning. That day the squadron made nineteen sorties, mainly dive-bombing attacks on enemy gun positions. The first two days' operations were intensive, and unique in the history of the RNZAF in that ground crews were given a grandstand view of the aircraft they were servicing dropping their bombs on enemy positions only 700 yards distant from their camp area. Being able to see the dive-bombers hitting back after being impotent and on the receiving end for so long boosted their morale. This continued to be true even through more enemy shelling. For example, a total of fifty-two shells arrived in the camp area on the day of the squadron's arrival. Usually the shelling started at dawn. The SBDs would start up in the midst of it and, once airborne, would stooge around Japanese positions to pick up the flashes of the guns and so pinpoint them. They did not have to venture very far; during the first two days eighteen aircraft and aircrews were operational out of eighteen. Thereafter the availability of units was kept high, despite all the difficulties. On average, the requirement was for some twelve aircraft, out of a normal total of fifteen, always to be kept serviceable. This objective was achieved and maintained for a three-month period, except for one single day when they were one aircraft short.

On the first day it was Squadron Leader de Lange who, along with Flying Officer L.T. Sewell, made the first operational sortie, an artillery-spotting mission at first light, and five more such missions were flown over the next three days. The first true dive-bombing strikes were also very successful. Four SBDs co-operated with twelve from the Marine Corps VB-305 squadron on 24 March with an attack on the enemy supply area at Tavera at the southern end of Empress Augusta Bay. Each New Zealand Dauntless placed a single 1,000lb bomb on the target and left a satisfactorily large pall of black smoke behind. A further twelve sorties were flown in support of the same Marine unit on another supply area to the east of Karno Hill, which overlooked their airstrip at Piva. During the first day's missions the squadron embarked Lieutenant Second Lieutenant Cyril Wynne Viggers, an artillery officer from 1st Fijian Infantry Battalion, who was familiar with the island and who pointed out the target area to the flight leaders. Two dozen 1,000lb bombs on the hill left this officer very satisfied with No. 25 Squadron's first mission while in a second attack the same day, although NZ5062 with Flight Sergeant Kelly and Flight Sergeant B. Cullen, received a shell through her rudder, the day's efforts were deemed totally successful.

On 25 March the eighteen aircraft flew two dive-bombing sorties of nine planes apiece against local enemy gun positions and troop concentrations, the SBDs pushing on down in a 75-degree attack angle to within 2,500 feet before releasing their single 1,000lb bomb loads. One Japanese artillery battery was completely destroyed this day, 25 Squadron being credited with two direct hits. It was subsequently leant that one of the Japanese colonels in charge of the attacking units on Bougainville was killed in these strikes.

From the third day, 26 March, onward the New Zealand SBDs began to range farther afield for, as well as defending their own base, they and the US Marine dive-bombers, were increasingly to assume the role of reducing Rabaul and nearby enemy-held island airstrips. From this time onward, although their work on Bougainville never ceased, their main strike efforts were directed more and more against Rabaul's several airstrips. Flights of six to twelve aircraft were sent in with the US Marine Corps squadrons every day, except during periods of bad weather. Vunakanua and Tobera airstrips were the targets most frequently attacked[7] From the very start No. 25 Squadron was expected to act as a United States unit, assimilating identical aircraft, weapons, tactics and language, with the same command. This process had commenced in May 1943 with four pilots, with wireless operator/air gunners and technical staff, attending courses run by the US Navy and was continued with USMC instructors both at Seagrove and Espirtu Santo. RNZAF sent personnel to the States for training, returning in September.

On 26 March also, the New Zealanders assisted the Americans in carrying out an attack on Kavieng, New Ireland, in support of the US landings at Emirau, some seventy-five miles distant, to neutralize the enemy airstrip there. The attack was staged through Green Island to co-ordinate with further USMC dive-bomber units there but, on taking their departure, bad weather was encountered and No. 25 Squadron's aircraft, along with six Marine SBDs, missed the rendezvous. After flying for two-and-a-quarter hours they were forced to return to Green island. It was one of the very rare operations that the New Zealanders were forced to abort.

On the following day one aircraft from a flight of six again had to return to base but the remainder carried out an attack on a Japanese supply area at Talili Bay in eastern New Britain. The enemy AA fire encountered there was moderate in scale but accurately delivered but, although hits were taken, and damage received by individual machines was only minor in nature. All their bombs were reported as landing within the target area and many fires were started and a large column of smoke resulted as they left the area. That same day Japanese supply and personnel areas inland from the mouth of the Mafririci river at the south-eastern extremity of Empress Augusta Bay were

---

7 See Map 00 p. 00.

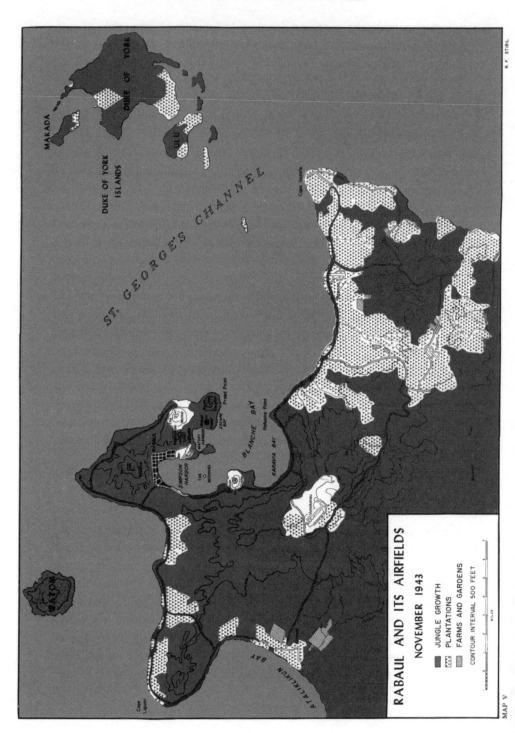

RABAUL AND ITS AIRFIELDS

NOVEMBER 1943

JUNGLE GROWTH
PLANTATIONS
FARMS AND GARDENS

CONTOUR INTERVAL 500 FEET

MAP V

attacked by six further SBDs. The actual target area was covered in dense foliage and results were therefore hard to make out; nonetheless ten of their bombs detonated within the assigned target zone. The dive-bombing attacks were followed with a strafing run made against the same area and also against an enemy supply barge which was spotted on the river itself.

Rabaul was again struck the following day, the target being Lakunai airfield. Thirty-six aircraft took part with No. 25 Squadron contributing their usual dozen planes, but, again, three of these were forced to abort with engine trouble. The remaining nine made confirmed hits on both the runway itself and AA positions in the face of intense fire, which left one Dauntless with her tail-plane full of machine-gun-bullet holes. Anti-aircraft positions were again the targets of six of No. 25 Squadron's aircraft in an attack on the enemy supply area at Vunapope, (Wunapope) at the north-eastern extremity of New Britain, on 29 March when three direct hits were confirmed.

An established routine was beginning to emerge as these strikes against Rabaul and its environs grew apace. The squadron's own Battle Report details the methods employed thus:

> The targets in the Rabaul area were, in the main, gun positions surrounding the aerodromes and supply areas. On four occasions the target was the supply area itself, and on three occasions the runway.
>
> The task of the SBDs during the attack is to knock out or quieten gun positions in order that the TBFs (Grumman Avenger torpedo bombers being used by both the US Marines and 30 Squadron RNZAF as shallow dive-bombers) may have a clear run through to destroy the strip which is the primary target. This is accomplished by dive-bombing the gun positions which each aircraft is allotted and strafing further gun positions on the line of retirement.[8]

Typical of such flak-suppression missions conducted by the SBDs was that carried out against Vanakanau airfield, which was the target for thirty-six Dauntless and two dozen TBFs on 30 March, with twelve of No. 25 Squadron's aircraft not only participating but providing the lead force. There was heavy cloud over Rabaul, which partly obscured the target area, and two SBDs suffered from bomb 'hang-ups'. Another Dauntless was

---

8   RNZAF Historical Branch, *Operational Room Log, 25 Dive Bomber Squadron RNZAF, and Operational Log Book, No. 25 Dive Bomber Squadron RNZAF*, AIR 160v3, 1944.

hit by small-arms fire on the way down. Ten direct hits were nonetheless scored despite the difficulties. Next day it was the turn of gun positions on Lakunai airfield. Twelve RNZAF SBDs again joined with a total of fifty-three bombers, each contributing a 1,000lb bomb. The New Zealand aircraft were credited with three direct hits on the airfield and two damaging hits on adjoining gun positions.

The initial Japanese land push against the beachhead had been halted, but the enemy was still very active, and No. 25 Squadron had again to turn their attentions inland on 1 April. Six SBDs made local bombing strikes on Japanese supply and bivouac areas near the Mafririci river during that morning, and this was again the target zone for the remaining six sent out the same afternoon. Once more the weather intervened effectively with showers and clouds making identifying targets difficult in the extreme and no resultant fires or smoke plumes were observed after either strike. It was the same story on 2 April when another large attack was put in with a total of sixty-six SBDs and twenty-four TBFs against Rabaul. Yet again the joint attack was forced by heavy cloud to divert to the secondary target of enemy barracks and store buildings at Raluana (Schulze) Point, between Blanche and Keravia Bays, where the Japanese had a heavy gun battery emplaced. There, an estimated forty-one bombs hit the target area, resulting in the destruction of many buildings, one of them a very large one, and caused many small fires. Supply barges at Keravia Bay were hit twice and other buildings along the beach were also obliterated.

This particular attack was notable, or notorious, as being the only occasion that the New Zealand dive-bombers were partly bombed-up with 120lb fragmentation (cluster) bombs. One of these was fitted beneath each wing carried on the Type-5 wing racks. They were designed to be used against parked aircraft on enemy runways, but their deployment against other targets proved to be far from a great success which is probably why they were not subsequently used again. One aircraft returned to base with both clusters 'hung-up' and one with a single cluster retained despite all efforts to free it. Both aircraft returned safely to base but, unfortunately, all those weapons were jolted free of the mounting by the landing. As a result, the safety devices of the M110 nose fuses shattered on contact with the metal strip and the resulting explosions wrecked both aircraft (NZ5054 and NZ5059) and injured the pilot of the latter machine, Sergeant Peter Robert Bryan Symonds, and W/OpA/Gs, Flight Sergeants Billie Boden and Thomas Edward Price. Both aircraft were wrecked beyond repair but all three men, along with the pilot of the first machine, Flight Sergeant Leslie Hunter Jolly, survived the experience.

On 3 April No. 25 Squadron again provided the lead unit in an attack against gun positions at Vunakanua but again heavy cloud cover forced some pilots to turn their attentions to the AA guns at Tobera instead, where a direct hit on one gunsite was confirmed. Those that did attack the main target found that the weather conditions prevented them from making accurate assessments of just what damage they had inflicted. On the following two days the weather closed right in, preventing any attacks being delivered at all. It did not, regrettably, prevent the squadron further losses. These came about in the following fashion. Two new Dauntless, still carrying their original US markings and codes (14 and 176), were awaiting collection at Henderson Field, Guadalcanal, to replace the three written off earlier. Accordingly, on 4 April, three SBDs were notified as awaiting collection at Henderson Field. Three of No. 25 Squadron's pilots were sent to collect them, these being Flying Officers Leslie Alexander McLellan-Symonds, Bruce Nelson Graham and Graham Cargill Howie respectively, the first named as a passenger in an American aircraft, the latter pair in NZ5048. Making a hop via Munda they arrived at Henderson and all three departed on the return flight at 1400, with McLellan-Symonds piloting 176, Graham 14 and Howie returning with NZ5048. This time they were due to make a refuelling stop at the Russell Islands.

Unfortunately, the new aircraft's radio equipment proved unreliable as they flew northward and, after a short time, all three lost audible contact with one another. That didn't matter so much so long as visual contact remained, but the weather again began to close down, and night was coming on. The trio of SBDs on this ferry flight somehow missed their way heading up 'The Slot', on the 7th, overshot and ultimately recognized the coast of New Britain while there was still light. Immediately they turned back toward Green Island but aircraft 176 broke away, still uncontactable, and was never seen again. Both Graham and Howie eventually got their mounts down safely after a hairy night landing on Green Island and later re-joined their squadron.

Sadly 32-year-old Flying Officer Leslie Alexander McLellan-Symonds, from Dunedin, one of the oldest pilots in the Squadron, flying Dauntless 176 (not yet allocated an official RNZAF number, her BuNo. being 28452) was of course without his usual W/Op A/G, Flight Sergeant Robert Francis Bailey, ran out of fuel and made a forced descent in enemy-held territory. It later transpired that he survived the crash landing but was captured by a Japanese patrol, one of whom shot him in the left thigh. He was taken to a prisoner of war camp, but his wound was neglected by the camp authorities with typical callousness and, despite being examined by a Japanese doctor, remained untreated as the camp commandant refused to sanction action. McLellan-Symonds was awaiting transfer to another camp when he finally died of neglect on 25 May.

Apart from this tragedy, during the period from 15 March to 5 April (covering two weeks of the squadron's combat activities) the SBDs achieved a great deal with little loss. The following was No. 25's official summary of guns they had been confirmed to have destroyed:

5-inch Dual Purpose Navy Type - 4
105mm	4
77mm	16
Automatic weapons	25
Light weapons	42

One report read:

> In four instances heavy gun batteries have been brought closer together so as to utilise one set of fire-control equipment for two batteries of guns. This indicated that there has been great destruction of fire-control equipment such as height finders, long-range telescopic sights and speed and angle of course indicators. In addition, the entire fire-control system of two batteries of 5-inch guns has been destroyed. Although no official figures for the period 15 April to 15 May have as yet been issued, the number of guns destroyed is greater, as is evidenced by the comparatively few remaining still to be destroyed.

When the weather lifted on 6 April combat operations resumed once more and the SBDs returned to the task of neutralizing the Rabaul airstrips. Vanakanua[9] was attacked by sixty-six SBDs including the usual dozen from No. 25 Squadron, along with twenty-four TBFs. Although cloud cover over the target again made the force switch targets to the Talili Bay supply area, the strike was subsequently considered a very successful one and many Japanese gun emplacements were destroyed.[10] The same areas were

---

9 See Map?

10 After earlier air raids some 31 Allied PoWs were taken from Tunnel Hill to Tulili Bay and executed. This, the Talili Bay Massacre, was falsely blamed on the Allied air attacks at the time, but many of the bodies were exhumed post-war and were found to have been shot or bayoneted, so thus revealing the truth.

struck again the following day, but this time only six SBDs from the New Zealand unit participated, and these made their mark by hitting six different gun positions and had three guns confirmed as destroyed. On 8 April No. 25 Squadron again contributed six aircraft to an attack with forty-eight SBDs and seventeen TBs on Rataval Ridge. Five direct hits were recorded on gun positions, three of them by the RNZAF Dauntless. Five further SBDs mounted an attack the same day against Japanese artillery positions some 1,000 yards west of the Mamgata river on Bougainville itself, scoring one direct hit and placing all their other bombs in the general target areas.

While many saw the Bougainville Campaign as a futile political exercise which achieved little, there was an element of attrition attached to it. The Japanese had committed a large percentage of their limited carrier aircraft ashore at Rabaul in January, only to see them waste away day after day in fruitless missions until these highly-skilled naval aviators were reduced drastically and were thus unavailable when they were direly needed in the naval battles of the Philippine Sea and Leyte Gulf later in the year when they might have achieved something worthwhile. The Allies could afford and absorb their small losses; the Japanese simply just could not. Finally, the emaciated IJN squadrons had been pulled out of Rabaul on 20 February, leaving the island airfields almost empty, mere targets to divert the Allies' attention while they pulled back to Truk in the Carolines many miles to the north. The few Japanese aircraft that did remain to Admiral Jinichi Kusaka were approximately thirty damaged Mitsubishi Zero fighters and twenty-six bombers. Kusaka was told to hold out notwithstanding and his resolute response was 'Let's get to work'. So, the Japanese garrison dug in and held on grimly as air attack succeeded air attack in a relentless and remorseless pounding. As an unsinkable aircraft-carrier, or as a bottomless sponge soaking up Allied aerial bombardment that might have been better employed elsewhere, Rabaul still remained effective. More, Kusaka and his men not only endured this but managed to repair eleven of their 'written-off' aircraft to make audacious, if largely ineffective, harassing air attacks as far afield as Manus while still retaining aerial communications with their by-passed garrisons on Bougainville and New Ireland, as well as Truk Atoll itself. It was a highly praiseworthy effort.

One eyewitness to the Allies' saturation raids was Father Jean-Baptiste Poncelet, a Belgian Catholic priest from the Tunboiru Mission near Buin, who had been interned at Vunapope. He recorded how the daily attacks continued. Clouds of American aircraft, bombers and fighters, arrived each morning. The sirens announced them with their strident whistling noise … . From time to time we witnessed aerial battles when the Japanese fighters dared to sally out to the attack. We could see aircraft falling in flames, either diving off to the right or turning away slowly to disappear finally into the sea or the bush ... . One day I saw five aircraft swallowed up into the sea near Vunapope in several minutes.[11]

By the time No. 25 Squadron had joined in these raids the sight of any defending Japanese aircraft over Rabaul was becoming a novelty. One such occasion was on 9 April when a solitary Zero was sighted off Cape St George by the twelve New Zealand SBDs which were leading a strike against the Vunakanua airfield gun positions once more. This Zero made no attempt to tangle with this mass of bombers, or their eight escorting USMC fighters. Another enemy plane was sighted during the actual dive-bombing attack, this being a twin-engine machine squatting on the runway. Although most of the usual gun positions remained mute, four new batteries opened fire and these duly received the bulk of the Allied bombs planted that day. No less than eight of the SBDs were hit, including two of the New Zealanders: NZ5051, which had its starboard wing and tail-plane badly peppered and the radio aerial shot away; and NZ5048 which took a cannon shell through the rear fuselage. All the aircraft made it back to base, however.

The next day twelve SBDs from No. 25 Squadron were part of a forty-plane force that struck at Raluana Point and Vunapope. They made their approach from 12,000 feet and this time no fewer than four Zero fighters were sighted quite clearly by two of the squadron's wireless operators, Flight Sergeant D.W. Gray (NZ5058) and Flight Sergeant Robert Francis Bailey (NZ5060). This enemy quartet were seen some 1,000 yards off to the left of the Dauntless formation but, strangely, the enemy pilots made no attempts to even harass the SBDs and broke away after briefly weighing up the odds against them.

With this threat behind them, the dive-bombers continued with their normal attacks, pushing over from 9,000 feet and diving down to a bomb-release height of 2,500 feet. Three aircraft were hit by flak during their descent, before breaking clear at 1,500 feet and carrying out the usual strafing attacks as they exited the area via St George's Channel. As they did so they sighted another solitary Hamp fighter which proved equally unheroic. Three damaging hits were reported on the target buildings while the damaged aircraft (NZ5047 Flying Officer L.H.F. Brown and Flight Sergeant G.D. Ashworth; NZ5049 Flight Lieutenant T.R.F. Johnson and

---

11 Father Jean-Baptiste Poncelet Diary included in O'Reilly, Patrick and Sedes, Jean-Marie Jaones, *Noirs et Blanc: Trois Annee de Guerre aux Les Salomon*, Editions du Monde Nouveau, Paris, 1949.

Flight Sergeant R.J. Howell; and NZ5061 Flight Lieutenant J.R. Penniket and Flying Officer L.H.F. Brown) all reached Piva North safely.

On the following day a fifty-bomber attack targeted gun positions to the west of Simpson Harbour but were unable to see the results of the attacks. They did, however, spot a solitary Kawanishi H6K 'Mavis' flying-boat tethered to her buoy during the attack. What was probably the same aircraft was observed leaving the area the next day when the Kiwis led in another strike of thirty-six SBDs and two dozen TBFs against gun positions along Talili Bay. They scored one direct hit and five near misses, without loss. And so the work continued day-in, day-out, with little variation. No. 25 Squadron was operating under the direct control of US Strike Command, COMAIRSOLS (Commander Air Operations, Solomons). Its US Marine Corps' squadrons were from VC-40, VB-305 and VMSB-235, and later VB-306 and VMSB-241, all from MAG-24 commanded by Colonel Lyle Harold Meyer. Although the normal tour of operations during this period was six weeks, No. 25 Squadron kept going for more than two months. Moreover, during this time the squadron conducted double the operational sorties per head of their US Marine flyer equivalents. The official report attributed this fact to the lack of sufficient aircraft in the area, which both enforced the use of all available planes and required the squadron to provide twelve aircraft for missions daily. Secondly, it appeared that Japanese fighter opposition, as already noted, was practically negligible. Previously the Allied air strikes had been limited mainly by the weather conditions. If the weather between base and target was at all doubtful the strikes were cancelled, or the aircraft returned to base if already airborne. This was because their own fighter escorts were unable to keep track of the SBDs and TBFs when flying through clouds and would therefore have been unable to provide sufficient protection in the event of Japanese fighter interceptions. With the dramatic decline of any meaningful enemy fighter opposition even the weather became a secondary consideration and only a solid front between Bougainville and whatever target was selected, or was encountered in the immediate vicinity of such targets, prevented any attacks from reaching their primary destinations. The average flight time for a strike against Rabaul, for example, varied between three-and-a-half and four hours.

There was also the basic factual position that there was simply no relief unit available for the Kiwi dive-bomber aircrews anyway. The formation of the second dive-bomber force, No. 26 Squadron, had been authorized to be sure, and Flight Lieutenant Peter Robert McNab, with two companions, Flight Sergeant James Henry Pope and Sergeant Jack Roberts Sparrow, had been posted to a Dauntless unit working up stateside to learn the ropes.[12] Unfortunately, although the squadron formed in January at Ardmore airfield, near Auckland, it only remained in existence for two weeks before being disbanded. The bland reason given at the time was that there were too many different types of planes already equipping the small RNZAF. One of No. 26 Squadron's intended pilots, Flight Lieutenant James Robert Penniket and Flying Officer John Hamilton Brady had joined No. 25 Squadron in December 1943 to gain experience and they remained with them, flying Dauntless NZ5063, throughout their war tour. Under a fresh agreement between the Americans and RNZAF, No. 26 Squadron was instead equipped with yet another new type of aircraft, the Chance Vought F4U Corsair.

No. 25 Squadron therefore soldiered on alone as the sole Dauntless outfit. Their routine continued for the next few weeks. Their losses remained minimal but, on 17 April, another Dauntless was lost. Eleven SBDs formed part of a forty-seven SBD and thirty TBF attack on gun positions adjacent to Lakunai airfield on Matupi Island, Hospital Ridge, on the Lakunai runway itself, and against the causeway between Lakunai and Matupi Island on the Gazelle Peninsula, jutting out in Simpson Harbour. This strike was met with heavy AA fire but was considered successful with many damaging hits confirmed on the guns. One Dauntless, NZ5059, crewed by Sergeant Pilot Alfred Charles Linton Forsberg and Flight Sergeant Edward George Leatham, received so much damage from flak on this mission that, although she reached Piva safely, the aircraft had to be written off as not worth repairing.

Worse by far was the fate of Pilot Officer Geoffrey Haughton Cray from Hawke's Bay, Napier, and Flight Sergeant Frank Desmond Bell, from Canterbury, flying 'Prune's Progress' (NZ5050) which was last seen releasing her bombs over the target. The Squadron Memorandum Book completes the story as far as it can ever be told:

> 10:30 – SBD Operations advised me that all aircraft had returned from strike with the exception of one of ours, 5050.
>
> 10:45 – SBD Operations asked AAC5 to signal Green Island and inquire whether 5050 had landed there.
>
> 12:50 – Inquired from Fighter Control whether any information had been received regarding 5050. They told me that this aircraft had not landed at Green Island and that

---

12 Duxbury, David, *Come in From the Cold, Number 26!* - File, with additions and corrections 11 August 2011 and *The Very Brief Life and Times of No. 26 (Dive Bomber) Squadron, January 1944* – Notes created for the Author, 6 March 2010.

the Dumbo [a Consolidated Catalina PBY Flying Boat
used for Air-Sea Rescue (ASR) work] had searched
for two hours in the vicinity of a position given to
them by Major Todd[13] without result. The position was
given over the radio by an aircraft intending to make
a water landing.

It later transpired that the Dumbo aircraft had rescued crew from a ditched
Grumman TBF Avenger, so this report was a red herring. Later interviews with
surviving squadron members who were on this mission were of the opinion
that NZ5050 crashed in a ravine near to Tobera airfield with no survivors.

On 18 April a thirty-seven-plane mission was mounted against Simpson
Harbour, led by six New Zealand SBDs, but, once more, conditions over the
target led to a switch against the supply area at Rabanga Bay. Although five
Japanese fighter aircraft were observed on the Rapopo runway, these made
no attempt to take off and challenge the dive-bombers and the attacks were
conducted having to face only light flak. Some thirty-one 1,000lb bombs
were reported as scoring direct hits on the runway itself. Next day the weather
proved even more unfavourable over New Britain and a forty-eight-aircraft
attack led by nine from No. 25 Squadron's aircraft had to be aborted when
they were still 100 miles from the target on Matupi Island. Local attacks on
20 April were followed by a repeat of the Matupi attempt on 21 April, but both
were 'weathered out' and all planes remained grounded. When a big strike
did manage to get airborne on 22 April, with a dozen New Zealand SBDs of
No. 25 Squadron leading forty-two USMC Dauntless and twenty-four TBFs
against Vunakanua, cloud cover prevented them attacking either this or the
secondary target of Lakunai, and they had to turn their attentions against
Rapopo airfield, with eleven out of twelve bombs scoring direct hits there.

Since they were working so closely with the US Marine Corps units and
were using the same aircraft, it was inevitable that No. 25 Squadron should
adopt their methods of attack. The V formation was abandoned for the US
Diamond-Box configuration, comprising fours during the approach period,
made at a normal height of around 14,000 feet. The initial descent would be
made some distance from the target down to around 9,000 feet at speeds of
about 270 knots. Over the target itself the final attack dive would begin from
this altitude and be made at a 75-degreee angle with dive brakes extended,
while bombs were released at heights of between 2,500 to 2,000 feet, with
the pull-out at around 1,000 feet.

---

13   Major Glenn L. Todd of VMSB-235.

Almost all the attacks carried out by No. 25 Squadron were made with a single 1,000lb bomb, and were designed to crater the runways and smash gun emplacements and associated equipment. Fusing, of course, depended on the type of target pre-selected, usually with a one-tenth-second delay. The underwing 100lb bombs carried instantaneous fuses. Fragmentation targets were, as we have noted, rare and, anyway, the bomb carriers themselves proved unsatisfactory in use. Occasional strafing runs were made as part-and-parcel of the attack exit routine to keep the enemy AA-gunners' heads down at this critical juncture.

The week that ended on 23 April had seen sixty-three bombing sorties flown but only thirty of these, less than half, had reached the target because of the weather and on 23 and 24 April there was no flying possible whatsoever. The next day twelve SBDs led a strike by four dozen dive-bombers and two dozen TBFs against Lakunai airfield and the adjacent gun positions on Matupi Island and Hospital Ridge, scoring many damaging hits. One aircraft, NZ5061, piloted by Flying Officer Ford Gillies McKenzie, with Pilot Officer G.H. French as his rear-seat man, was hit on this occasion, but not seriously. No less than sixty-two direct hits were recorded on their old target of Vunakanua next day and, out of the regular twelve New Zealand dive-bombers committed, only one, NZ5049 with Flight Lieutenant Thomas Randall French Johnson, was hit, taking a splinter in the propeller which meant he had to force land on Green island. Two days' restricted weather conditions were followed with a strike on Lakunai being forced to return on 28 April. The following day the primary target for four dozen SBDs and two dozen TBFs was once more Lakunai, with, as secondary target, Matupi Island. Yet again the weather prevented attacks being conducted on either of them and instead this mass of aircraft assaulted a military barracks and a native village on the east coast of Buka Island off the north-western coast of Bougainville. All save twelve of their bombs landed in the target zone and several direct hits on buildings were reported.

Local flying was conducted on 30 April with twelve SBDs airborne to carry out artillery spotting for counter-battery work during the day, and the same schedule occupied them on 1 May 1944. The weeks that followed were generally of the same pattern with over 231 hours' flying time being clocked up by the squadron during which sixty-six sorties were mounted. Tobera airstrip was hot on 2 May. Here, one aircraft suffered a bomb 'hang-up' but the other eleven aircraft hit the runway. Vunakanua was re-visited on 3 May and one of the New Zealand SBDs varied the routine with a direct hit on the bridge at the mouth of the Warango (Adler) river on the eastern Gazelle Peninsula of north-eastern New Britain. In return three of the twelve aircraft were damaged by flak – NZ5060, NZ5063 and NZ5066. Tiny Sohana (Schane) Island to the south of Buka Island, and controlling the Buka Passage, had become a Japanese seaplane base and was scheduled as the target for the next day but bad weather aborted the mission. On 5 May six Dauntless bombed through a gap in the thick cloud against local targets on Bougainville itself. A heavy AA gun site in a clearing some three miles south of Sorum village overlooking the Buka Passage was one objective with another such position located near the Muguai Mission and Mount Boeder the other, but the results could not be observed in any detail.

On 6 May a spectacular result was achieved when a direct hit was scored in an attack on the Rataval supply area of Rabaul by Flight Sergeant Charles Morgan O'Neil, along with Flight Sergeant David William Gray in NZ5056. The 1,000lb bomb 'started an immense fire, thought to be a petrol dump.' There followed a great upspurt of flame, then thick black smoke rolled up to an estimated height of 4,000 feet which remained visible at twenty-five miles from the target.

On 7 May, while several RNZAF aircraft provided missions for local artillery spotting, a six-plane strike was launched against Rattan Island, to the south of Bougainville. Four of the bombs fell in the target area but results were not observed even though two US Marine Corps' Dauntless, with photographers on board, accompanied the strike and circled the area. A new target provided itself for their attention the following day, however, in the form of formidable heavy coastal guns (5-inch naval guns) in a battery mounted at the ironically named Cape Friendship at the southern end of the island. But 'nothing of a military nature was seen' during the attack, although three bombs fell in the required target area. One SBD from the five sent out had to abort due to engine failure.

After another idle day work resumed on 10 May with a dozen New Zealand aircraft as part of a strike by eighteen SBDs and twelve TBFs against gun positions on Matupi Island and on Hospital Ridge. They were met with heavy and accurate AA fire, as if the enemy had been husbanding his strength and waiting for them. A four-engine flying boat observed in the harbour may have been used to fly in fresh stocks of AA ammunition from Truk but, be that as it may, it was the hottest welcome they had received for a long period and two aircraft, one SBD and one TBF, were lost. The Dauntless, NZ5051, piloted by Flight Lieutenant J.W. Edwards with Flight Sergeant Lou Andreas Hoppe, from Auckland, was seen to drop its bombs on the gun positions allotted to it at Lakunai and to pull out of the attack dive very low over the runway. A few second later a large splash was seen in the middle of Greet harbour. When the aircraft failed to rendezvous with the rest of the force afterward it was assumed it had been hit during the retirement and had crashed without survivors.

The final momentum of attack continued remorselessly, right to the end. On 11 May twelve New Zealand SBDs were again part of a large force (forty-eight Dauntless and twenty-four Avengers) directed against Vunakanua. Once more bad weather conditions were encountered over the target and the attack force divided itself over a variety of secondary targets. Eight from No. 25 Squadron hit supply dumps at Marawak, south of Piva, scoring hits with seven bombs; 5-inch air-to-ground rockets were also used in this attack for the first time by the Marine aircraft. Some of the others hit Tobera airfield while three more attacked a bridge over the Warangoi river in New Britain. The remaining machines from this quartet, being forced to abandon the attack with engine trouble. One jettisoned his bombs over the sea and made an emergency landing on Green Island.

A more ambitious sortie took place on 12 May, a double strike in fact. Out of a total force of four dozen SBDs and two dozen TBFs, No. 25 Squadron contributed the normal twelve Dauntless and hit targets in the Rabaul region. After hitting objectives from Talili Bay to Raluana Point, they landed at Green Island to replenish fuel and bombs and then attacked native villages south of Sorum, the north-east coast of Bougainville, on their return flight. Slight damage to one Dauntless was the only result from light return fire. No strikes were conducted the following day, although two SBDs did some artillery spotting work, but it was back to Vunakanua on 14 May as part of a forty-eight-strong strike from which photographic reconnaissance later revealed that direct hits had again been made on the runway. Once more a rare sighting of half-a-dozen suspected enemy fighters was made some five miles distant during the retirement but these reluctant warriors contented themselves with aerobatics at a safe distance, as though they were small boys jeering a bully but keeping well out of arms' reach!

The squadron's period of combat action was fast approaching its end. Long overdue for a rest after constant operations in the most trying of circumstances, it mustered itself for a few days' more operations. It was already known that they were due to pull out and most of the men were by then ready to do so. On 15 May six aircraft attacked the supply area at Chabai, in the north of Bougainville, ten miles east of Bonis where the Japanese had constructed an airstrip close to Matchin Bay. They are recorded as scoring four direct hits on this strip. Eventually the Japanese were forced to give up attempts to use their new airstrip due to continued Allied attacks. The following day four RNZAF Dauntless led a glide-bombing assault against positions close to Tovera when the main target, Talili, was closed in with clouds. That same afternoon the target was Bonin airfield once more where they made three direct hits on AA gun sites on the airfield perimeter,

And so came the final strike conducted by No. 25 Squadron which was carried out on 17 May, six aircraft taking part in a total force of thirty-five, three of which bombed gun positions at Lakunai airfield while the others bombed supply dumps at Buka and oil barges in Simpson Harbour. The mission has been preserved for posterity on cine-film as a photographer flew as a passenger in NZ5049 (*WinniPu III*) with Flying Officer Leonard Henry Ferris Brown. All the aircraft returned safely.

During the next two days all available aircraft were brought up to maximum serviceability for the flight home and, on 20 May 1944, seventeen SBDs lifted off from Piva for the final time. First stop was Renard Field in the Russell Islands, thence to Guadalcanal, where they handed the mounts back to the Americans 'as good as new'. From there the crews were flown in Douglas Dakota (Skytrain) transports to Tontouta and Whenuapai.

Unfortunately, the squadron was never again employed actively, being officially disbanded on 19 June 1944.[14]

There was no connection between the SBD Squadron and the new No. 25 Squadron which was formed in October 1944 under Squadron Leader G.M. Fitzwater, for this latter formation was established as a fighter-bomber unit equipped with the powerful Chance-Vought F4U Corsair. This squadron served at Santo Espiritu, Guadalcanal, Los Negros, and Emirau until it, in turn, was disbanded in July 1945.

Although its active life was short, (the unit had only originally been authorized for a single tour of duty) No. 25 Squadron's achievements, both in organization and in striking at the enemy on its very doorstep, were worthy of the highest praise. Against the loss of six aircraft, only two on operations, the Douglas SBD Dauntless of New Zealand's only dive-bomber force could set these results: 498,800lb of bombs had been dropped and 108,000 rounds of .50 calibre and 217,000 rounds of .30 calibre ammunition had been expended. They had a total of eighteen confirmed direct hits on enemy aircraft, and thirty reported direct hits, plus seven confirmed damaging hits and six reported damaging hits. They also totalled 252 hits in the target area,

---

14 Administrative Instruction No. 89, dated 23 June 1944. 'Establishment No. WAR/150 (25 Squadron) will be cancelled.'

with 106 unobserved and bombings, and only suffered forty-six 'hang-ups'. The hits in the area applied to targets like supply areas, machine-gun nests and various automatic-gun positions which were difficult to pinpoint from photographs and where it was necessary to bomb by geographical location.

In total No. 25 Squadron flew thirty-two combat missions. They reported destroying dozens of Japanese artillery pieces and also thirty aircraft on the enemy airstrips around Rabaul, of which eighteen were confirmed. New Zealand should be proud of its dive-bombers and the air and ground crews that kept them flying during that critical period, even if their achievements were largely overshadowed by subsequent Australian operations in the battle, which began a few months later, to clear Bougainville of the Japanese.[15]

One of the ironies of that episode is that, having withdrawn the only specialized Commonwealth dive-bombers from the island because it was wrongly believed that their role was declining in the Pacific, the Allies were forced to use the SBD, yet again, in the conquest of the Philippines later and also to use, yet again, obsolete and makeshift substitutes in the form of the eighteen Commonwealth Boomerangs and four Wirraways of No. 5 Squadron RAAF which flew into Piva in November 1944 to take up the work so well initiated by No. 25 Squadron.[16]

---

15 They never totally succeeded and General Kanda fought a stubborn rear-guard action right up to the end of the Pacific War. Earlier, Major Otsu, Kanda's envoy, had spoken to 3 Division (AIF) HQ in Southern Bougainville on 18 February 1945, regarding a rendezvous between Allied representatives and General Kanda in order to arrange a formal surrender. The RAN corvette *Lithgow* accompanied by a motor launch, arrived at the pre-arranged rendezvous point five miles off the coast on 20 May but Kendra failed to turn up. Instead a subordinate officer came with a message that no formal surrender could not take place until word was received from Rabaul. Otsu stated that some 20,000 Japanese soldiers remained on Bougainville rather than the Allied estimate of 11,000.

Kendra finally surrendered his remaining troops to the Allies on 21 August 1945. The Japanese had suffered enormous casualties on Bougainville and adjacent areas but had held on to two enclaves to the bitter end. It was estimated that the Japanese lost 16,700 men to combat, and a further 26,400 to disease and malnutrition on Bougainville. See – Long, Gavin, *Australia in the War of 1939-45, Vol. VII, The Final Campaigns*. Canberra: 1963. Australian War Memorial.

16 One of the Author's proudest possessions is a copy of my book *Jungle Dive Bombers at War*, London, 1987, John Murray, on which this chapter is based, signed in May 1990 by thirty-five of the surviving members of No. 25 Squadron RNZAF and forwarded to me by their Commanding Officer, the then Air Commodore Theodor Jasper MacLean de Lange at Rotorua.

Chapter 8

Vindication at the Philippine Sea

Task Force 58 under the overall command of Vice Admiral Raymond Ames Spruance, with Vice Admiral Marc Andrew Mitscher in charge of the fast carriers, steamed out from its anchorage to take the fight to the enemy in the Mariana Islands. Amongst that awesome array of power was Task Group 58.3 with the carriers *Enterprise* and *Lexington II* with VB-10 and VB-16 respectively embarked. They were the last shipborne SBD squadrons in this fleet, the prolonged teething problems with their bigger and faster replacement, the Curtiss SB2C Helldiver, having finally been overcome and replacing all other dive-bomber units for this battle. Between them VB-10 and VB-16 were to write the Douglas dive-bomber's final page in the great carrier duels of the Pacific War.

For the third and final time, the carrier aviation strength of the Japanese fleet had been built up sufficiently to man the air groups on their remaining carriers. The overall commander for the Japanese Fleet plan, Operation A-GO, was Vice Admiral Jisaburō Ozawa, with Vice Admiral Kakuji Kakuta in command of the 1st Air Fleet. There were three heavy carriers remaining to the Japanese, *Shōkaku* and *Zuikaku* having been joined by the new *Taihō*, and these formed A Force, along with two heavy and one light cruisers and seven destroyers. Supplementing these ships were six light carriers, each with their accompanying escorts, and, of these, three – *Hiyō*, *Junyō* and *Ryōhō* – formed B Force while the remaining trio, *Chiyoda*, *Chitose* and *Zuihō*, formed the Mobile Force vanguard. In support was an oiling force of five tankers with five escorting destroyers in two groups, while twenty-five submarines were deployed in a scouting line ahead in the usual manner. The Japanese, therefore, felt some confidence in tackling the American fleet again, in pursuit of the chimera that bedazzled them for the whole war, the *Kantai Kessen*, the *decisive* engagement, that was destined to be the Tsushima[1] of the current war. For this Operation A-GO was set in

---

1 The Battle of Tsushima, Admiral Heihachiro Togo's overwhelming victory over the Imperial Russian Fleet in 1905.

train in June 1944. A nine-carrier fleet was indeed a formidable power, but they would be up against an American fleet composed of *fifteen* carriers, seven heavy and eight light, organized in four task groups.

For surface strength the Japanese had five battleships, eleven heavy cruisers and two light cruisers to oppose seven US battleships, eight heavy cruisers and thirteen light cruisers. In ships alone then the Japanese were outnumbered by almost two-to-one, but in aircraft the ratio was even more marked; in fighters the Americans would field 475 against Japans 225; in torpedo-bombers 190 against half that number, 81, while in dive bombers 174 Curtiss SB2c Helldivers and 59 of the new Douglas Dauntless SBD-5s, 233 in total, were opposed by just 126 Aichi D3A2 Vals and Yokosuka D5Y Judies. Nor was that the end of Japanese naval inferiority, because in airborne and surface radar they were totally outclassed, while in experience and training the Japanese flyers were, in the main, but half-trained youths against, generally, experienced veterans; even the most junior American navy pilot had two or three times the number of flying hours under his belt than his Japanese opposite number.

The Japanese were not fools, of course, and acceptance of these kinds of odds was made only after careful deliberation. Okawa's aviators were not to be alone in the 'decisive' battle; even before they became involved and delivered the key strikes from the sky so the giant *Yamato* and *Musashi* could then follow up and complete the rout with their 18.1-inch shells, the US carriers and battleships would, in theory, have been heavily punished and their numbers depleted vastly by attacks from more than 500 shore-based naval aircraft held under the command of Vice Admiral Kakuji Kakuta's Base Air Force, with its headquarters on Tinian. Japanese naval aircraft continued to outrange their American opposite numbers and they also hoped to gain advantage from the prevailing easterly trade winds of the Central Pacific. In fact, the Japanese land-based aircraft, sent out from the Japanese-held islands of Guam, Rota and Yap airfields, contributed little or nothing at all to the battle. Much of this impotence was brought about by the pre-emptive strikes that the US fast carriers themselves launched against these airfields, and also against the staging posts on Iwo Jima and Chichi Jima, between 15 and 19 June, which reduced the Japanese numbers to a minimum at trivial loss to themselves. The American battleships and cruisers were formed into a separate task group and placed out ahead of the carrier groups to form a wall of steel and anti-aircraft artillery through which the attacking Japanese had to fly, and which culled them significantly before the superior American fighters chopped down the survivors wholesale.

The resultant massacre was given the title of 'The Great Marianas Turkey Shoot', so one-sided was it, ten Japanese aircraft falling for each American.

With the plotting of the first incoming Japanese attacking air fleets at 1005 on the 19th most of the SBDs were scrambled off the flight-decks of both *Enterprise* and *Lexington* and sent to safe waiting positions on the eastern – disengaged – side of the US fleet. There they remained for an hour, circling and watching the slaughter. Admiral John Walker Reeves, commanding Task Group 58.3, thought they could have been better employed than this by making search-and-attack sorties along 'meridian line 260 degrees true' and suggested as much at 1003 in a signal to Mitscher. At 1010, however, those aircraft were ordered to strike at Guam instead and not at their opposite numbers.[2]

This switch was not really thought out, because all the Dauntless were bombed up with 1,000lb (450kg) armour-piercing (AP) and 500lb (227kg) general purpose ordnance for use against the enemy fleet; nonetheless it was duly complied with. The SBDs from *Lexington* took Orote Field on Guam as their target and discovered between twenty and thirty Japanese aircraft on the ground there. Joined by the SBDs from *Enterprise*, they made their attacks at 1300, though heavy flak, losing one of their number; but their bombs drippled holes in the coral rather than devastating the enemy planes.

Similar dive-bombing was also carried out against Agana airstrip. But the 19th was the day of the Hellcats and the Dauntless pilots had to wait until the following day to make a more meaningful contribution and leave their trademark on the wooden decks of the Imperial aircraft-carriers for the last time. Searches were flown throughout the morning of the 20th resulting in a series of sketchy reports and it wasn't until 1557 on this second day of the battle that Spruance finally obtained detailed information as to the exact whereabouts of his enemy, and while Ozawa was retiring westward at slow speed, refuelling from his supporting tankers in readiness to strike again with his remaining 120 aircraft on 20 June, Marc Mitscher ordered the very risky long-range strike against Ozawa's force. This decision was done after some hesitation for the enemy was at the extreme edge of the American aeroplanes' range. Mitscher consulted his Operations Officer, Commander William John Widhelm, who had been in a similar situation leading VB-8 from *Hornet* at the Battle of Santa Cruz. There he himself had had to ditch and be rescued, so he knew the risks first-hand. After carefully

---

2 The *Taiho* had already been hit by submarine torpedo and was later to be totally lost by
   inept damage control conducted by an almost untrained crew.

double-checking the data he informed Mitscher, 'We can make it, but it's going to be tight.' Mitscher's response was 'Launch them'.

Thus the 216 American aircraft took off in the full knowledge that not only would they have to attack at extreme range and therefore might not have sufficient fuel to return, but that even if they made it, know that it would involve a night deck landing, which, although being a night carrier specialist group, was never an easy operation at the best of times. Doubts there may have been; nonetheless, go they did.

The Dauntless had the shortest range of all the US carrier aircraft sent off in that historic launch and was thus the limiting factor. The first reports placed the Japanese carriers some 200 miles distant, but this was later to be found in error and the true distance from Task Force 58.3 to the target was 275 miles (442km). The SBDs launched at 1624[3] as part of a large strike that included eighty-five Grumman Hellcat fighters, fifty-four Avengers – only twenty of which carried their designed armament of torpedoes, the rest being armed with four 500lb (227klg) bombs – and fifty-one Helldivers. One of the VB-16 Dauntless, the mount of Lieutenant Jack Lovel Wright, accompanied VB-10's aviators, having had to make an emergency landing aboard *Enterprise* the day before with an oil leak. He volunteered to go on the mission with them and then land back aboard *Lexington* on its completion. In view of the state of his aircraft, a very brave decision indeed.[4]

Both Dauntless squadrons were very experienced, having almost reached the end of their normal combat tour period. The SBDs launched into a clear blue sky and climbed initially at 100 feet per minute to about 10,000 feet (3,000m) at a speed of 140 knots and all were aloft by 1636. Because of the distances involved, it had already been decided to adopt a 'running rendezvous' for the initial form up; instead of circling over the carriers in the usual way, the aircraft gained their cruising altitude slowly in task group formations to save precious fuel. The strike departed at 1645, but a second strike, already up on the flight-decks of the two carriers and being prepared to follow them, was cancelled due to the lateness of the hour; they were therefore disarmed and defueled, and struck back down below once more.

In total twenty-six SBD-5s were despatched. VB-10 launched eleven from a total complement of twenty-one, with the addition of one VB-13 aircraft, and VB-16 launched fourteen from a complement of twenty-three, but one

---

3 According to W.D. Dickson, *The Battle of the Philippine Sea*, Annapolis: 1975. Naval Institute Press. However, combat reports and personal memoirs time it at 1610 or 1615.

4 The SBD-5 had a range of 1,115 miles or 970 nautical miles (1,794 kilometres) against the Curtiss SB2C-1C Helldiver, which formed the bulk of the American dive-bomber forces, and had a range of 1,200 miles or 1,045 nautical miles (1,930 kilometres)

of these Dauntless, piloted by William Williams with rear-seat man Hank Collins, was forced to abort the mission due to engine problems and had to return to *Lexington* early. All the Dauntless committed were SBD-5s. The strike lasted from 1630 to 2200 with an estimated 297 miles to target, and a 270 miles night-flight return.

VB-10 Pilots and Radiomen/Gunners	
FIRST DIVISION	
Pilot	**Aircrew**
Lieutenant Commander James David Ramage USN	ARM1c David John Cawley
Lieutenant (j.g.) Carl Nicholas DeTemple USNR	
Lieutenant (j.g.) Oliver Wayne Hubbard USNR	ARM2c Jack Glass
Lieutenant William George Schaefer	ARM2c George A. Santulli Jr
Lieutenant Aubrey Earle Fife	
Lieutenant (j.g.) Albert Amiel Schaal Jr USNR	
SECOND DIVISION	
Lieutenant Louis Lee Bangs USNR	ARM1c Howard F. Honea. *
Lieutenant (j.g.) Cecil Ralph Mester USNR	
Lieutenant (j.g.) Donald Lewis USNR	ARM2c John A. Mankin USN
Lieutenant (j.g.) Hubert Frederick Grubiss	
Lieutenant (j.g.) Jack Lovel Wright USNR (of VB-16)	ARM2c Willard Newman Fellows USNR
Lieutenant (j.g.) Charles Vincent Bolton Jr	

* Known to be at the battle but pilot not confirmed.

+ VB-10 Radiomen whose actual participation or not in this battle has yet to be confirmed were AOM1c Jack A Bailey, ARM1c James William Patterson Jr and ACOM Wayne A. Wright (both of whom were awarded the Silver Star); and also ART1c Earl H. Morin Jr, AWCA Charles Henry Otterstetter, ARM1c Clyde V. Mayer, ARM1c Milton C. Smythe and ARM2c Ralph W. Whittaker.

N.B. I have a copy of the Aircraft Action Report but it contains no Order of Battle details. The squadron war diaries are missing from the National Archives and do not resume until September 1944 when VB-10 was reformed in the USA. Both factors make a full listing impossible to confirm at the time of going to press.

VB-16 Pilots and Rear-Seat Men (16 Listed)	
FIRST DIVISION	
Lieutenant Commander Ralph Weymouth USN (CO)	ARM1c William McElhiney USN
Lieutenant (j.g.) James Albert Shields Jr USNR	ARM2c Leo Ovila LeMay USNR
Lieutenant (j.g.) Thomas Roy Sedell USNR	ARM2c Anthony Charles Maggio USNR
Ensign Eugene Vincent Conklin USNR	AOM3c John William Sample USN
Lieutenant Thomas Earl Dupree USNR	ARM2c Daniel David Dowdell USNR
Lieutenant (j.g.) George Thomas Glacken USNR	ARM2c Leo William Boulanger USN
Ensign Orville Melvin Cook USNR	ARM2c Theodore Henry LeMieux USNR
SECOND DIVISION	
Lieutenant Donald Kirkpatrick Jr USNR	AOM2cRichard LeRoy Bentley
Ensign William B. Barry USNR	ARM2c Henry Francis Kelly
Lieutenant (j.g.) John Donald Reichel USNR	ARM2c John Albert Landaker Jr USNR
Lieutenant Henry Harrison, USNR	ARM2c Raymond Alfred Barrett, USN
Lieutenant Cook Cleland	ARM2c William Joseph Hisler
Ensign Hank Moyers	SEA1 Lee Van Ettan
Lieutenant William Williams *	ARM2c Hank Collins *
Ensign Joseph Franklin Caffey	ARM2c Dala Estrada
Lieutenant (j.g.) William Lee Adams	ARM2c Harold Kelly

*Aborted the mission, mechanical problems.

The original course set was of 279 degrees, but at 1715 Lieutenant Commander James David Weymouth, leading VB-16, took in a signal from one of the Avenger scouts giving a corrected enemy location which placed Ozawa's flat-tops a further sixty miles (100km) away, and course was therefore adjusted to 284. In the interim, one VB-16 aircraft, crewed by Lieutenant William Williams and ARM2c Hank Collins, was forced to abort the mission due to a malfunction in its fuel supply. Of the remaining SBD-5s all toted 1,000lb (450kg) bombs, half being AP and half GP.

Ramage had already decided that his squadron would use manual lean fuel control for the mission, with a setting of 1,750rpm, and would stay at a low altitude in order to avoid using the highly precious pint of avgas. With 252 gallons (1,146 litres) of fuel in their tanks and fifty to seventy-five nautical miles less combat range than the other American aircraft, it was essential for the SBDs to eke out every precious pint of avgas.

Eventually, however, Ramage had to abandon this plan due to the presence of enemy fighters, and the Dauntless finally climbed to an altitude of 15,000 feet (4,500m). Another precaution taken, the result of long experience, was gradually to move what fuel remained from tank to tank to even out its distribution; this would give the Dauntless greater balance and aid the dive attack, but a further factor was the knowledge that any tank that was completely drained would build up residual vapour and therefore be more vulnerable to a lethal explosion if hit by enemy fire.

American signals had already been intercepted by the Japanese heavy cruiser *Atago*, which relayed them to Ozawa's flagship, and, by 1615, he was well aware of what was coming. He abandoned what was left of his refuelling programme, increased speed to 24 knots, and proceeded to put more miles between himself and the US aircraft. The Japanese fleet was formed into three groups, each containing carriers and protecting warships. At 1754 the whole force went to action stations and some forty fighter aircraft, reinforced by twenty-eight other types, were scrambled to intercept the four groups of incoming US attackers.

The first Japanese ships actually sighted by the American airmen, at 1825, were of course the big tankers of one of the oiling forces and their guarding destroyers. These six oilers of the supply group were easy and tempting targets, being well within range, proceeding at a relatively slow speed and steering a straight and steady course of 270 degrees, with six destroyer escorts. They left an oil slick in their wake. One Helldiver commander decided to hit this target[5] However, the SBDs scorned such a

---

5 This unit being VB-14 from *Wasp,* commanded by Lieutenant Commander John Devereux Blitch Jr USN. As a result of their attacks the oiler *Hayasui* was hit by one bomb and near-missed by two more and set on fire. Her damage control party extinguished the fire with only slight damage and she survived to reach Balikpapan, Borneo, safely. The oiler *Genyo Maru* was damaged by one bomb and two near misses which split her sides and, after her survivors were taken off, the destroyer *Uzuki* sank her with torpedoes. Finally, the *Seiyo Maru* was also so severely damaged by bombs that she, too, had to be abandoned and was sunk by torpedoes from the destroyer *Yukikaze.* The other three tankers were not struck.

target and pressed on looking for the Japanese carrier forces.[6] The SBDs were then flying at an altitude of 16,000 feet (4,900m) and, at a range of about forty miles (65km), they were duly rewarded with a carrier force sighting at 1830.

The weather at the point of contact was cumulus scattered clouds from 2,000 up to 6,000 feet with unlimited visibility.[7]

The first carrier force taken under assault, between 1810 and 1930 according to Japanese records, was A Force. As with Midway, there is considerable confusion in all accounts about which aircraft attacked which ships. Lieutenant Commander Jackson Dominick Arnold's report for Air Group Two has it that VB-10 joined his attack on *Zuikaku,* but Lieutenant Commander Ramage's account is in absolutely no doubt that it was B Force that he attacked. The majority of reports mention the fact that there were three carriers, but widely separated, and that these were in an *echelon* formation from north-east to south-west – most probably *Junyō, Hiyō* and *Ryōhō* and it is a fact (unknown at the time of the strike) that *Zuikaku* was all on her own, the only carrier surviving with the more north-westerly of the three Japanese groups, her two companions having already been sunk the previous day by submarines, as related above. The remaining trio of carriers, *Chiyoda, Chitose* and *Zuihō,* were with the main force to the south-east which would confirm Ramage's accuracy. Some eyewitness accounts, Ramage's among them, identified a *Zuihō-*class carrier, which would appear to indicate that it was indeed this group that VB-10 attacked. All reports are confused by the fact that the American airmen were incorrectly recording their targets as vessels of a completely mythical *Hayataka-*class carrier; there never was, nor ever would be, such a carrier, or indeed any type of warship in the Imperial Japanese Navy. VB-10 came round to a course of 350 degrees in order to

---

6 Ramage was scathing about Blitch's choice of target, recalling how 'About two hours out (300 miles) I sighted a strike group off to our port in an attack situation. Beneath them I could see four oilers and several escorts. I broke radio silence calling to Lt Van Eason, [Lieutenant Van Vernon Eason Jr of VT-10.] our torpedo element leader, "85 Sniper from 41 Sniper. We will not attack. The Charlie Victors (CVs = carriers) are dead ahead." I then opened up on VHF guard channel saying, "Unknown Strike Leader from 41 Sniper. The carriers are dead ahead. What are you trying to do? Sink their merchant marine?" The other strike group continued with the attack despite the information that the Japanese carriers were the prime targets. I was exasperated. I later found out that their commander stated that his SB2Cs were low on fuel! Who wasn't?'

7 Aircraft Action Report VB-10 USS *Enterprise.* Report No. H-13. Dated 20 June 1944. RDT2 Archives, NARA, College Park, Maryland.

be in better position to dive on the carrier force. Two carriers, evidently untouched, were in clear view, the first a *Zuiho* class and second, 10 miles to northwest, one of the '*Hayataka* class'.

The location of the targets was logged as $015^0 14$'N; $134^0 11$'E with the bright sun setting and unlimited visibility. As the Dauntless dropped down to 12,000 feet (3,600m) in preparation for the actual attack, VB-10 split into its two divisions in order to divide their payloads equally between two of the enemy carriers. At this point the SBDs were met by what remained of the enemy's fighter defenders, eight Zeros (and she apparently launched nine more) but they were mainly ineffectual in their defence of the ships. The Zekes were described as being of 'mustard' colour, with red balls on wings. And ten of them made long-distance attacks on the Dauntless, both during their dives and on retirement. The Zeros showed 'little aggressiveness and had no effect. However, they did follow during the dives.' Only one of VB-10's aircraft, piloted by Lieutenant (j.g.) Cecil Ralph Mester, was hit by them, taking a single 20mm hole in her left wing and about twenty 7.7mm holes in the hood between the pilot and the gunner.

All the Japanese warships opened a fierce fire with their weapons, which ranged from full 8-inch (20cm) gun salvoes from the heavy cruisers, described in the report as 'intense', down to 1-inch (25mm) and 0.5-inch (13mm) light flak. The resulting pyrotechnics were a multi-hued display of firepower as the Japanese used different colour-bursting charges to help the gunners determine range, height and accuracy calculations. The American airmen therefore had to penetrate a screen of shell-bursts, not only of the normal black, white and yellow variety, but of reds and pinks and more exotic variations, burgundy and lavender, to carry out their dives. The heavy guns of the cruisers were described as 'accurate for altitude but off by about 200 yards to starboard in deflection'.

As pre-arranged the first division attacked the nearest carrier, *Zuiho*, while the second division, led by Lieutenant Louis Lee Bangs, continued to its target to the northwest, some ten miles distant.

Ramage himself selected the rear ship of the three-carrier formation, splitting his flaps at 10,000 feet (3,000m) and targeting what he called a *Zuihō*-class carrier for his division's objective, attacking her from downwind from east to west in a standard seventy-degree dive, and opening fire with his forward wing-mounted machine guns at 8,000 feet (2,400m) to help line up the target in the gathering gloom. He lined up on the ship's forward lift and released at low level, 1,800 feet (550m), so determined was he to make certain that he would score a hit. A defending Zero fighter (one of six shadowing the force at this time) followed him down but overshot as he pulled out at 300 feet (90m), and the Dauntless itself was also rocked by the detonation of his own bomb.

In fact he had missed as the Japanese ship had made a hard-starboard turn at the last minute; the second man down in the stack, Lieutenant (j.g) Carl Nicolas DeTemple, was able to confirm that Ramage's bomb had detonated close to the carrier's stern, while his own 1,000lb (450kg) bomb had similarly exploded hard in the ship's creamy wake. Next man in was Lieutenant (j.g.) Oliver Wayne Hubbard, and his bomb was also a near-miss, off the carrier's port beam, while his wingman, Lieutenant William George Schaeffer, suffered the frustration of having his bomb 'hang-up' on him.

So far the carrier had been very fortunate, and this luck continued, with Lieutenant Aubrey Earle Fife placing his bomb just off the starboard quarter of the still swinging vessel. The concussion from this series of near-misses close astern of her shook the ship's steering and rudder considerably, but did not affect her speed. Finally, one 1,000lb (450kg) bomb did just about hit her, that being the one aimed by Lieutenant (j.g.) Albert Amiel Schaal, attacking last of this division, and again it was the after-part of the carrier that took the blow. Schaal claimed that his SAP bomb had clipped the port after-edge of the flight-deck, had then pushed on through the overhang and again spent its force in the water close astern. 'A spurt of smoke and flame indicated that the explosion was below decks, aft.' All this division were heavily engaged by all the ships of the Japanese force as they made their low-level exits over the screen of *Terutsuki*-class destroyers which immediately opened up with 20mm and 40mm fire, intense but inaccurate. Swinging around to east at a varying attitude of 200 to 500 feet, the flight making violent evasive tactics, passed through AA from cruisers of the *Atago*, *Tone* and *Mogami* classes and several destroyers. The cruisers brought main batteries to bear as well as AA, and appeared to be using a volley type of phosphorus shell.

The second division of VB-10, led by Lieutenant Louis Lee Bangs, had taken the next carrier in line as their target, a ship they described as a '*Hayataka*-class' carrier; the six Dauntless therefore steered to the north and then pushed over. However, due to a misunderstanding, only the first section – Lieutenant Bangs, Lieutenant (j.g.) Cecil Ralph Mester and Lieutenant Donald Lewis – attacked the chosen target, 'a *Hayataki*-class carrier', which was the leading Japanese ship, while Lieutenant (j.g.) Hubert Frederick Grubiss, Lieutenant (j.g.) Charles Vincent Bolton and Lieutenant (j.g.) Jack Lovel Wright of VB-16, hit the second, or middle, carrier, 'thought to be a *Zuiho* or *Chitose* class, thinking this carrier was the target chosen for the whole division'. So it came about that two Japanese carriers were attacked by two three-plane strikes instead of just one.

Making a fast approach down to 9,000 feet (2,4740m) and firing their wing guns as they made their final attack dives on the most northerly carrier, all three SBDs of Bangs' section released their 1,000lb (450kg) bombs at about 2,000 feet (600m). The first bomb was claimed by Bangs to have been a direct hit on the rear of the carrier's flight-deck, and the resulting explosion was said to have blown several planes spotted right aft over the side. Mester's bomb went to the left of this one, also aft. Finally, Lieutenant Lewis claimed his bomb to have been a direct hit just behind the ship's small island superstructure. These three direct hits left their target ablaze as the Dauntless made their way out across the enemy fleet to the rendezvous point. They were again intercepted by Zeros waiting for just such an opportunity, and Mester's mount took hits from both cannon and machine-gun fire at this stage; however, she survived it all. Lewis had taken a different exit route and also got out unscathed.

Almost at the same time, the final three SBDs were pulling out after delivering their bombs against the second ship in the line, which Grubiss reported as an 'unidentified light carrier'. They had met very little anti-aircraft fire as they strafed this ship's flight-deck on the way down and made their releases. Of the three 1,000lb (450kg) bombs, the first was claimed by Grubiss to have been a very close miss astern; Wright's missile also went into the sea of the carrier's port side aft, and the fate of the last bomb, aimed by Lieutenant Charles Vincent Bolton, was unobserved by his rear-seat man. At 400 feet (120m) they recovered from their dives and headed out to the rendezvous point, unhindered by enemy fighter aircraft.

The Japanese B Force was sighted by VB-16 at 1845, and they estimated that it contained two *Hayataka*-class carriers, one light carrier, two *Kongo*-class battleships, two to four heavy cruisers of the *Tone*- and *Mogami*-classes and four to six light cruisers and destroyers. They could also make out a second group (A Force) twelve miles (19km) further northward, with a third group beyond them (the Vanguard Force). Despite this somewhat erroneous assessment, there was no doubt that they had found a juicy enough target. Seeing that everybody's favourite target the *Shōkaku*-class carrier (in fact *Zuikaku*) in the middle group, was already under attack by American forces – including, Weymouth reported at the time, the *Enterprise* dive-bombers – Weymouth directed *Lexington*'s dive-bombers against the nearest group.

VB-16 therefore passed north of B Force, the protecting Hellcat fighters skirmishing with eight Zeros that attempted to intervene in the process, but only one of the SBDs took damaging hits, the aircraft of Lieutenant (j.g.) William Lee Adams, which was struck in the rudder and right-hand fuel tank. Weymouth then turned to make his strike against 'the southern *Hayataka*' at 1904. Most of the Dauntless apparently concentrated their attacks against *Junyō*, while others went for *Hiyō* and they claimed no fewer than seven 1,00lb (450kg) bomb hits on the former and two on the latter, for the loss of just one SBD.

Boring down through the flak, Weymouth attacked along his target's flight-deck out of the setting sun, finally releasing at 1,500 feet (450m) and pulling out at 800 feet (240m). His bomb was claimed to have scored a direct hit by his rear gunner William McElhney, who saw black smoke erupting from alongside the ship's island structure. Five direct hits were claimed in total on this vessel, plus four near-misses and one unobserved – and more was to come. Both of the last two aircraft in the attack, flown by Lieutenant William Adams and Ensign Hank Moyers, also claimed to have hit this target, rear-seat man Harold Kelly stating that one bomb went down through the exact centre of the flight-deck, and noting that Moyer's missile hit soon afterward.

Lieutenant (j.g.) George Thomas Glacken was 'wooded' by the preceding section and could not complete his initial dive, so he switched target to the next carrier along, which was then commencing a hard-right turn. Unable to get a clear shot at her either, he saw his bomb miss. He was joined in his assault by Lieutenant Cook Cleland and Ensign John Franklin Caffey, the last two VB-16 Dauntless down off the stack. However, they were given the full benefit of the enemy flak gunners' undivided attention, and Cleland's mount took three direct hits. Notwithstanding this, he rolled with the punches and completed a low-level attack and was certain that his bomb had punched into the carrier's deck planking dead centre and towards the stern.

The very last Dauntless dive-bomber to attack a Japanese carrier that day was piloted by Ensign John Franklin Caffey, but the result of his strike was not observed. Meanwhile the Zeros had again closed in, although Cleland's gunner, Hisler, claimed to have shot one enemy fighter into the sea and also to have engaged an Aichi Val dive-bomber apparently acting in a defensive role over her parent ship as the SBDs themselves had done on several previous occasions.

From the enormous number of direct hits that were claimed as 'certains' by the returning US pilots in their various combat logs, the enemy casualties were, in truth, incredibly light. The Japanese records stated that *Junyō* was hit by two bombs which both detonated close to her bridge, and that there were six very near misses scored; this made operating her aircraft very difficult, although her engines remained undamaged. *Hiyō* was not apparently hit by a bomb at all in this attack and suffered only slight damage superficially. She did finally succumb to two aerial torpedo hits by the Avengers and eventually she blew up and sank at 2032 that same evening.

As for the other Japanese carriers, *Zuikaku* of A Force took heavy punishment. Direct hits were scored on her, one which penetrated down into her hangar deck, as well as five very near misses, themselves described as 'damaging' in this well-delivered attack. These caused dangerous hangar deck fires in the ship's aviation gas stores and she was left on fire from end-to-end. It looked like a repeat of the Midway result for the SBDs and at one time her Japanese captain, Rear Admiral Kaizuka Takeo, ordered 'Abandon Ship'. Somehow or other the very experienced and well-trained damage-control parties did not panic and reported at this time that they were making progress in fighting the blazes. The order was therefore cancelled, and the ship was ultimately saved; she eventually arrived back at Kure Naval Base on 23 June and was dry-docked on 14 July until 2 August for repairs. Considering the number of hits and close misses she suffered, this was a remarkable achievement on the part of the Japanese dockyards and she was ready for action again by 10 August.

Chiyoda was hit by two 500lb (227kg) bombs aft, credited to *Wasp's* air group and these destroyed or damaged several planes parked there, and these hits and splinters from the many near-misses killed and wounded fifty of her crew, but *Chitose* and *Zuihō* were not attacked at all.

As the SBDs of VB-16 withdrew, they were again subjected to persistent fighter attacks by eight Zekes and these were often pressed home well. Lieutenant Donald Kirkpatrick had his rudder, fuselage, wings and cockpit all hit, but somehow survived it all, but Lieutenant (j.g.) James Albert Shields' aircraft was not so lucky, and his SBD was lost with both her pilot and rear gunner, Leo Ovila LeMay. In reply VB-16 tail gunners claimed two Zeros destroyed and others damaged. Finally, the Dauntless survivors started their withdrawal at 1918 on a course of 100, estimated distance 270 miles. In total, nine Dauntless made the rendezvous and were then joined by five more which had avoided crossing the heavy flak zone over the enemy fleet, but only at the cost of using up yet more precious extra fuel.

It was a similar story for VB-10. Ramage somehow survived a full 8-inch (20cm) salvo from all eight guns of a *Tone*-class heavy cruiser at a range of a quarter-of-a-mile (402m) by diving down to thirty feet (9m) and making a 45-degree right turn. Once he had safely cleared the outer ships of the Japanese destroyer screen he made a gentle turn to the left at a height of 1,000 feet (300m) and from 1930 onward collected first six, then another three aircraft. As he headed back into the darkness to try and find his carrier at a speed of 150 knots, other formations joined up with the SBDs, which had their running lights turned on, and then left them behind.

If the outward flight had been a slow affair, the return was pedestrian. The average height was kept to 1,000 feet (300m) to conserve fuel, with again lean throttle settings. VB-10's overall flight time turned out to be 5.8 hours. Those with action damage were in dire straits very soon and faced a lonely death out in the vast expanse of the dark Pacific Ocean.[8]

Ramage's VB-10 had been highly drilled in night operations by their previous air group commander, Commander Roscoe Lee Newman, so the night held relatively fewer fears for them than many of their inexperienced colleagues. Like the equally experienced VB-16, their SBDs had their engine exhaust ports fitted with flame dampers for night operations, but *any* light would have been welcomed on that lonely voyage back into blackness. This was apparent from the chatter that broke out among other air groups as they winged their way home through the night with falling fuel gauges. Ramage's disciplined unit maintained a dignified silence in the midst of this babble, and then at around 2030, ARM1c David Cawley managed to pick up the ZB/YE homing signals from *Enterprise* by radar at ninety miles (145km) range. All around them other aircraft were running out of fuel and going down into the sea, but VB-10 remained intact, and, at 2120, locked onto Task Force 58 located some thirty miles (50km) distant.

Admiral Mitscher had ordered every carrier group to make the maximum illumination in order to guide the aircraft home, but for some this proved more of a hazard than a help. Ramage recorded that with all ships, including destroyers, lit up like Christmas trees, and with some cruisers firing star-shell bursts as well, the problem was not so much finding the fleet, but identifying an aircraft carrier amidst the myriad of lights. While it was not surprising that many aircraft landed back aboard the wrong carrier – it had, after all, been so ordered by the C-in-C – others inadvertently made persistently desperate attempts to touch down on other types of warship,

---

8   Mitscher had determined *before* the launch of the strike that if Task Force 58 could close the distance to the north-west at 23 knots while the aircraft were in the air by about seventy-five miles or more it would reduce the return flight distance sufficiently to be a practical proposition – however, while the aircrew were manning their aircraft, word came in from a scout that the enemy was actually sixty miles farther on, which nullified this calculation; nonetheless the first strike was allowed to go ahead but the second strike was cancelled.

even destroyers! Some air group leaders decided to land their whole squadrons on the water en masse; others, like Ramage, made every attempt to get their SBDs down on a carrier deck, come what might.

By 2140 VB-10 was over the home base intact, but a bad deck crash, by Lieutenant William Edward Harrison of VB-16, caused them to be waved away and Ramage ordered them to land on any deck they could find. Most were down to their last thimbleful of gas. Ramage himself and another VB-10 pilot, Lieutenant (j.g.) Donald Lewis, both eventually got down aboard the *Yorktown*. They found that, up to that time, only two of her VB-1's fifteen SB2C Helldivers had got back – but this was typical, and all save one VB-10 Dauntless made it home; beside the pair on *Yorktown*, two got aboard *Enterprise*, five more landed on *Wasp* and one on *Bunker Hill*. Only Dauntless 36129, piloted by Louis Bangs, had been forced to ditch, although one of the survivors went into a barrier and became a write-off. Bangs and his rear gunner were rescued by the destroyer *Cogswell,* (DD651), Captain Harold Thomas Deuterman, whose ships' doctor, Lieutenant (JG) Warren Samuel Kelly, MC-V(S), USNR, put six stitches into Bangs' head where he had struck his bomb-sight on hitting the water. Seven of these 'strays' were flown back aboard *Enterprise* the following day.

Of the VB-16 Dauntless, one had been lost over the target, that of Lieutenant (j.g.) James Albert Shields Jr, while two more, those flown by Lieutenant Thomas Earle Dupree (28304) and Lieutenant (j.g.) Henry Harrison (28419), had run out of fuel and gone into the sea, but their crews were saved.

***

Weymouth and five more finally got back down on the *Lexington,* while six others ended up aboard *Enterprise*, including Jack Lovel Wright who had apparently grown attached to her. Thus, out of twenty-six SBDs, one was lost to enemy action, three to ditching and one to a crash-landing, a ratio which compared very favourably with the thirty-nine Helldivers lost from the fifty-one launched. In summary then, one SBD was lost due to enemy action, Lieutenant (j.g.) James Albert Shields with his gunner ARM2c Leo Ovila LeMay USNR. One Dauntless, piloted by Lieutenant Henry Harrison with rear-seat man ARM2c Raymond Alfred Banett USN, crash-landed aboard *Enterprise*. Lieutenant Louis Lee Bangs USNR of VB-10 was forced to ditch, as was Lieutenant Thomas Earl Dupree USNR with ARM2c Daniel David Dowdell USNR of VB-16, but both these aircrew were rescued by destroyers. On the 21st the 'strays and orphans' returned home, seven SBDs had landed back aboard *Enterprise* at 1015.

167

Most aviators were disappointed when the final authenticated results were made known. As usual, many more carriers were claimed sunk than the one that actually went down, and although the two submarine successes made the score line respectable, some of the veteran Dauntless pilots considered that the American strike forces, as a whole, ought to have done much better.

So, the Japanese fleet lived to fight another day; but their nemesis was not long in arriving, because in October the Battle of Leyte Gulf brought about the almost total annihilation of their now useless carrier fleet, used as mere decoys, and also many of their proud battleships and heavy cruisers which had been husbanded for the final main battle but just frittered away pointlessly on the very brink of success off the beachhead. Sadly, the Dauntless was not there to see it happen or to take part. Ramage later recorded what happened later this way:

> When our task group entered port in Eniwetok on 9 July, I was summoned by Admiral Mitscher to visit him on his flagship, USS *Lexington*. While I had met him when he presented medals to us, I didn't know quite what to expect. As I entered his in-port cabin, he arose and came to the door to meet me. I remember those blue eyes looking at me. Right off I could feel the warmth that he had for his pilots. His first words were, 'Tell your boys that they did a good job.' We then proceeded to go into details about the strike. It became obvious that what he wanted was information on the relative performance of the two SBD squadrons – VB-10 and VB-16 – compared to the SB2C squadrons. He mentioned that we had more hits with far fewer losses. I mentioned that Air Group 10 was night qualified. I refrained from expressing some rather subjective views which I think were quite obvious to him. A discussion ensued about returning to the SBD as standard equipment for the bomber squadrons. I told the Admiral that so far as the pilots were concerned, there would be no difficulty. The staff pointed out the logistical problems, which were insurmountable in the forward area because of time.

So, there was to be no reprieve for the carrier-born Dauntless.

But in four years of air/sea warfare the SBD had left an indelible mark, one that would never be equalled, let alone bettered. Those who say the Pacific War was won by the Dauntless dive-bomber exaggerate – but only by a little!

Chapter 9

US Marine Corps Dauntless in the Philippines 1944-45

In the steady closing of the ring about the conquered territories held by the Japanese, from the Solomons in the south, round to the distant Chinese and Burmese borderlands, the dive-bomber played a leading role. The conditions of fighting in that vast zone, much of it covered by jungle, meant that accuracy counted for far more than overwhelming air strength. Attacking jungle-covered targets required that the bomb loads be delivered exactly on target to be effective, and only the dive-bombers of the various nations involved could regularly and unfailingly guarantee to do this. Among the leading exponents of this method of attack were the US Marine Air Groups (MAG), operating initially from Wake, Midway and then Guadalcanal, subsequently on Bougainville and later in the Marshall Islands. It is no surprise, then, that the same aviators were in the lead when the basic techniques for close-support 00.operations, using the dive-bombing method for accuracy, were absorbed, modified and then encoded; and it was into the re-conquest of the Philippines that the Marine Corps put all the lessons that had been learnt in the preceding three years into impressive practice.

With the MAGs the American had, for the first time in the Pacific War, an equivalent integrated dive-bomber force that could instantly and accurately respond to the needs of the men on the ground in the same way that for years the German Luftwaffe had operated their Ju.87 Stukas in close harmony with their Panzer forces. It had been a long hard road for the Marine Corps flyers to cover, shackled as they were by USAAF indifference and lack of funding, but the spectacular achievements of the various German blitzkrieg tactics in Poland, the Low Countries, Yugoslavia, Greece, Crete, North Africa and finally in the opening stages of the war against the Soviet Union in the years 1939-41, patently demonstrated the power of the dive-bomber if accompanied by effective radio communication links with the troops on the ground.

Even the USAAC had been impressed and German conquests had re-kindled their abandoned interest from the 1920s, largely due, it must be said, to the influence of General Henry Harley 'Hap' Arnold. Almost single-handed he had comprehended the lessons thus imparted by the Germans and was the driving force behind the ordered of large numbers of dive-bombers for the USAAC. However, after twenty years of neglecting this subject, the American air force found itself in the same position as the RAF had been and, as a result, had to poach its equipment, ideas, methods and aircraft from other sources, mainly naval. Thus, the USAAC (later the USAAF) had, perforce, taken over batches of A-31 Vengeance from existing RAF orders, 300 machines in all, but then imposed so many modifications on them that they became virtually a different aircraft, the A-35, of which huge numbers were ordered. So many modifications were insisted upon that production was continually delayed while changes were incorporated, and this resulted in turn in a largely unskilled workforce being unable to cope, thus delaying its entry into service and the air force was eventually forced to abandon it in its designed role.

The USAAF also ordered 100 land-based equivalents of the US Navy's Curtiss SB2C Helldiver, under the Army designation of A-25A Shrike. By string 1941 a procurement order for another 3,000 had been placed and a new plant had been built in St Louis, Missouri, simply to construct the type. The first A-25A flew on 29 September 1942 and the first batch of ten aircraft was completed in March 1943, by which time the USAAF had just given up on specialized dive-bombers almost totally.

Similarly, the Army ordered 192 of the new Brewster SB2A dive-bomber, as the Type 340, which was also under development for the RAF as the Bermuda (750 aircraft) and the Dutch East Indies Air Force (162 aircraft later taken over by the USMC as the SB2A-4). The RAAF ordered 243 of these dive-bombers, hoping to equip eleven squadrons with eighteen aircraft apiece, but delays saw them replaced by the Vultee Vengeance. The Americans re-christened the Shrike as the A-34 Buccaneer and in had ordered 140 aircraft (increased to 203 later). At least one squadron was formed and apparently performed very well, but, again, development work was so slow, and the Brewster works were chaotic due to expansion, that the contract was finally cancelled after only a few hundred had been delivered.

Meanwhile the Army had ordered land-based equivalents of the SBD Dauntless under the designation A-24 Banshee and equipped 8 and 91 Bombardment Groups with it. These were sent piecemeal to Australia, then up to the final stages of the Dutch East Indies shambles. They also operated with 27 Bomb Group from Australian bases against targets in the

Timor Sea and New Guinea areas, at Lae and Salamaua, early in 1942. But having such aircraft did not mean that the Army pilots knew how to employ them, and none of the operations proved very effective. The last straw came when six out of seven A-24s were lost in an attack on Buna carried out on 29 July 1942. The Army thereafter claimed that the A-24 was old, obsolete, not manoeuvrable and was slow, but, in truth, they had no 'feel' for dive-bombing and with General Henry Harley Arnold, Chief of the Army Air Corps and the main proponent in that force of the dive bomber concept, by-passed, little interest in learning the skills required was shown. The A-24 was withdrawn from combat.

The only effective dive-bombers that the USAAF finally received and used successfully in combat were the North American A-36A Apaches. Some 500 of these single-engine derivatives of the famous Mustang fighter aircraft had been built and used to great effect in Italy, (also being used to great effect at the Cassino battle in re-supplying the Gurkhas on Hangman's Hill, the only way they could receive vital equipment and ammunition); a limited number also saw service in the Burma-China theatre. But, apart from these comparatively few aircraft, the USAAF experience of dive-bombing had been far from a happy one. They concluded that it was not effective, was too dangerous (to the troops being supported as well as the aircrews) and too expensive.[1]

An official report commented:

> It is easy now to criticize the Army airmen for their lack of foresight, but their reactions must be placed in time and context. Striving for their independence they recoil from too close ties to the ground forces – the idea was separation, not closer amalgamation. Even the very term 'Air Support' was an anathema to them. 'Support' implies a secondary role – and through the war the preferred terms for tactical missions in direct support of ground troops were 'air-to-ground co-operation' or 'air-to-ground co-ordination'.

In this their feelings matched exactly those of the RAF whose upper echelons remained convinced to the very end that heavy bombers laying waste to enemy cities would win the war unaided.

---

1 AAF/War Department, Command and Employment of Air Power, FM100-20, 20 July 1943.

Army airmen considered control by infantry officers on the ground, later to become Forward Air Controllers, 'an attempt to shackle the air to the ground and therefore a failure to realize the full capabilities of air attack'. They could still enshrine their concept of close support thus:

> In the zone of contact, missions against hostile units are most difficult to control, are most expensive, and are, in general, least effective. Targets are small, well-dispersed, and difficult to locate. In addition, there is always a considerable chance of striking friendly forces.[2]

It was therefore left to the Marines to show the way. Robert Sherrod has recorded that the main lessons learnt by Marine Corps flyers up to that period were:

1. Adequate and reliable radio communication from air to ground was essential. One-channel radios were entirely inadequate and later two-channel installations were not much better.
2. Panels and pyrotechnics (i.e. light signals and Very lights,[3] respectively, for example, were inferior to radio communications but often had to be resorted to because of poor radio equipment and radio discipline. Their use required thorough air-ground co-ordination.
3. An airborne co-ordinator was required for liaison between scout bombers in the air and infantry assault on the ground.[4]

---

2 AAF/War Department, *Command and Employment of Air Power,* FM100- 20 July 1943. Washington DC. This finding had become totally reversed by 1945 when the AAF Evaluation Board then admitted that 'The above doctrine is in error'. POA Report No. 3. Its findings in 1945 were that that in comparison with the Army doctrine, it was the Navy methods that were 'effective, safe and well practised and rehearsed, while the Army doctrine of close support had no system, lacked control, practice or rehearsal and was dangerous', but by then it was too late for the Army Air Forces to put things right in time.

3 Martha Coston had been granted a patent for such a signal device, the Coston gun, in 1859. Lieutenant Edward Wilson Very, US Navy, made small improvements to it and the American Navy thereafter named them Very lights, although the term Verey also became widely used worldwide.

4 Sherrod, Robert Lee, *History of Marine Corps Aviation in World War II,* Washington DC:1952. Combat Forces Press.

It is interesting to compare these requirements with the practice of the Luftwaffe Stuka pilots throughout the war. It is almost identical. Stuka pilots were sent in rotation to act as ground liaison officers to co-ordinate attacks, often leading Panzer columns in specially-equipped tanks and calling in the Ju.87s whenever the enemy tried to make a stand.

Tentative experiments had been carried out by the US Marines to put into effect some of these ideas during the Solomons and Bismarck Barrier campaigns, as we have seen. These lessons were to be built upon. It was known that the campaign to clear the Philippines would be a very tough one. The jungle was still there as a hazard but there was also an urban element as well, which demanded house-to-house fighting with similar calls for precision, as the Germans had experienced at Stalingrad where Luftwaffe pilots conducted missions with maps in hand. There was confidence aplenty; when one Marine pilot was asked if he would like to dive bomb German targets, his response was, 'If they asked me to bomb a factory my first question would be – What department?' But the coming campaign would require much more than this innate skill if they were to convince a cynical Army, well-used to being bombed by their own airmen, to trust them implicitly. Because Army flyers had no such expertise, or interest in developing it since 1942, it was decided very early on in the planning stage to leave this work to the Marines. A much-expanded Marine Dive-Bomber Wing was to be formed and trained up especially for the job.

This unit, MAW-1, was to be put under the command of Major General Ralph Johnson Mitchell, USMC, who had taken over the wing from Major General Roy Stanley Geiger in April 1943. During the complex original planning for the re-conquest of the Philippines, MAW-1 had expected to participate in the initial landings which were to have been at Sarangani Bay, southern Mindanao. However, during the working out of details, it had been decided that the enormous calls on shipping and supplies meant that MAW-1, based far away in the Solomons, was one of the units the invasion would have to do without, if only because of the hard dictates of logistics. Mitchell was so informed on 26 August. A second blow to the Marines' hopes of participation was received on 15 September when the planners had changed the sequence of landings because of Admiral Halsey's carrier strikes in the South China Sea which had surprisingly revealed that the Japanese was far weaker in the area than assumed initially. Mindanao, therefore, instead of being the first stop of a rung-by-rung, south to north stage of liberation, was abandoned and the Americans would go straight for Leyte. Ralph Mitchell, his command's main mission in tatters, decided to go on leave.

While Mitchell was away in the States, however, at some unspecified date in September his deputy commander, Brigadier General Claude Arthur Larkin, received an unexpected visitor at his HQ on Bougainville. This officer, from General George Churchill Kenney's staff, informed Larkin that the sequence for the Philippines was now to be Leyte, then Mindoro and then Luzon, and that for the latter assault *all* seven of MAW-1 dive-bomber squadrons had been designated for participation. This was welcome news but as it was only transmitted verbally, without any detail and 'unofficially', with no written confirmation, required delicate handling by Larkin. Fortunately, he proved up to the task and began to assemble an all-SBD wing from his widely-scattered command. MAG-24 had two fighter squadrons transferred and replaced by two dive-bomber units (VMSB133 and VMSB-236 (Bougainville), VMSB-241 (Munda) and VMSB-341 (Green Islands). Also on Green islands was VMSB-244 under MAG-12; VMSB-142 and VMSB-243 were under MAG-12 on Emirau.

It was not until 10 October 1944, with General Mitchell still away[5] . Further oral confirmation of the Marines' future role was received from a mission from Kenney's HQ which arrived at the Army HQ of Major General Oscar Woolvereton Griswold, commander of XIV Corps on Bougainville, whose own force was also assigned to the Luzon landings. Larkin was present and was told that MAW-1 was to provide close support for the Army and that transport shipping sufficient for two MAGs was to be made available for their conveyance. Larkin duly advised his closest MAG commander that it was 'go'. To co-ordinate the other three SBD Squadrons, MAG-32, at that time in Hawaii, was ordered (again verbally) on 14 October to transfer into MAW-1. It took three days to organize LSTs [6] to load up with fifty officers and 600 men, under veteran dive-bomber ace Lieutenant Colonel John Lucian Smith, and sail for Emaru. Finally, written orders for all these movements were received on 12 October![7] They confirmed that one dive-bomber group of seven squadrons was to be in the Lingayen area of Luzon, with a landing date of 20 December and with the SBDs' operational date set for fifteen days after that. Follow-on detail included that fact that the MAW-1 was to be attached to Fifth Air Force.

Meanwhile Colonel Lyle Harold Meyer USMCR, commanding MAG-24 on Bougainville Island, had assembled his key men and

5 Mitchell had returned from leave but was with the Leyte invasion fleet as an observer at this date.
6 Landing Ship, Tank.
7 Operations Instructions No. 73, General HQ, SW Pacific.

announced the crucial part that they were to play in the forthcoming battles to free the Philippines. He informed them that they were to be joined by MAG-32, placed under the command of Colonel Clayton Charles Jerome, with veteran Marine dive-bomber pilot John Lucian Smith returning from the Hawaii as his executive officer. This gave the new dive-bomber wing a total of seven SBD squadrons acting in concert. As senior officer, Colonel Jerome Jones became overall commander of the wing when both groups worked together in combat. The various Marine Corps squadrons (VMSBs – V = Heavier than air; M = Marine; S = Scout; B = Bomber) were allocated to the MAGs which in turn made up the MAW.

The total composition of 1 MAW, later nicknamed the *Diving Devil Dogs of Luzon* (and, unofficially, as the *Pickle Barrel Bombers* in reference to their accuracy), was as follows:

Table 31: USMC SBD Squadrons Providing Close Support in Philippines 1944-45

VMSB-133 – Commanded by Major Lee Aird Christofferson. MAG-24. Christofferson was later relieved in command by the Executive Officer, Major Floyd Cummings at Malabang on Midanao. Nicknamed *The Flying Eggbeaters*.

VMSB-142 – Commanded by Captain Hoyle Redman Barr. MAG-32. Nicknamed *Wild Horses*.

VMSB-236 – Commanded by Major Francis John Frazer.[8] MAG-24. Nicknamed *Black Panthers*.

VMSB-241 – Commanded by Major Jack Lambert Brushert. MAG-24.[9] Nicknamed *Sons of Satan*.

VMSB-243 – Commanded by Major Joseph William Kean Jr. MAG-32. Nicknamed *Flying Goldbricks*.

VMSB-244 – Commanded by Major Vance Hobert Hudgins (later relieved by Major James William Poindexter). MAG-32. Nicknamed *Bombing Banshees*.

VMSB-341 – Commanded by Major Christopher Findlay Irwin Jr. MAG-24. Irwin was later relieved by Major Robert J. Bear, a veteran of the Battle of Midway on 4 May 1945.] Nicknamed *Torrid Turtles*.[10]

---

8 Frazer, awarded the Purple Heart for his services, was later to be killed in action flying a night sortie mission in Korea on 20 November 1950.

9 Brushert actually took over command from Major Benjamin Brown Manchester III on 19 February 1945, the latter assuming the role of ALO.

10 For the most part these various nicknames were not adopted by the squadrons until shortly before their arrival in the Philippines.

Assembling the aircraft and the men was the first stage. As we have seen the wing's various component squadrons had been widely dispersed around the Pacific battle zones, at Ewa, Oahau, the Marine Corps Air Station seven miles west of Pearl Harbor; Nissan island airfield, Green Islands; Munda on New Georgia island, Solomons; and Emirau Island as well as Bougainville. All these units had to be concentrated as an integral whole in the Philippines as quickly as possible after the initial assault, and meanwhile had individually to assimilate the new policy and practices as soon as possible to meet a very tight schedule.

The second was the detailed assimilation of every close-support technique and theory known at that time and its formulation into a positive policy.[11] All these facets had to be studied and the best practice drawn from them, and this had to be done quickly and, when approved, disseminated to the squadrons and practised. Initial classroom lectures had begun on Bougaianville as early as 23 October and continued over the following two months. This vital work was entrusted to a team of experts headed by Lieutenant Colonel Keith Barr McCutcheon, MAG-24 operations officer. He was to become the Marines' guru or 'don' of close-support systems.

The personnel involved were given a basic course of no less than thirty-seven different lectures ranging from how both Japanese and American infantry units were organized and the differing tactics they favoured in the field of combat, the varied terrain likely to be encountered in the Philippine Islands, the weather in the likely combat zone, and other local factors as well as refreshing such essentials as map-reading, artillery spotting and targeting methods. The lecturers included such relevant operatives as Air Liaison Officers, six Combat Intelligence Officers who been involved in direct assault operations at Saipan and Tinian, similar representatives from the 7th Fleet which acted in support of MacArthur's ground forces, as well as officers from the 5th US Air Force[12] and representatives of both the

---

11 'close air support had grown to have almost as many definitions as there were units which had made use of it.' 'Close air support was progressing rapidly in 1944, but there was still no unified approach to the problem. There existed in the various doctrines many differences of procedure and nomenclature.' Boggs, Major Charles William Jr, *Marine Aviation in the Philippines*. USMC Monograph. Washington DC, Historical Branch, HQ USMC.

12 the Army flyers agreed to lay on Support Air Parties, but had no intention of employing direct communication between the ALPs and the aircraft in order to *direct* each sortie. In this the Army differed significantly from the Marine flyers and the latter decided to go ahead on their own and train their own ALPs to adopt the latter dual-purpose method as both request responders and direction attack controllers, which they deemed far more relevant. Special training was therefore adopted for such teams during which co-ordination of the correct procedure was emphasized and exhaustively practised.

Americal (23rd) and 37th Divisions of the US Army who were themselves in active preparation for the invasion. Once the course had been assimilated by the various VMSB squadron representatives, these returned to the units at Emirau, Green Islands and Munda to pass on what they had absorbed to around 500 Marine pilots and air gunners.

One of the positive advantages of this arrangement was that the seven squadrons could devote their whole time and energy to this one subject. There was no need to break up the specialized training to cope with other eventualities, and, as in so many other war activities, it was found that one specially trained and close-knit unit was worth many generalized and all-purpose ones. Morale and understanding became indivisible, and there was the 'pride in unit and achievement' bonus that they were experts undertaking a vital job of work. Thus, the dive-bomber wing dismissed long-range bombing missions and its associated problems, from their minds, likewise air defence, all of which could be left to others.

The Marine Wing had another advantage in that the US Army 37th Infantry Division on Bougainville had experienced something of what they could do in harmony, and thus already had faith in what they might be able to expect to improve on in the future. They therefore co-operated fully in the Marines' training programme.

Although the newer Curtiss SB2C Helldivers and big Chance-Vought F4U Corsairs were generally available, the Marine flyers initially stuck with their faithful SBDs. These machines were well-liked, familiar and reliable, and, as speed was not a vital element in close support, a fact which the Junkers Ju.87 was continuing to prove in Europe (and as the Douglas AD Skyraider in Vietnam and later the Fairchild-Republic A-10 Thunderbolt-II in the Middle East continued to down the decades). Accuracy was the *real* essential element here, the ability to loiter and deliver the required ordnance where it was needed – these were the true vital components of close air support, something which many Allied Air Chiefs, and Website 'experts' alike seem never to understand.[13]

Those on the spot at the time, and charged with doing the job, had no such doubts, fortunately. They began work quickly. The tactics were studied, written out with diagrams and lectures, and printed for special courses for aircrew. No less than forty of these lectures were thus prepared in three days. Then, on 8 December 1944, study began for a total of 500 pilots

---

13 The USAF, despite the experiences of Korea, Vietnam and Afghanistan, still today recoil from the Close Air Support role as being 'subservient to the Army'.

and navigator/gunners who went through and absorbed all 'Professor' McCutcheon's strictures. A basic close-support manual entitled *Close Support Aviation* was issued, which codified these methods and tactics.

The principle used by McCutheon was that such close dive-bomber support was 'an additional weapon to be employed at the discretion of the ground commander' and was to be used by him as he saw fit 'against targets that cannot be reached by his other weapons or in conjunction with the ground weapons in a co-ordinated attack.' The guiding principles were that such close support should be 'immediately available' and should be carried out 'deliberately and accurately' and 'in co-ordination with other assigned units'. This called for the teams to go forward with the lead troops in any assault so that they could familiarize themselves with the actual battle terrain because working just from maps and photographs was of insufficient use. Acting on bitter experience re-learned hardily, special emphasis was placed on radio communications and not less than four communication nets were set up to cover all eventualities. These were worked in conjunction with the improved Air Liaison Parties (ALP) which comprised an Aviation Intelligence Officer (AIO) and several Aviation Communication Technicians, who were to be allotted the latest radio-equipped jeeps. Their role was signal 'requests' for aerial firepower, to direct any subsequent attacks. They could assist a Support Air Controller (SAC) to brief and direct strikes on required pinpoint targets.

The radio nets themselves are perhaps best summarized as follows:

SAR   (Support Aircraft Request): this linked the ALP to the Support Aircraft Commander (SAC) and the Airborne Air Co-Ordinator (AAC).

SAD   (Support Aircraft Direction): this was a two-way channel to link the SAC, the AAC and the supporting aircraft.

SADE   (Support Aircraft Directional Emergency): as the name implied, this was an emergency channel linking the ALPs directly with the supporting aircraft.

SAO   (Support Aircraft Observation): this was another two-way channel to link the SAD with the airborne observers in scout planes.

There were also four very high frequency (VHF) and two medium high frequency (MHF) channels available to each SBD and to each ALP jeep. On the ground each Marine division had by this date a Joint Assault

Signal Company (JASCO) but the Army was late in following suit. Mobile communications ground hardware also included two KI-51 trucks kitted out with the US Army standard SCR-299 mobile communications outfit, which included a 350-watt HT-4 transmitter with a range of over 200 miles, and a BC-242 receiver, along with aerials, converters, integral power supply and associated equipment.[14]

The new tactics were given a pre-embarkation workout with the help of 37th Division while the Marine flyers were still on Bougainville. The soldiers simulated infantry attacks on an enemy pillbox and the ALPs in close attendance were able to tune in their nets as the SBDs conducted mock dive-bombing attacks in conjunction, but without dropping any ordnance. Quite what the Japanese defenders thought about it all is hard to imagine but it was their colleagues defending the more important Philippines who were to 'benefit' from the lessons imparted. The exercise also increased mutual respect between the dive-bomber crews and the infantry, a vital ingredient if the work was ultimately to prove worthwhile in battle. Another factor that experienced ALOs felt was vital was that, in the interests of speed of response being applied at the point of battle, they should be able to talk *directly* to the CAS pilots rather than having to refer to a remote controller, with the resulting inevitable time-lag (not to mention possible blurring of information) this would entail in a fast-moving battle scenario.

Everything, then, was as ready as it could have been for the ultimate test of combat. Meanwhile, the first army units had waded ashore on the disputed islands on 17 October, the main landings following up three days later on Leyte's east coast. On 21 October the first Marine ground force joined in the fray when Brigadier General Thomas Eugene Bourke's V Amphibious Corps Artillery disembarked with 1,500 Marines at the Leyte bridgehead, not made fully secure until after the tremendous air/sea battles offshore had largely crippled what remained of the Japanese Navy's surface fleet and the first *Kamikaze* attacks began. The first Marine aviation unit ashore was the Night Fighter Squadron VMF(N)-541 which occupied Tacloban Field on 3 December. Meantime the Dauntless crews were still assimilating their lessons and awaiting their chance to put them into practice.

Concentration of the Marine squadrons was initiated on 22 November when VMSB-241 moved from Munda to Bougainville. Difficulties encountered ashore led to a re-adjustment of the Philippines timetable

---

14 SCR-299 - Signals Corps Radio – Type 299. The vans were custom-adapted by the Hallicrafters Company of Chicago, and had been used successfully in North Africa and at Normandy.

and it was not until December that the various Marine air components' move toward the combat zone finally got underway with the Bougainville ground echelons commencing embarkation on 12 December, Green islands on 16 December and Emirau-based units three days later. The flying components, after a combined combat operation against Kavieng in New Guinea with 108 SBDs on 19 December, then began island-hopping flights on their way northward in succession.

We can here use the example of VMSB-341 as typical of the preparatory work conducted prior to the assembling of the various squadrons on Philippine soil. This unit, working under MAG-14, had been withdrawn to Green Islands in June 1944 and had been mounting combat sorties against Vunapope on New Britain, hitting bridges, villages, artillery positions and enemy surface vessels caught off there and New Ireland. The original aircrew members of the squadron had mostly been relieved as they had completed their allotted tour of overseas duty, but the ground crews were retained intact ready for the Luzon operations. Various ordnance experimentation had been carried out while at Green Islands Lagoon, including air-to-ground rockets, both 3.5-inch and 5-inch, the racking together of clusters of 100lb GP bombs on underwing racks and .50-calibre machine-gun pods also carried under the wings. However, whether successful or not, none of these were finally taken to the Philippines.[15]

On 5 October VMSB-341 was officially transferred to the administration of MAG-24, 1 MAW co-incidental with the introduction of the new close-support programme. The ground crews sailed from Green Islands aboard the cargo ship *Julian* on the 6th and took a leisurely route via Hollandia, New Guinea, and Lae, not arriving at Leyte until 16 January. They finally disembarked on 21 January, and set up base at Mangalden airfield adjacent to the beachhead, in Pengasinan province as part of MAGS-DAGUPAN.[16] Until the base was ready to receive them the flying echelon remained at Green Islands until 22 January absorbing the new doctrine as best they could; they then flew in a series of island hops – Ovia Emirau (Lorengau)

---

15 In the Philippine Campaign the use of napalm (jelly mixed with petrol/gasoline and carried in underwing fuel tanks) was widespread in the Army air forces, but was hardly ever used by MAW-1. The auxiliary fuel tanks of the SBD were in constant use in their proper role and stocks were too limited for experimentation with napalm. A few Japanese belly tanks were adapted and tried out in two experimental missions conducted on 15 and 20 March 1945 by MAG-32, but they proved unsuitable and highly inaccurate and further tests were then abandoned.

16 Dagupan town was on the 'Blue Beach' landing site at Lingayen Gulf for MacArthur's second landing in the Philippines on 9 January 1945 and became his HQ.

in the St Matthias Islands, Manus and Los Negros, in the Admiralty Islands, Oui Island and then out to the tiny speck of Peleliu Island, east of Mindanao and the scene of the USMC's most recent and bloodiest fighting to date – finally reaching Malgaldan, which was an improvised 6,500-foot runway built on impacted paddy fields[17] on 30 January to commence combat operations.

The principle Marine air units, including the newly-readied dive-bombing squadrons from 1 MAW, began shifting their emphasis to one of preparation for the army's forthcoming invasion of Luzon. On 9 January, the US Sixth Army landed on that island and, two weeks later, units of MAG-24 arrived. Shortly afterwards they began flying combat missions in direct support of the advancing troops. At the Lingayen landings the combat missions increased in intensity.[18]

The sequence in which the various Squadrons of MAW-1 reached their destination was as follows:

> VMSB-133 and VMSB-141 at Lingayen on 24 January. VMSB-133 was subsequently re-deployed to Mindanao on 21 April. VMSB 241 at Luzon on 25 January. The squadron was subsequently re-deployed to Mindanao on 10 April. VMSB-341 – at Lingayen on 26 January. VMSB-236, VMSB-244 and VMSB-244 all arrived on 27 January.

A large-scale test of their technique took place on 31 January when the Marine aircraft were ordered to give their aid and assistance to 1st Cavalry Division's drive to take the city of Manila itself. In the sixty-six-hour dash, and during the subsequent severe street fighting for control, the Marine aviators demonstrated fully their newly-honed proficiency in the use of dive-bombing support at close quarters. This practical application of the air-to-ground team proved to be very effective indeed and finally won over the army doubters. One account read: 'The air support given by the Marines forced the enemy to remain under cover, helped to thwart his potential to establish effective resistance, and facilitated the rapid advance of 1st Cavalry Division.' Brigadier General William Curtis Chase, commanding 1 Brigade during the advance on Manila stated: 'I have never seen such able, close, and accurate close support as the Marine flyers are

---

17 From the Malay *Padi* = rice, anglicized to Paddy.
18 Santelli, BA. James S. – *Marines in the Recapture of the Philippines*, 1965: Washington DC. Historical Branch, HQ USMC.

giving us.' Another distinguished army officer was of the same opinion. In an interview given after the Americans had entered Manila, Major General Verne Donald Mudge stated:

> I can say without reservation that the Marine dive-bomber outfits are among the most flexible I have seen in this war. They will try anything and from experience with them I have found that anything they try usually pans out. The Marine dive-bombers of the First Air Wing have kept the enemy on the run. They have kept him underground and enabled us to move up with fewer casualties and at greater speed. I cannot say enough in praise of these men of the dive-bombers … for the job they have done in giving my men close support in this operation.

The Japanese had not been caught totally flat-footed or in disarray by the Lingayen landings – after all they had themselves invaded the same spot three years earlier and so did not really expect the American troops to come ashore in Manila Bay itself. Their plan was to concentrate the bulk of their 250,000-strong Fourteenth Army inland, in three groups, and to restrict the US advance to the plain where they could counter-attack the Americans to good effect. But, in a dilemma similar to the German commander Erwin Rommel in Normandy, they had not realized just how much command of the air would dictate movement on the ground.

The construction crews quickly got to work, and two airstrips were already in operation on Mindoro from 23 December onward. As a result, when the Japanese attempted to switch their divisions to oppose the Americans on Luzon, they found that their columns were dive-bombed off the roads north of the capital and into the dubious sanctuary of the jungle, where Filipino guerrillas, loyal to the US, awaited them. Totally confused, the Japanese defence organization dissolved under the hail of bombs, among the casualties being the only armoured division the defending general, Tomoyuki Yamsahita, possessed. By 27 January all six airfields at the massive Clark Air Base had been liberated and the capital itself finally fell after three weeks' fighting on 23 February. In all these operations 1 MAW played a full part.

Another personal recollection of how the army became convinced of the merits of dive-bombing was recounted by a historian of the American 24th Regiment. One trooper had become cut off from his comrades and isolated by Japanese patrols:

It was quiet for a long time. Dive-bombers woke me up next morning. Plane after plane dove into the Nip positions. They dropped napalm and high-explosive bombs all around me. I was covered with dirt and leaves by the explosions and I guess that helped to hide me. The Japs were excited and afraid, and they ran all around my position. Maybe they thought I was dead. Maybe they were too busy getting out of there to care. Most of them were killed by the bombs or by the bullets when the planes came back. [ibid.]

During February 1945 the Marine Dauntless formations flew no fewer than 4,000 combat sorties in the Philippines. Despite the abundance of Japanese heavy and light anti-aircraft weaponry all over the islands, the losses taken by the SBDs were minimal; only three Marine Dauntless flyers were killed in this period. Of aerial opposition there was little or none, the last Japanese fighter aircraft having long since been shot out of the sky or bombed on their runways or expended in suicide dives against the massed Allied fleets off the beachheads.

Despite all they had done, and even though the commanders and men on the ground were won over completely, the feeling grew that the Army Air Forces Commander, General George Churchill Kenney, was deliberately keeping the Marine dive-bomber wing under-employed. Embarrassed by its success and their own failures, and ever mindful of the importance of self-promotion of the USAAF itself, this became blatant. Indeed, Fleet Admiral William Frederick 'Bull' Halsey Jr, never one to mince words, and whose own carrier dive-bombers had been attacking the remnants of the Japanese fleet continuously from Indo-China to Tokyo Bay, made a pithy written complaint on just this fact. He told the Commander-in-Chief, General Douglas MacArthur, bluntly that Army Air Forces General Kenney, when not keeping 1 Marine Air Wing idle, 'was assigning it to missions far below its capacity'.[19]

Representative of the work of one squadron was VMSB-341 who flew their first combat sorties on 12 February in direct support of 9th Airborne Division advancing on the Philippines capital and against targets in Tarlac province. The SBDs were called also upon to aid 1st Cavalry Division, and in particular the memorable 'Dash to Manila' by the flying column under

---

19 Halsey, Admiral William Frederick, and Bryan III, Lieutenant Commander J., USNR, *Admiral Halsey's Story*, 1947: New York. McGraw-Hill Book Company Inc.

Brigadier General William Curtis Chase, whose third serial, the Provisional Reconnaissance Squadron (Lieutenant Colonel Thomas H. Ross)[20] contained a Marine Air Control Group under Captain Samuel H. McAloney USMC, which for the first time demonstrated their direct communications links with the MAW and acted as the column's flank and rear guards. The column was ordered by General MacArthur to liberate more than 4,000 American and Filipino captives and to 'rush' Manila without getting involved in heavy fighting. Speed was of the essence and the SBDs from the wing provided the flexible heavy back-up throughout the three-day, one-hundred-mile dash from Guimba to the capital, which commenced on 1 February. In the words of one history, the Dauntless dive-bombers 'roamed over valleys, searched every road and track for signs of enemy resistance. Whenever a roadblock was spotted they reported on the situation and, when permission was granted, cleared the area by precision bombing ....'

Another report by Combat Correspondent Staff Sergeant William Allen was filed on 7 April. He described a typical operation thus:

> The hills guarding the approaches to San Fernando la Union had presented a bloody barrier to ill-equipped but determined Filipino guerrillas. Bodies sprawled in the rice paddies to the north of the slopes bore grim evidence of the price paid for a few precious yards of advance. Today, dive-bombers of the 1st Marine Air Wing were out to chop a path through the Japanese hill positions and mole-like fortifications. Target time was 0800. Promptly at 0815, a low-flying Marine SBD, piloted by battle-wise Major Benjamin Brown Manchester III of Providence, R.I., circled Reservoir Hill. Below, crouched along the northern embankment of a destroyed railroad, hard-bitten guerrillas waited to advance. Communications were established quickly between Benjamin Brown Manchester and Captain Samuel H. McAloney of Cos Cob, Conn., Air Liaison officer attached to Guerrilla Headquarters on the ground with his two-way radio jeep. The directions were short and concise. The Japs, with mortar and machine-gun fire on Reservoir Hill positions, had stopped the Filipino advance into their once colourful San Fernando. The guerrillas had outlined their advance positions with land panels – white strips of cloth – and were fighting a holding action, waiting for the dive-bombers to open the way for their advance.

---

20 Ross himself was killed by enemy fire early on in this mission.

As Captain McAloney outlined the targets to Major Benjamin Brown Manchester, who was flying as co-ordinator of the strike, eighteen dive-bombers circled 12,000 feet overhead. Major Benjamin Brown Manchester made the first dive, dropping a bomb to mark the spot. 'You're on target now', the voice from the ground said. It was the cue for the bombing runs. The Marine bombers were sure and accurate. Peeling off three at a time, they plastered the area with nine and a half tons of high explosives. The guerrillas moved forward as the bombs fell. They were as close as 200 yards behind the bomb blasts, taking cover from flying bomb fragments. Although it was impossible to hear anything except the roar of the motors, the pounding of machine guns, and the blasting crash of bombs as they hit home, the guerrillas were cheering as they ran forward, waving their weapons and spoiling for a good fight. This time they had air power on their side. 'Sounds like a football cheering section,' Captain McAloney reported to the pilots. The diving runs were executed in exactly four minutes. The dive-bombers, apart from Major Benjamin Brown Manchester who stayed over to see the results and direct Army fighters in on the target in a second sweep, winged their way home.[21]

The column achieved its main mission, but Manila itself proved a harder nut to crack and was not finally liberated until 3 March. The US Army pushed forward after Manila eventually fell with 1st Regimental Combat Team (RCT) of 6th Division, under Colonel James Conway Rees, taking San Jose to the north of the city on 4 February. On this same day Army Air Forces aircraft had tried their hand at close-support strafing with the unhappy result of 1st Division taking several casualties from 'friendly fire'. This not only had an adverse effect on the troops, but their commander was reluctant to repeat the experience, no matter how difficult things became on the ground.

The change in attitude came on 28 February, when a squad of soldiers under a wounded lieutenant became cut off from the rest of their unit across a Japanese-dominated valley. The terrain was wild and difficult, and the enemy were entrenched in positions as close as 200 yards from the encircled Americans. Any attempt to reach them, it was estimated, would take at least an hour under heavy fire. The Marine Air Wing radioed an offer of help and, after a detailed briefing on the situation via the communications net,

---

21 Allen, Staff-Sergeant William, *Marine Corps Chevron,* Vol. 4, No. 13, 7 April 1945.

the soldiers' commander, Colonel Rees, gave them his permission to go ahead, but only the dropping of a solitary wing bomb from each aircraft. It had to be right or not at all. The Marine flyers grabbed their opportunity and one SBD was despatched to the target. The assembled and anxious army watchers, including many of the regiment's top brass, including the commander of 6th Division, Major General Edwin Davies Patrick, had a grandstand view of the attack as they were located on one side of the valley atop a high cliff. Visibility was perfect as the Dauntless dived in, etched against the brilliant blue sky, and released its single bomb. It hit, right on target, the enemy detachment. Colonel Rees, suitably relieved and impressed, radioed the go-ahead for the plane to drop its main under-belly bomb and its other wing bomb also.

In acknowledgement, the Marine pilot pulled his Dauntless up to regain sufficient altitude, which took some twenty minutes. Meanwhile the rest of the seven SBDs stooged around overhead awaiting their chance. The second dive-bombing run was even more precise if anything, with both bombs landing right in among the Japanese. From that moment on 1st Regiment, anyway, was sold on the Marine flyers and permission was given immediately for the rest of the squadron to join in the attack. Of the twenty-seven bombs that they released, the farthest off-target was thirty yards away.

Colonel Rees now became an enthusiastic exponent of dive-bombing, according to an eyewitness, Captain James L. McConaughy, ALP, so much so that 1 RCT was to have a permanent stand-by daily requirement of nine flights a day, each of nine SBDs, for the rest of the campaign.[22]

This sortie was influential as it was witnessed by so many senior Army personnel and it confirmed the flexibility of the radio organization that enabled the army commander, the ALP and the squadron commander in the air to co-operate, right down to the individual bomb drop. The range of the communications net almost proved its worth, until the air waves became swamped with Allied chatter as the campaign wore on. When the VHF channels became too jammed solid with Army Air Forces aircraft signals, the Marines were able simply to switch over to MHF.

By the end of January 1945, 168 SBDs along with 472 officers and 3,047 men were in situ at Mangaldan. Not a single aircraft had been lost in transit although Second Lieutenant S.L. Hammond of VMSB-241, transiting from Leyte had his engine cut out on him while at 10,000 feet over Manila

---

22 Boggs, Major Charles William Jr– *Marine Aviation in the Philippines, op cit.*
    Unfortunately, Rees himself was killed by an artillery shell during on 11 March.

Bay. He jettisoned the wing tanks and associated equipment and, down to just 500 feet, fortunately the engine re-started and Hammond safely made an emergency landing at Lingayen. Another aircraft, from VMSB-133, piloted by First Lieutenant L.M. Carlson suffered engine problems at Peleliu which delayed arrival by just two days.

At this period the Marines came under the operational control of the Army's 308th Bomb Wing and their initial operations had to conform to their practices, which was in direct opposition to all they had trained for. Not only were its combat mission's long-range ones beyond the front line, but there was no ground liaison with the infantry on the ground and requests for air strikes had to be cumbersomely relayed right up the line to Sixth Army HQ for permission to act. By the time such OK was received the situation on the ground had changed as one day's requests were authorized for next day's missions! Not only were the squadrons allocated tightly controlled but the type of ordnance to be deployed was dictated and even the time they were to spend on the target. Moreover, often such radio requests were monitored and could be (and often were) vetoed by high command anyway. To the Marines it was an utter waste of resources and their skills.

The Marines' first mission of this type was mounted on 27 January with eighteen Dauntless from VMSB-241 led by Major Benjamin Brown Manchester. The target was thirty-five miles distant from their airfield and was designated as heavy and medium gun positions, bivouac areas, oil dumps, and some specified buildings at San Fernando La Union. These targets were duly hit. That same afternoon VMSB-133, under Major Lee Christofferson, was assigned supply dumps and buildings at the much-bombed Clark Field, north of Manila, which was also adjudged a successful mission.

After this auspicious start, despite the cramping Air Force restrictions, the Marines got to work in earnest. Their attack methodology employed was described as follows. The take-off formation was usually made in three-plane sections, (although six and, on one occasion, nine-plane rolls off occurred.) Once aloft the SBDs formed up in as close a formation as possible to give mutually-supporting firepower. The preferred maximum height maintained to the target was 15,000 feet but once near the objective they would lower down to a third of this altitude for target identification. Once confirmed, the lead section entered the dive followed by the rest of each flight, attacking singly at an angle of approximately 70 degrees with dive-flaps extended to reduce speed to 250 knots. The reflector bomb-sight was calibrated for a 2,000-foot bomb-release height and the ordnance was usually a single 1,000lb bomb. Either instantaneous or with a two-tenths-of-a-second-delayed fuse setting, pull-out was completed at around 1,000 feet. The dive-brakes were closed and low-altitude zig-zagging evasion was practised until rendezvous made for a re-forming away from the target area and flak concentrations. Sometimes, if the Japanese ground defences were weak, low-level strafing runs were also conducted prior to the Dauntless forming up and making their departure.[23] On the debit side of the ledger, it was in this area on 28 January that 1 MAW took its first loss, when the Dauntless of First Lieutenant Gordon Rhys Lewis, with Corporal Samuel Patrick Melish as his rear-seat man, took a 20mm shell into the engine just after bomb-release and dived in.

On 29 January a call was made from the 158th Regimental Combat of I Corps, after they had been brought to a halt by determined enemy defences on the east bank of the Bued river, to the east of Rosario town. After a thorough reconnaissance, VMSB-133 and VMSB-241 despatched twenty-nine SBDs to make what was, up to that date, the nearest thing to a close-support mission; they directed fifty-five bombs into the enemy bunkers.

On 30 January VMSB-236 and VMSB-341 combined to make a thirty-six-aircraft attack on enemy positions at Tuguegarao, Cagayan airfield and its environs, which Japanese aircraft had been using as a staging post for reinforcements flown in from Formosa. The following day saw the last of seventeen such attacks conducted by the Marine Air Wing's five squadrons, with 207,800lb of bombs dropped that month.

Lack of enemy air opposition saw the small-scale fighter escorts provided by the Army fighter aircraft discontinued in February as the American ground forces, having consolidated their Lingayen beachhead, taken Clark Field, and opened up Subic Bay to shipping, concentrated on the liberation of Manila. The MAW SBDs were called upon during the initial stages of the Luzon operation in supporting 11th Airborne Division. South of Manila Bay and the daring airborne drop on Tagaytay Ridge.

The Dauntless flyers were also finally allowed to lend their unique expertise to 6th Division of XIV Corps, once the former's commander, Major General Edwin Davies Patrick, had grudgingly consented to their value. On 27 February for example some seventy-five sorties had been made including one by nine Dauntless against Japanese ammo dumps and artillery positions at 0810 in the Wawa approaches to the mountains east of Manila in the Wawa Dam and across the Lobac (Loay) river in Bohol province. The dam built across the Wawa Gorge on the Mankina river,

23 See USMC Monograph – *Marine Aviation in the Philippines,* op. cit.

in Rizal province south of Shimbu, was believed by the US Army to be the main source of water supply for Manila itself. It was not until after two months' hard fighting that it was belatedly realized that Wawa Dam had, in fact, been abandoned in 1938 and that water for the capital came principally from the Ipo Dam. The Japanese had an estimated 30,000 troops along this front and they fiercely fought for the powerful Shimbu Line defended by the IJA's Fourteenth Army under Lieutenant General Shizuo Yokoyama, which put up hard resistance to the advancing Americans. The SBDs made positive contributions to the early advances, with strikes of thirty-six, forty-six, forty-eight, fifty, sixty-three and culminating in a massive dive-bombing by eighty-one SBDs on 10 February. Next day in support of 11th Airborne, thirty-six Dauntless from VMSB-133 and VMSB-341, hit enemy pillboxes at Nichols Field with 1,000lb bombs and exploded an ammunition dump. Another loss was taken, however, with Second Lieutenant Edward E Fryer and his gunner, Sergeant John Henry King, crewing an SBD which was shot down into Manila Bay.

Again, on 27 February, for example, some seventy-five sorties were made including one at 0810 by nine Dauntless against Japanese ammunition dumps and artillery positions; another at 1420 by eight SBDs against an estimated 100 enemy troops on a knoll and a third at 1540 which struck the Japanese holed up in caves south-east of Wawa.[24]

Meanwhile, what of a typical individual unit of the wing? Nine Dauntless from VMSB-341 had conducted diving attacks on Corregidor on 9 February, starting many serious fires, and supported the rescue mission carried out by the 6th Ranger Battalion led by Lieutenant Colonel Henry Mucci and Captain Robert Prince, of 513 Allied PoWs from Cabanatuan internment camp[25] VMSB-341 made repeated attacks on the HQ buildings and support facilities of the Japanese commander, Fourteenth Army, General Tomoyoki Yamashita, IJA, at Bagulo City during 33rd Infantry Division's advance there.[26] Fort Stotsenburg, adjacent to Clark Air Base, was also among the earlier targets struck in quick succession by the SBDs.[27]

From 1 February the Marines had been reacting to 308th Bombardment Wing's 'Air Alert' missions. They gave 1 MAW at least *some* of the flexibility

---

24 The Ipo Dam was not finally to be taken until 17 May while the redundant Wawa Dam was not captured until 28 May.

25 See Hilliard, Sergeant Clayton Paul, VMSB-341 in Bright, Richard Carl, *Pain and Purpose in the Pacific: True Reports of War*. 2014: Victoria BC. Trafford Publishing.

26 The city finally fell to the American 37th Infantry Division in April.

27 Fort Stotsenburg fell to 37th Infantry on 31 January.

that they had trained for. Under this system a standing patrol of nine SBDs was to be maintained over the 1st Cavalry Division during all the hours of daylight with direction in the hands of front-line observers. In effect the airborne Marines covered Chase's left flank for three days for thirty miles ahead and twenty miles astern, and broke any enemy concentrations that might hinder progress, as they did at Angat and San Jose del Monte on Day One, and San Isidro on Day Two. At the latter place, VMSB-133, VMSB-144 and VMSB-241 contributed a force of forty-five SBDS which flattened a specified area box of just 300 x 200 yards. They also conducted a series of skilful feint attacks very close to the column's head which had run into a dug-in Japanese battalion and so diverted the enemy that the Americans broke through. Two radio jeeps accompanied Chase's force, manned by Captain Francis Richard Borroum Godolphin [28] and Samuel Holt McAloney and their teams respectively. The column reached the university building on the night of 3 February and released 3,000 starving internees. The cost to the Marines was just one Dauntless, the aircraft of Captain Glen Harold Schluckebier and Sergeant Donald Martin Morris, which took a hit in its engine. After jettisoning his bomb, the pilot managed to make a wheels-up landing in a paddy field where the aircrew were almost instantly rescued by the cavalrymen they were supporting.

Attention meanwhile shifted to new landings on the by-passed islands of the group where it was finally decided to eventually deploy both Marine Groups, but in the end only MAG-32 was moved initially. Meanwhile MAG-24 remained to support Sixth Army from Mangaldan, for the time being at least, while their executive officer, Lieutenant Colonel Smith, visited the various army units and tried to persuade them to use the SBDs to help them, but was received with distrust by most of the soldiers. Colonel Jerome's hoped-for shift of HQ from Bougainville, was, however, cancelled and he was forced to make only fleeting visits to his front-line units.

On 19 February Second Lieutenant Donald Milton Johnson of VSMB-133 was lost when his SBD was shot down during a forty-eight-plane strike by MAG-24, led by Colonel Lyle Harold Meyer, against derelict shipping being used as sniper and machine-gun nests in Manila Harbor, in aid of 37th Division. On 12 February VMSB-341 sustained their next aircraft loss when Second Lieutenant Eiton Arthur Barnum was hit by AA fire. This pilot was reported as MIA but managed to land at a small Allied airstrip safely. Once the Americans had entered the outskirts of the capital itself SBDs began

---

28   Post-war Dr Godolphin became Dean of Princeton University.

to operate from a makeshift airstrip that was actually a specially-widened boulevard of Quezon City. It was not the ideal operating airstrip but, for *some* vital missions, and in order to maintain a nominal force at the front closer than Mangaldan which was 110 miles to the rear, it sufficed. Throughout February, therefore, this city street also acted as an emergency landing strip which received an average of one Dauntless in difficulties per day.

From 19 February onward, the use of airborne co-ordinators was gradually increased as confidence in the MAW's abilities increased from 'proof-of-the-pudding' deeds in action. Dummy runs were gradually abandoned and the time from request to strike drastically improved more in keeping with how the Marines had trained. The use of SBD pilots in the air-to-ground liaison role also increased, it being found that such pilots were obviously more in tune with what the SBDs were capable of carrying out, the downside being that they, naturally, lacked the regular Marines' awareness of ground tactics. On Luzon there were now four VHF channels in use by all air forces, a fact which tended to cause a lot of 'overcrowding' of the airwaves with so many aircraft using them simultaneously. This was compounded by the fact that while the more modern Dash-6 Dauntless were equipped with both the four-channel VHF and the two-channel MHF set, the older Dash-5s, which still equipped squadrons VMSB-243 and VMSB-244, only had the MHF. To partially overcome this every flight of Dash-5s was assigned a similar number of Dash-6s for close-range missions. When acting alone the Dash-5s were sent against more distant targets where there was less aerial 'clutter'. Once the VHF channels became clogged, however, the Marines used MHF almost exclusively.

Another unexpected problem was the lack of detailed maps for the greater area of the Philippines; this was puzzling for, even though they had been under United States administration for fifty years or more, only those areas of Luzon adjacent to Manila and in the central plains had satisfactory charts; and this was further compounded by the duplication of place names, from province to province across the country.

Once it was decided to use MAG-32 initially in the Mindanao landings, it was specified that four squadrons were required. This required some considerable re-assigning of the various squadrons as some had many personnel whose transfer home to the States was imminent. The solution was for MAG-32 to comprise of VMSB-142, VMSB-236, VMSB-243 and VMSB-341 while MAG-24 was to become a three-squadron force with the transfer of VMSB-244 from MAG-32. On 20 February Colonel Lyle Meyer was assigned as Commander, MAGs Dagupan *and* Commander Mangaldan.

On 2 March a daring night attack was made on Mangaldan by three Mitsubishi G4M Betty twin-engine bombers at 0200. While one Betty flew high and attracted the base's entire AA attention (in vain) two more swept low over the base at about 300 feet and showered over 250 anti-personnel bomblets across the Marines' encampment, killing four men and wounding seventy-eight. Eleven 500lb bombs were also dropped on the airfield itself, destroying one Dauntless and damaging a second. Total surprise was achieved.

Notwithstanding this surprise, MAG 24 continued to support both the regular army I, XI and XIV Corps and the guerrilla forces fighting behind enemy lines in northern Luzon; some 186 attacks were made by the SBDs in this latter regard between 5 and 31 March. In support of the US Army's drives into northern and eastern Luzon, the Dauntless were prominent, flying eighteen-plane strikes as well as three-plane 'Air Alert' missions, despite their reduced numbers. Thirty-eight attacks were made at Solvec Bay in the north-west Rocos region, thirty-five at the bitter fighting at the Balete (Dalton) Pass in Nueva province, and fourteen more around Baguio, Cordillera, in the central mountains and later the site of the final Japanese surrender. The last sortie was flown on 2 April and then MAG 24 ceased operation in readiness for joining their colleagues on Mindanao, to which we now retrace our steps.

Following the American landing at Zamboango, Mindanao, on 1 March the VMSB-341 Squadron was split on 21 March with eight pilots with supporting ground personnel, sent to San Jose, Mindoro, which they reached four days later. The ground team sailed from Mingalden Bay on 25 March for San Roque airfield, Zamboango, disembarking two days later and moving on to the airfield,[29] the next day to establish MAGZAM. The rest of the pilots from VMSB-341, along with 134 crew and all aircraft remained at Malgalden until 25 March when they were flown by USAAF C-46 transports to Zamboango while the Dauntless dive-bombers flew into Moret to join the re-united squadron.

The first ground support sortie was made on 17 March and the SBDs continued to give their assistance to Major General Jens Doe's 41st Infantry Division, that officer warmly welcoming the Marine dive-bombers in contrast to the initial reaction of most of his fellow generals who had to be converted.[30]

---

29   which Colonel Clayton Jerome had renamed as Moret Field on 13 March.
30   Hammel, Eric. *Coral and Blood: The U S Marine Corps' Pacific Campaign*. e-book.

Between 11 and 23 March SBDs also operated from a makeshift dirt strip at Dipolog, north-east of Zamboango City.

While those of the ground personnel whose tours were completed were shortly afterward returned to the US, the Squadron continued combat mission assignments, supporting 31st Infantry Division and Filipino guerrillas as they pushed forward up the Sayre Highway toward Malaybalay, meeting fierce resistance from General Gyosaku Morozumi's defending troops and suffering from the limitations of the dirt road, which made bringing up artillery difficult in the extreme. The SBDs substituted and were much in demand. Even so, Malaybalay was not finally to fall to 155th Infantry Regiment until 21 May.

Meanwhile MAG 24 had been delayed in its move to join its compatriots and not until 12 April did the ships carrying the ground teams for VMSB-133, VMSB-241 and VMSB-244 reach San Jose, Mindoro; they moved up to Mindanao on the 14th. In the interim there had been repeated calls on the aircrews left behind on Luzon to continue their close-support work in aid of 37th Division, still bogged down along the Balete Pass, and attacks were continuous from the 10th to the 14th but the increasingly heavy rain was fast turning the rice-paddy strip into a morass. Accordingly, the SBDs were concentrated back at Clark Field, this being done by 17 April; the next few days were spent in refurbishment of the aircraft. In their last period of combat operations on Luzon between 5 February and 14 April, some forty-five days, the Dauntless had conducted an average of 159 sorties per day. In total the Luzon campaign had seen 1 MAW conduct 8,842 combat sorties during which they delivered 19,167 bombs into the enemy's lap. The once-reluctant Army commanders were won over, the commander of Sixth Army, Lieutenant General Walter Krueger, stating that his subordinates 'have repeatedly expressed their admiration for the pin-point precision, the willingness and enthusiastic desire of [Marine] pilots to fly missions from dawn to dusk and the extremely close liaison with the ground forces which characterized the operations.' Finally, MAG-24's hop from Clark to Malabang was undertaken in sections between 20 and 22 April.

MAG-32 had not been idle. In April the Dauntless were called upon to mount close-support missions for the 163rd Infantry and Filipino guerrillas against the only major concentration of Japanese left between Zamboanga and Tawitawi, which was Jolo Island. There the Japanese 55th Regiment had 2,400 soldiers, along with 350 IJN Marines and 1,000 air force personnel. The Americans landed on 9 April and the Japanese withdrew to prepared positions, the toughest of which was Mount Daho, six miles south-east of

Jolo town. The SBDs gave continuous support and when the attack went in on the 22nd gave sturdy assistance to the men of the 163rd.

From 5 April the SBDs of Major General Ralph Johnson Mitchell's 1 MAW, moved from Dipolog to Malabang field which had been seized by guerrilla forces a few days earlier. Immediately the Dauntless began flying combat sorties from that airstrip and within five days the Japanese began retreating to Parang, but an American landing there on the 17th followed. The Marine flyers were heavily involved at Malabang where once again the SBDs joined in the general naval bombardments to soften up the area. The opportunity was taken to sail a convoy of gunboats and landing-ships up the thirty-five-mile Mindanao river itself to take Kabacan, forcing the Japanese to withdraw. Malabang was rapidly reinforced by 31st Division and MAG-24 and 24th Division advanced toward Davao City, while the 31st attacked up the Sayre Highway toward Macajalar Bay. By 3 May the Americans had entered the city and then two months of difficult, close-range and mopping-up warfare followed against elements of the Japanese 100th Division. On that same date 31st Division entered Kibawe. Heavy fighting followed at Maramag and Malaybalay finally fell on 21 May.

Marine flyers' attacks were continued on the Kibabwe Trail north of that Davao. Between 8 and 12 July the focus of Dauntless attacks became enemy troops at Saraganin Bay in southern Mindanao, aiding 21st Infantry in the clearing of the enemy, working from Diplog with the final sortie of VMSB-341 being flown on the 31st. Between March and the end of July the squadron took zero combat or operational losses of pilots.

Fighting was to continue on the ground but in August VMSB-was transferred out of MAG-32, this being done on the 15th, and they were shipped back to the States via Seattle. By 13 September they had arrived at Marine Corps Air Depot, Miramar, California, and it was there that the squadron was decommissioned

The Marine Dauntless Squadrons flew some 255 sorties and dropped 104 tons of bombs for the loss of just one SBD shot down by AA fire, on 28 January. Despite the negative attitude of the USAAF, the Marine Corps dive-bomber wing continued to apply its now perfected technique of close-support where it was allowed throughout the remainder of the Luzon campaign. The missions in support of the troops on the ground continued until the final sortie, which was carried out on 14 April 1945. However, by that date some of 1 MAW component squadrons had already been shifted to a new area of combat, with the plans to retake most of the southern Philippines. From March 1945 SBDs were flying yet further dive-bomber missions in this, albeit subsidiary, region.

The first of the new assignments was backing the US 41st Division whose own main task was to clear the Sulu archipelago; to facilitate this, American troops waded ashore on the south-eastern tip of Mindanao on 21 March to re-occupy the Zamboanga peninsula. It took a fortnight's hard fighting for them to get a decent toehold there but, with the dive-bomber support from the Marine air wing, Sirawai fell on 21 March. They then turned their attentions to the chain of islands that spanned the northern end of the Celebes Sea from the Philippines to Borneo. In the centre of this chain was the island of Jolo and 163rd RCT went ashore there on 9 April to find it garrisoned by 4,000 resolute Japanese troops. The fighting there, grim and dour slogging, continued for three weeks before the main area of the island was cleared of the enemy; and even so certain Japanese units held out until July. The SBDs were in continual demand to break strongpoints of resistance during a bloody, and not widely-known, episode.

Finally came Cebu, in the central Philippines group, which guarded the south-west approach to the vital supply route of the Visayan Sea. There Marine veterans joined hands with army veterans, for the American division assigned to take Cebu was formed from divisions that had fought at Guadalcanal and Bougainville. They knew each other well and worked well as a team. These troops landed close to Cebu City on 26 March and immediately ran into formidable defences which stopped them dead. Even the beaches were extensively mined. Two weeks' hard fighting ensued, but some Japanese units were still resisting as late as June. The bulk of the American dive-bombing sorties were carried out in support of regular ground forces, but some were highly specialized missions to bring airborne firepower to Filipino guerrilla forces behind enemy lines. These taxing operations continued until the war's end.

The faithful Douglas SBD Dauntless was now reaching the end of its American combat life. One of MAG-24's dive-bomber squadrons, VMSB-244, had its Dauntless aircraft replaced by Curtiss SB2C Helldivers towards the end of May. The other two, VMSB-133 and VMSB-241, were de-commissioned on 16 July, near the end of the fighting. Finally, on 1 August 1945, the four SBD squadrons that made up MAG-32 reached the end of their operational tour also and prepared for their return home two weeks later.

It was the end of an era, but the Marine SBD pilots had picked up the proud traditions of their forebear, Major General Ross Erastus Rowell, and his companions whose diving attacks in Nicaragua many years before had started the ball rolling for US close air support. The work of 1 MAW in the Philippines not only honed the weapon to perfection and demonstrated its efficiency but had laid the foundations for the future role of the US Marine Corps aviation. The full significance was that, for the first time during the Second World War, they were able to demonstrate America's whole concept of close-support as it is understood right to this present day.

Although Marine aviators had in other battles, like those conducted in the Solomons and later, at Okinawa, used certain facets of the doctrine, the real test of the adaptability of close air-support was manifested in the Philippines campaign. As one Marine historian recorded 'This employment was a notable milestone in the formulation of Marine Aviation's post-war mission'.

Appendix 1

The Emperor's New Clothes

In 1873 a short story by the Danish author Hans Christian Andersen was published. It was entitled *Kejserens nye Klæder* (*The Emperor's New Clothes*). I sometimes feel like the child in that story who blurted out, when nobody else dared, that the Emperor was naked! In the so-called 'Flight of Fantasy' scenarios, first propagated by Major Bowen Pattison Weisheit USMCR (Rtd) in 1993,[1] the *Hornet* strike force, led by Stanhope Ring, was declared not to have flown the course of 240 degrees to locate the *Kido Butai* on the morning of 4 June 1942, as declared in the official report of the battle, but instead flew an entirely different course of 280 degrees, almost due west. Since then Bowen Pattison Weisheit's scenario, based on the flimsiest of evidence and an enormous amount of speculation, has taken hold like Japanese knotweed in a garden and appears to become an accepted 'fact' even by some of the most respected of historians. Theories are fine, as *theories*, but if they pertain to be taken as *facts* then proof is required, especially if several people's reputations are ruined. Of course, such a theory *might* be true, but, should that be the case, an awful lot of otherwise respectable people lied at the time and continued lying until they died.

I prefer authenticated facts that can be substantiated and, until these are produced and verified, I retain my doubts about the validity of this theory. I am more than willing to be proven wrong but, to date, have not seen any such printed evidence. So, while perfectly happy for others to believe wholeheartedly that *Hornet*'s report was 'doctored', that Marc Mitscher, and all his staff; Ring and his many colleagues, even those with high antipathy toward him personally; that Lieutenant Commander Ernest McNeill Eller Jr, who was at Pearl Harbor, and who, in his own words 'interviewed all the flag officers, captains of ships, gunnery officers,

---

1 Weisheit, Major Bowen Pattison – *The Last Flight of Ensign C. Markland Kelly, Junior, USNR: with a New, Corrected Charting of the Flight of VF-8 from USS* Hornet *During the Battle of Midway*. 1993: Annapolis, MD. Self-published.

squadron commanders of planes, and others'[2]; that Under-Secretary of the Navy James Vincent Forrestal, who flew out to consult shortly after the battle in order to produce an accurate report and get to the truth, who studied the draft report; and that Admiral Nimitz himself who delayed publication until he was satisfied that it was accurate and who, again in Eller's words 'wanted it just right and I did too' were all somehow complicit in a cover-up? Eller, as rear admiral, later became the highly-respected Director of Naval History at the Naval History Division between 1956 and 1970. Are we to believe that he acceded to the wholesale distortion of official records, and that he, and indeed any eyewitness who disagreed with Bowen Pattison Weisheit's view, are *all* mistaken? I prefer to believe those self-same eyewitnesses unless it can be proven otherwise. Here are some reasons for my reservations.

1: Lieutenant James Seaton Gray who commanded the *Enterprise's* fighter section, VF-6, failed to locate his own charges, VT-6,[3] for whom his fighters were to provide protection, but instead found VT-8 and flew top cover on them. Now, if VT-8 and VT-6 had been flying widely differing routes as they took departure, Gray would have certainly noticed and commented on the fact. He did not. Instead he happily went along with VT-8, knowing they were steering, at the outset anyway, much the same course as VT-6 would have been.

This squares with Ring's immediate post-war description, in which he stated that his attack was made on a 'pre-estimated interception course'[4] and that, in due course his force arrived *'at the line between the last reported position of the enemy and Midway Island.'*[5] If one takes these two datum points and projects them from *Hornet's* position on departure of her striking force, then the heading that results is approximately 240 degrees, or, as VB-10's war diary faithfully records, Lat 30-35 (N) Long 178-35 (W).[6]

2 *Eller, Rear Admiral Ernest M, U.S. Navy (Retd) Volume II.* Based on seven interviews conducted by John T. Mason Jr from December 1974 through August 1978. 1990: Annapolis, MD. U S Naval Institute; also, Ernest McNeill Eller Papers, 1880-1991, Manuscript Collection #618 held at the Pritzker Military Museum & Library, Oral History Room, V63.E55, Chicago. Il.
3 The SBDs after circling for a considerable time, had already been sent off alone on the orders of Spruance.
4 Linder, Captain Bruce Rich. *Lost Letter of Midway.* Naval Institute *Proceedings,* August 1999 Edition. pp. 29-35.
5 My italics.
6 *VB-8 War Diary 4 June 1942,* filed at the Office of Naval Records and Library on October 2 1942. FVB8. No. 62849.

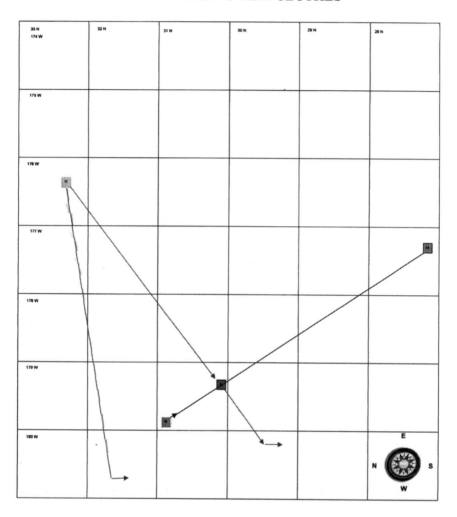

2: It is alleged that radar tracked *Hornet's* attack group taking a route 'almost due west' on the morning of 4 June 1942. During my various researches into this subject between 2000 and 2018 I was informed by officials at College Park that 'none of Task Force 16's radar logs were retained post-war.' It would appear that this information still remains the case. So the radar tracking question remains without positive confirmation. However, a hitherto unreleased report from *Hornet's* Air Operations Officer has recently been brought to light. The document in question, although finally and belatedly 'De-Classified', (sixty to seventy years after the event!), in 2012 was located in the archives recently by George M. Walsh who kindly sent sent me a copy.[7]

---

7 Confidential Report CV8/A16, U.S.S. *Hornet*. OF29-AS.

From: Air Operations Officer.[8]
To: The Commanding Officer.[9]
Via: The Air Officer.[10]

Defects Observed During the Action off Midway on June 4, 1942. Dated June 12, 1942. Declassified – Authority E.O. 13526, By: NDC NARA Date: Dec 31, 2012.

However, it proved of no help at all in resolving the radar tracking question relating to the outward *Hornet* air striking force's initial departure course as it might well have done.[11] Nonetheless, we are able herewith to glean some useful information by citing various other points that do have some considerable relevance on the matter, as follows.

Foster confirmed that:

(a) The 2 hour and 19 minute delay on the Fox schedule of the original contact of enemy planes reported approaching Midway is entirely too great a time lag and indicates that only direct communication is sufficient. This is especially so where aircraft are involved.

(b) The period of 2 hour and 33 minutes between the sighting of enemy planes approaching Midway and the report of enemy surface force position, course and speed was entirely too long and inadequate under the conditions obtaining and especially so *in as much as the enemy's position confirmed to prior estimates.*[12]

(c) The lack of information on the enemy's surface forces … was serious and jeopardized the tactical advantage we enjoyed over the enemy. The delay of the *Enterprise's* Air

---

8 Lieutenant Commander John Gold Foster Jr, US Navy.

9 Captain Mark Andrew Mitscher, US Navy.

10 Commander Apollo Soucek, US Navy. This document was nonetheless illuminating in its own way. It should be noted that Lisle Abbott Rose had access to this document at a much earlier date as he included extracts from it in his book *The Ship That Held the Line*, Naval Institute Press, Annapolis, 1995.

11 There is no information whatsoever on the outward direction taken. As George wrote with the enclosure, 'I see nothing about Ring's course, but much hand-wringing about communication and reconnaissance woes. Also repeats that "closing the enemy" was given in lieu of a Point Option.' Walsh, George M., to the Author, 19 October 2018.

12 My italics.

Group attack against the enemy carriers and the failure of the *Hornet*'s VSB planes to make contact with the enemy *can be attributed to this lack of information.* Further, the loss of planes from the *Hornet* and *Enterprise* by water landings from lack of fuel can be partly attached to this unfortunate lack of information on the enemy's movements.[13]

(d) It appears that the enemy was most certainly ignorant of the presence of Task Forces 16 and 17 until radio silence was broken.

The summing-up was damning: 'As the tactical situation was in our favour, it was only through errors on our part that we did not gain a more impressive victory.'

However, the deck log of *Hornet*, and those of several accompanying ships, *were re*tained and are available for study. I reproduce a copy of *Hornet*'s deck log here.

Now, if the deck logs are correct (*all* of them) we are asked to believe that Mitscher deliberately despatched his main air striking force to the west, entirely off his own bat, but then immediately steamed a course of 240 degrees to recover them! Nagumo launched his strike force, then steamed along their route to recover them, and did so easily; Fletcher launched his abortive search the same morning and was forced to steam away from Point Luck to recover them; *Enterprise* launched her strike force in dribs and drabs and steamed along their route to gather them in; but Mitscher, we are asked to believe, sent his aircraft one way and then steamed *away* from them. One must ask whether an aviator as experienced as Mitscher, would adopt such a strange and callous procedure, especially such a commander as Mitscher who, history records, deliberately switched on his fleet's lights, despite the risks, to gather in his aircraft not once, later at Midway, but twice, as recorded, during the Battle of the Philippine Sea. I cannot accept such an outlandish notion. *Enterprise* and *Hornet* stayed in visual contact as they ran down their 240-degree course, and for good sound reasons – because that is the direction in which *Hornet* had finally despatched her aircraft at 0806. Finally, there is the fact that the 'expected point of interception' was shown on the report map as being about the same for both the *Enterprise* and the *Hornet* striking forces, indicating that they must have flown near identical courses.

---

13 My italics. Remember these words were written on 12 June 1942, not decades later.

N Nav 43
(Mar 1929)

UNITED STATES SHIP ___HORNET___   Thursday   4   June ,19 42

                                           (Day)   (Date)   (Month)

ZONE DESCRIPTION Plus 10   **REMARKS**

0 to 4

Steaming darkened on base course 210 true and pgc at 13.5 knots, 130 rpm, in company with Task Force 16 in cruising disposition 11-V, fleet axis 270 true. Guide in ATLANTA, OTC in ENTERPRISE. Ship in condition of Readiness III, Material Condition Baker modified. 0110 Changed speed to 15 knots, commenced zig-zagging in accordance with Plan #7. Average R.P.M. 143.8.

R. R. BOETTCHER,
Lieutenant (jg), U.S. Navy.

4 to 8

Steaming as before. 0441 Cut in boilers No. 1,2,6 and 8. 0540 Held General Quarters. 0635 Secured from General Quarters, set Condition II, Material Condition Baker modified. 0640 Ceased zig-zagging, changed course by ships turn to 040 true and pgc. 0737 Let fires die out under boilers No. 1,4 and 7. Average steam 400. Average R.P.M 145.7.

R. J. KOSHLIEK
Lieutenant (jg), U.S. Navy.

8 to 12

Steaming as before. 0800 Cut in all boilers on the main steam line. Formation turned left to 300 true. Mustered crew on stations. Absentees: WESTFALL, O.W. SC3c, USNR., McGEE, E.W. SC3c, USNR., and PAGE, W.T. SC3c, USNR., Absent Over Leave since 1830 May 27, 1942. 0807 Went to General Quarters on order of the O.T.C. 0811 Formation changed course to 270 true. Changed speed to 20 knots (196 rpm). 0814 Formation changed course to 240 true. Changed speed to 25 knots (246 rpm). 0855 HORNET, MINNEAPOLIS, NEW ORLEANS, ATLANTA and screening destroyers left formation and turned into wind to launch aircraft. Steadied on 158 true. Launched combat air patrol. Launched attack group of 34 scout bombers, 15 torpedo bombers, and 10 escorting fighters. Mission is enemy concentration approaching Midway from the northwest. 0954 Recovered 8-F-17 (deferred forced landing). 1006 HORNET task group turned to 240 true, keeping in sight of the ENTERPRISE task group. 1035 Received signal to form disposition 11-V. Before we could form, the YORKTOWN was attacked by enemy aircraft. For the next hour the ENTERPRISE fighter director directed the combat air patrol on various suspicious contacts. Our radar screen picked up many contacts, but all enemy planes concentrated on the YORKTOWN, which was sending up dense smoke. At about 1130 the radar screen was clear of enemy planes. 1130 Relieved combat air patrol. The base course for the rest of the day was 280 true, speed was 20 knots. We steamed on the base course at 30 knots, closing the ENTERPRISE except when conducting flight operations. Average steam 400. Average R.P.M. 265.5.

A. H. HUNKER,
Lieutenant (jg), U.S. Navy.

12 to 16

Steaming as before. 1241 Recovered some fighters who were low on gas. 1300 Picked up large group of planes bearing 260 true, distant 56 miles. 1312 Sighted planes of our group returning from morning flight. 1312 Turned into wind and commenced recovering aircraft. Steaming on various courses and speeds. Steadied on course 130 true. 1409 Completed recovery of aircraft. The following planes failed to return: 15 (all) torpedo bombers, 14 scout bombers, and 10 fighters. Note: At about 1400 we received word from Midway that 11 scout bombers from the HORNET had landed there. They were to be re-fueled and sent out again. Our air group which returned did not find the enemy. They searched until their gas was low, then jettisoned their bombs and returned. It is believed that the torpedo planes made their attack. However, nothing has been heard of them since. 1409 Resumed base course. Radar reported much activity ahead of us in the direction of the YORKTOWN. 1410 YORKTOWN reported that she was being attacked by aircraft. The sky in her direction was filled with anti-aircraft bursts. 1419 On orders from O.T.C. the NEW ORLEANS and VINCENNES plus two destroyers proceeded to the aid of the YORKTOWN. HORNET launched five fighters to augment combat air patrol. At this time the attack seemed to be over. All fighters short on gas and ammunition were ordered to land. YORKTOWN planes were

Hornet did not have an onboard of Combat Intelligence Unit (CIU) decoders embarked aboard cleared for receiving or transmitting the Class 5 Cryptographic code, even though both *Yorktown* and *Enterprise, having Flag Officers embarked,* did. Their updates were invaluable. Mitscher, by contrast, was forced to rely on the scraps of information *only* randomly passed over from *Enterprise.* Mitscher and his team were given *no* 'Point Option' by Captain Miles Rutherford Browning, Spruance's inherited Chief of Staff, *no* target designations and *no* group course. One thing all the commanders were broadly agreed upon was that Nagumo's Task Force would continue toward Midway until they had re-embarked their aerial strike force. At the time *Hornet*'s force took off, the last reported position of the enemy they were given was that *Kido Butai* was steaming on course 140 degrees (True) at a speed of 25 knots. Any subsequent intelligence, such as scraps of radio transmissions, relating to the enemy's location or movements, once departure had been taken, by Ring's force, was not, for radio security reasons, subsequently passed on to Ring. This is confirmed in *Hornet*'s after-action report of 13 June:– 'We did not break radio silence to report this to the planes'. This was why Spruance in his final report commented that, should there be any discrepancy in the reports, then *Enterprise* was more likely to be the accurate one, simply because Mitscher was not told everything and *not* for some nefarious plot. But nobody loves a conspiracy theory more than the American public.

Marc Mitscher and Stanhope Ring were professional naval airmen. The greater part of their careers had been training, and re-training, for the one great mission of their lives, the sinking of Japanese aircraft carriers. That had been their focus and that remained their focus. We are asked to believe that such men, when offered the location of the one enemy they had been desiring to meet and defeat, immediately abandoned that focus and flew off into the blue on a heading far removed from where that enemy was expected to be and, instead, opted to attack some nebulous force, that might, or might not, exist, in an area that could be anywhere but where the enemy was expected to be. It appears to me to be beyond the bounds of reasonable credibility that they would do such a thing, yet that is what we must believe if Bowen Pattison Weisheit's theory is to be taken as valid as many assert. We must also believe that they also took that decision, even though they were the most junior commanders present, without authorization from their senior commanders in the field! Without some written proof I just cannot buy such assumptions.

Dale Jenkins makes the following additional point.

Whether or not additional records or other facts eventually emerge, the simple logic is that no sensible commander would send an entire carrier air group on an unsubstantiated, speculative search if, as a result, it meant that the remaining air group of one carrier was sent to attack a force of at least two enemy carriers, and possibly four or five. No responsible person has had a serious doubt about Spruance or Mitscher being a sensible person. Nimitz himself at Pearl Harbor, receiving the scouting reports immediately by cable and virtually contemporaneously with Fletcher and Spruance, did not believe that there were only two carriers at the position where the PBY made its report at 0603.[14]

3: I interviewed Commander Clayton Evan Fisher USN (Retd) during a three-day visit at his home in Coronado in 2006. On that flight he was, of course, one of Ring's two wingmen, much to his chagrin. He personally did not like Ring as a man or a leader, so had absolutely no axe to grind. But he was crystal clear on what course they flew and what he had seen that confirmed his memory. I found him intelligent, clear of mind, lucid, and he had conducted much of his own research since the Bowen Pattison Weisheit theory emerged, which he totally disagreed with. He was eager to record his views which I tape-recorded extensively and answered all my subsequent later queries. What he told me during those interviews I duly recorded in *Midway Dauntless Victory*, so I will only repeat the most relevant comments here. 'Our navigation course was plotted by all the SBD pilots to the last reported position of the enemy carriers. Ring did not consider that the enemy carriers would need to change course to recover aircraft that had attacked Midway.'[15] of the limit Fisher continued. 'Flying the left wing position, I flew a loose position [he meant formation] and was able to observe a solitary vertical column of black smoke at my 10 o'clock position, which gradually appeared at my 8 o'clock position. I assumed the smoke was from a fuel storage tank on Midway.' He added, 'I have researched a time line off the *Enterprise* and *Yorktown* dive-bombers and have always been convinced that the enemy aircraft had not been hit when I observed the column of black smoke. Also, all the photographs I have seen of the burning fuel tank and the resulting column of smoke I observed were very similar.' He also added that 'I strongly

---

14 Jenkins, Dale, *Midway, the American Attack: First Stage,* to the Author, 1 September 2017.

15 Among the few pieces of the enemy SitRep that Mitscher and Ring had received via *Enterprise* was that the *Kido Butai* was expected to continue on *toward* Midway until their strike was re-embarked.

believe our flight must have been at least under fifty miles from Midway. If our flight was north of the Japanese carriers how could I see the Midway smoke column?' He added, 'There was no way I could have seen the smoke from Midway if we had flown the 265-270-degree course as alleged.'[16]

Fisher also informed me later that he had obtained a copy of VB-8's war diary for June 1942 and I reproduce here, the entry for 4 June 1942.

VB-8 war diary; June 1942.
Filed at the Office of Naval Records and Library October 2 1942.
(FVB8. No: 62849.)

4 June 1942:
Launched nineteen airplanes in company with Scouting Eight and ten airplanes of Fighting Eight to attack a Japanese force of carriers, battleships, cruisers and destroyers reported in Lat 30-35 (N) Long 178-35 (W).
The Group climbed to 19,000 feet.
The sky was five-tenths overcast at 2,000 feet with large patches of Strato-cumulus and small patches of cumulus cloud. No contact was made in the vicinity of the reported position and the Group turned south towards Midway to locate the enemy. Upon reaching Kure Island at 1215 with no contact, the return was started.

That entry, to my mind at least, states quite clearly that they were sent, and duly sought the enemy, towards Nagumo's last reported position and not in some imaginary and arbitrary location plucked out of the air, as the 'Flight to Nowhere' theorists would have it. Then, and only then, they turned south. Both Lieutenant Commander Mitchell and Lieutenant (j.g.) Gray of VF-8 reported that they overflew Kure Island, sixty miles east of Midway itself. To have reached Kure at 1215 from where the conspiracy theory *claims* they were looking, would not, in my view anyway, have been possible in the time concerned, considering the alleged distance involved.

Finally, Fisher commented on the Bowen Pattison Weisheit book as follows:

According to the official accounts, *Hornet* resumed a course of 240 degrees true after launching all her aircraft. *I am sure that is the course I plotted to the enemy position on my plotting*

16   Amplifying e-mail Fisher to the Author, dated 15 September 2006.

board. If Ring took on the 270⁰ course I sure as hell would have been aware of it. I absolutely do not buy the 270-degree theory. Also, I have read Bowen Pattison Weisheit's book many times and I feel like he was trying to fit a piece of a jigsaw puzzle into a space that it did not quite fit in. Ruff Johnson [17] stated that after not sighting the enemy carriers where they expected them to be he turned south toward Midway.

Bowen Pattison Weisheit made much in his book of a long-distance phone conversation he had with Rodee many decades after the event. Early in the exchange Rodee stated 'they gave us the bearing of the enemy which we (flew) down.' Later he said, 'We took the given course. I don't know what he [Waldron] took.' It was until later on in the phone conversation that Rodee changed this and claimed that he recorded the westerly route in his personal flight log book. Professor Craig L. Symonds accepts this without question, 'he [Rodee] did write it down in his flight log, *which he kept.*'[18] Professor Symonds does not state whether or not he has seen this entry, or indeed, the flight log itself. If he has, then that would be decisive. But, if he has, then he is the only one to have done so. Others have tried: James Sawruk, a meticulous researcher, called on Rodee before his death but was apparently refused sight of the flight log. Subsequently others, including Rodee's son and Clayton Fisher, tried to locate this elusive document, but without success. I myself also wrote requesting that if they would not wish to allow me to see it, or even reproduce it alongside Clayton Fisher's log in my book for a fair comparison, then at least, for sake of the American national interest, why not allow someone with official standing to examine that entry, if no other, but without eliciting any response.[19]

Fisher also commented that

> Normally a squadron clerk made the flight log entries after a flight, of the plane's serial number, length of the flight and a designation number of the type of flight. Unless Rodee's flight log was full after Battle of Midway and a new log book started, and Rodee sent the log book home, I feel his log book must have been lost when the *Hornet* was sunk.

---

17 Lieutenant Commander Robert Ruffin Johnson, of VB-8.

18 My italics. Symonds, Craig Lee, *The Battle of Midway.* Appendix F, p 390. 2011: New York. Oxford University Press.

19 Incidentally, Flight logs were not kept by the pilots themselves; they were maintained by yeomen in the squadron personnel office and returned to the pilot at the end of each tour or in the event of a transfer to another unit.

He added that his own flight log book

"…..was saved by a VB-8 pilot, Art Cason, when the *Hornet* Air Group abandoned before the ship's company personnel. Cason was able to step from the *Hornet*'s tilted flight deck to a cantilevered wing of a destroyer and therefore did not get the log books wet. I accidentally met Cason on NAS North Island in November of 1942 and he told me he had my log book."[20]

Of course, Rodee led a later *Hornet* air group attack, which Ring in his 'Lost Letter' graciously acknowledged was more successful than his own. After more three decades, and at the end of a scratchy long-distance line, might Rodee have remembered *this* mission as heading 'due west' rather than the original one Bowen Pattison Weisheit was quizzing him on? Who can say? But his log book remains unseen. Secret Information Bulletin No. 1, entitled *Battle Experience from Pearl Harbor to Midway, December 1941 to June 1942 including Makin Island Raid 17-18 August,* was prepared by the United States Fleet Headquarters of the Commander in Chief and released on 15 February 1942 by Rear Admiral Richard Stanislaus Edwards, Chief of Staff, after a period of deliberate consultation. It includes a map which shows clearly the *Hornet*'s first strike taking a 240-degree outward route, exactly the same as the *Enterprise* air group, but going slightly farther out and turning south not north.

After reaching Kure Island, Johnson made the decision to head for Midway and while his XO, Lieutenant Alfred Bland Tucker, headed for *Hornet*, Fisher re-iterated, 'I am convinced I could not have seen the smoke from Midway if we were as far north as we would have been had we flown a 270 degree course.'[21]

Clay Fisher also wrote his own memoirs which were later published in a very abbreviated form.[22] In it he confirmed what he had already told me:

Finally, I noticed a large column of black smoke to the southwest of our position which had to be coming from Midway Island. This column of smoke looked very similar to post-war pictures of the smoke bellowing up from the island. You can see large

---

20   Clayton Fisher to the Author, e-mail dated 9 September 2008 timed at 3:28.
21   Fisher to the Author, 27 September 2006.
22   *Hooked – Tales & Adventures of a Tailhook Warrior.* 2009: Denver, Colorado. Outskirts Press.

objects such as a mountain range from over a hundred miles, but our flight position had to be closer than forty miles from the Island for me to [be] able to see that 300-foot high smoke column.

It was *single* column of smoke he saw, so it was not the three columns from the burning Japanese carriers and anyway the time difference ruled the latter out anyway.

4: Also returning in the direction that they fondly thought was where *Hornet* lay were the ten F4F Wildcats of the fighter escort. Walter Lord personally interviewed their leader, Lieutenant Commander Samuel Gavid Mitchell, when he was researching his book on the battle[23] and was told that, while *en route,* 'they looked to the *north*' and there saw the enemy that they had been seeking earlier.

5: Robert Barde, in his book recorded that *Hornet*'s air group finally departed 'on a heading of 240⁰.' (Barde, Robert Elmer. *The Battle of Midway: A Study in Leadership*, transcript of dissertation. College Park, MD: 1971. University of Maryland and also 'Midway: Tarnished Victory', article in *Military Affairs, Vol. 47. No.4* 1983: Fredericksburg.]

6: Lastly, the only survivor from Waldron's doomed squadron, George Gay, probably the one person who had the least reason to agree with Ring's version of affairs, having personally witnessed the death of every one of his colleagues. A self-appointed 'expert' has stated that Gay 'never produced a report' on the action. Indeed no, but he went better and wrote a whole book,[24] which many other commentators also totally ignore. What Gay *did* write is certainly relevant and worth quoting verbatim:

> The first section, headed by Waldron, was four two-plane groups. The second, headed by Jimmie Owens, was two groups of two planes, and one of three planes. I was the last plane on the right side and the last one of three planes.
>
> He continued, 'I had been put back there *so I could concentrate on my navigation* more than flying close formation. *Our course was a constant 240 degrees* and the speed was 110 knots.'[25]

---

23 Lord, Walter, *Incredible Victory*. 1967: New York. Harper & Row.

24 Gay, George, *Sole Survivor: The Battle of Midway and its effects on his life.* p. 117. 1980: Naples, Fl. Midway Publishers.

25 My italics.

Nothing could be more unbiased, or clearer. Another report, from the Commander-in-Chief, Cruisers, Pacific Fleet to Commander-in-Chief, United States Pacific Fleet, dated 14 June 1942, confirmed this, stating, 'At 0910 Task Force SIXTEEN commenced launching attack groups and gave as their Point Option course 240^0.[26]

In one account Gay is accused of being 'confused' in his memory after 'thirty-seven years'; Likewise Mitscher's official report of the time, reproduced here, although checked and verified by an impartial third-party at the behest of Admiral Ernest King, is deemed a falsification, Ring's account, written only a few years later, is vilified as unreliable, Fisher's memory was, and still is, considered flawed and similarly disdainfully dismissed as incorrect, as is Gay's book. However, Rodee's memory over a long-distance telephone line, on which the whole shaky edifice is based, was, and is still, assumed to be crystal-clear after the same period of time. And with no known viewer, as far as I am aware, of his famous Pilot's Log that is cited, it remains unconfirmed, although apparently accepted as gospel.

CO USS *Hornet* (CV*). Action Report (exert).
CV8/A16-3.   June 13 1942.
Serial 0018.
SUBJECT: Report of Action – 4-6 June 1942
"At 0900 (all times given hereafter are Zone plus 10) commenced launching the Air Group for attack: VSB loaded with 500lb bombs, VTB with torpedoes and VF with M.G. ammunition only. The objective, enemy carriers, was calculated to be 155 miles distant, bearing 239^0T. from this Task Force.; one division of 10 VF Squadron (Lieutenant Commander S G Mitchell, USN) in charge, was sent with 35 VSB and VTB, to offer fighter protection. Deferred departure was used.
Sgd. M.A. Mitscher.

---

26 Commander in Chief, Pacific Fleet report, Serial 01849 of 28 June 1942, World War II action reports, Modern Military Branch, National Archives and Records Administration, 8601 Adelphi Road, College Park, MD 20740. Declassified E.O. 13526 by NDC, Dec 31, 2012. This was report was later altered by the NHHC to read 260^0 and duly posted as such at https://www.history.navy.mil/content/history/nhhc/research/archives/digitized-collections/action-reports/wwii-battle-of-midway/commander-cruisers-pacific-fleet-report.html. In all other respects the document is unchanged.

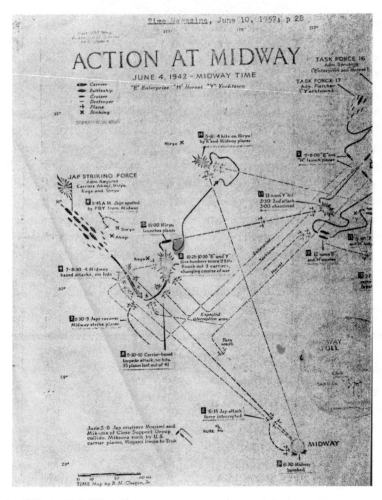

Action at Midway, R.M. Chapin Jr.

I make absolutely no claim to be omniscient in this matter, but, as an attempted recorder of *facts*, I personally cannot embrace such implausible speculation as that proffered by Weisheit, which is almost totally bereft of certified and authenticated documentation. Nor does It make any allowances for the tides and currents to which the Pacific is no less subject to than any other Ocean or Sea. Until there appears some written and verifiable proof to back it up, I will continue to regard the whole 'Flight to Nowhere' scenario as fantasy – a Shibboleth.[27]

27 'A worn-out or discredited doctrine' – Evans, Ivor H (Editor), *Brewers Dictionary of Phrase and Fable,* Cassel, London, 1992.

Glossary of Acronyms

1/c – 2/c – 3/c	First, Second and Third-Class Ratings
AA	Anti-aircraft
ACDUTRA	Active Duty Training Naval Reserve
ACIO	Air Combat Intelligence Officer
ACMM	Aviation Chief Machinist's Mate
ACOM	Aviation Chief Ordnanceman
ACRM	Aviation Chief Radioman
AD	Attack Douglas
ADF	Aerial Direction Finding
AG	Air Group
AGC	Air Group Commander
AM	Aviation Metalsmith
ALO	Air Liaison Officer
ALP	Air Liaison Party
AMM	Aviation Machinist's Mate
ANC	Aircraft Navigational Computer
AOIC	Assistant Officer in Charge
AOM	Aviation Ordnanceman
AC/S	Assistant Chief of Staff
'Angels'	Altitude in thousands of feet above sea level
AP	Armour-Piercing
ARM	Aviation Radioman
ART1c	Aviation Radio Technician (1st Class)
A/S	Anti-submarine

ATO	Air Tactical Officer
Avgas	Aviation gasoline (petrol)
A-D	USNR Flight Officers, Detailed to Active Duty
BB	Battleship
'Bogey'	Unidentified and Potentially Hostile aircraft
BuAer	Bureau of Aeronautics
BuNav	Bureau of Navigation
BuOrd	Bureau of Ordnance
CA	Heavy Cruiser (8-inch guns)
CAP	Combat Air Patrol
CarDiv	Carrier Division
C and R	Communications and Radio
CASU	Cooperative Administrative Support Unit
CB	Battle Cruiser
CEAG	Commander *Enterprise* Air Group
CHAG	Commander *Hornet* Air Group
CI	Communications Intelligence
CIC	Combat Intelligence Center
C-in-C	Commander-in-Chief
C-in-CPAC	Commander-in-Chief Pacific
CIU	Central Intelligence Unit
CL	Light Cruiser (6-inch guns)
CLAA	Anti-Aircraft Cruiser (5-inch guns)
CLAG	Commander *Lexington* Air Group
CNO	Chief of Naval Operations
CoAirSoPac	Commander, Air, South Pacific
CO	Commanding Officer
COMAIRSOLS	Commander Air Operations, Solomons.
COMB	Combined secure radio link
COMINCH/CINCH	Commander-in-Chief Navy
COMINT	Communications Intelligence
ComScoFor	Commander Scouting Force

GLOSSARY OF ACRONYMS

COS	Chief-of-Staff
CP(PA)	Communications Personnel (Photographers Assistant)
CruDiv	Cruiser Division
CV	Aircraft Carrier
CVE	Escort Aircraft Carrier
CVL	Light Aircraft Carrier
CW	Carrier Waveband
CWAG	Commander *Wasp* Air Group
CXAM	RCA-built search radar
CYAG	Commander *Yorktown* Air Group
DCNO	Deputy Chief of Naval Operations
DesRon	Destroyer Squadron
DD	Destroyer
D/F	Direction Finding
D/P	Dual Purpose
EM	Electrician's Mate
EO	Engineering Officer
FDO	Fighter Direction Officer
FO	Flight Officer (USN)
F/O	Flying Officer (RNZAF)
FRUPAC	Fleet Radio Unit, Pacific
GP	General Purpose
HF or H/F	High Frequency
HQ	Headquarters
IAP	Inner Air Patrol
IAS	Indicated Air Speed
IFF	Identifier Friend or Foe
IJA	Imperial Japanese Army
IJN	Imperial Japanese Navy
j.g.	Junior Grade
Jr	Junior
LF or L/F	Low Frequency

JASCO	Joint Assault Signals Company
KIA	Killed in Action
MAG	Marine Air Group
MAGZAM	Marine Air Group Zamoanga
MAW	Marine Air Wing
MCAS	Marine Corps Air Station
MHF	Medium High Frequency (Band) 1605k/c to 4,000k/c
MO	Medical Officer
MU	Maintenance Officer (RNZAF)
NO	Navigation Officer
(P)	Permanent
PO	Personnel Officer
P/O	Pilot Officer (RNZAF)
R/G	Radioman/Gunner
RI	Radio Intelligence
RIU	Radio Intelligence Unit (embarked)
RM	Radioman
RNZAF	Royal New Zealand Air Force
Rtd	Retired
SAC	Support Air Controller
SAD	Support Air Direction (USMC)
SADE	Support Aircraft Direction Emergency (USMC)
SAO	Support Assault Observation
SAP	Semi-Armour-Piercing
SAR	Search and Rescue
SAR	Support Aircraft Request (USMC)
SB2U	Scout Bomber, Vought
SBC	Scout Bomber, Curtiss
SBD	Scout Bomber, Douglas
SC	General Electric search radar
Sea	Seaman
SeeBees	CBs – Construction Battalions, US Navy.

GLOSSARY OF ACRONYMS

SOC	Scouting-Observation, Curtiss
SS	Submarine
(T)	Temporary
TAIC	Technical Air Intelligence Center
TBD-1	Torpedo Bomber, Douglas
TBF/TBM	Torpedo Bomber, Grumman
TBS	Talk Between Ships
TCO	Take-off Control Officer
TF	Task Force
TI	Traffic Intelligence
TV	Terminal Velocity
USAAC	United States Army Air Corps (to June 1942)
USAAF	United States Army Air Forces (from June 1942)
USMC	United States Marine Corps
USN	United States Navy
USSBS	United States Strategical Bombing Survey
VB	Dive Bomber Squadron
VF	Fighter Squadron
VHF	Very High Frequency
VMSB	Marine Scout Bomber Squadron
VSB	Scouting Bomber Squadron
VO	Observation Squadron
VSB	Scouting Bomber Squadron
VT	Torpedo Bomber Squadron
WO	Warrant Officer
WOP	Wireless Operator (RNZAF)
XO	Executive Officer
ZB	Zed Baker or 'Hayrake' homing beacon transmitting aerial.

Bibliography

Anon., *Aviation in the Fleet Exercises 1911-39. Administrative History, Volume 16,* 1956: Washington D.C. Office of the Deputy Chief of Naval Operations (Air).

_____, *Report of the Battle of Midway,* 7 June 1942. Marine Aircraft Group Twenty-Two, Second Marine Aircraft Wing, Midway Island T.H.

_____, Henderson, *Major Lofton: A Memoir.* 1949: Washington D.C. Office of US Marine Corps.

_____, *3rd Bomb Group, Operations; 3rd Bomb Group War Diary; 8th Squadron Composite Diary.* Maxwell AFB.

_____, *Operational Room Log, 25 Dive Bomber Squadron RNZAF & Operational Log Book.No.25 Dive Bomber Squadron RNZAF.* AIR 160 V3. 1944: Auckland. RNZAF Historical Branch.

_____, *Command and Employment of Air Power.* FM100. 1943: Washington D.C. AAF/War Department.

Barde, Robert Elmer, *The Battle of Midway: A Study in Leadership.* Transcript of Dissertation. 1971: College Park, MD, University of Maryland.

Boggs, Major Charles William Jr, *Marine Aviation in the Philippines.* USMC Monograph, 1945; Washington DC, HQ USMC.

Brazelton, David, *The Douglas SBD Dauntless. Aircraft Profile Nr 196.* 1967: Windsor. Profile Publications.

Bright, Richard Carl, *Pain and Purpose in the Pacific: True Reports of War.* 2014: Victoria, BC. Trafford Publishing.

Brown, Captain Eric Melrose RN, *Wings of the Navy – Testing British and US Naval Aircraft.* 2013: Manchester. Hikoki.

Bryan, Commander Joseph, USNR & Reed, Philip, *Mission Beyond Darkness.* 1945: New York. Duell, Sloan and Pearce.

Buell, Commander Dr Harold Lloyd, *Dauntless Helldivers.* 1992: New York. Random House.

BIBLIOGRAPHY

Burns, Eugene, *Then There Was One: The USS* Enterprise *and the First Year of the War.* 1944: New York. Harcourt Brace & Company.

Cales, James Hedge, *Remembrances of Guadalcanal.* Article in *The Hook,* Volume 18. 1990: Annapolis.

Dickinson, Clarence Earle (USN), *The Flying Guns: Cockpit Record of a Naval Pilot Pearl Harbor through Midway.* 1942: New York. Charles Scribner.

Dickson, W.D., *The Battle of the Philippine Sea,* 1975: Annapolis. Naval Institute Press.

Dull, Paul S., *A Battle History of the Imperial Japanese Navy.* 1978: Annapolis. Naval Institute Press.

Duncan, Admiral Donald B., *Oral Transcript.* 1969: New York. Columbia University.

Fisher, Clayton Evan, *Hooked – Tales & Adventures of a Tailhook Warrior.* 2009: Denver, Co. Outskirts Press.

Foosekis, Natalie, *Interview with Edward W Carmichael.* Oral History OH 368. 2007: Fullerton, Ca. El Toro Air Station/California State University.

Gay, George, *Sole Survivor: The Battle of Midway and its effects on his life.* 1980: Naples, Fl. Midway Publishers.

Halsey, Admiral William Frederick Jr & Bryan III, Lieutenant-Commander J. USNR, *Admiral Halsey's Story.* 1947: New York. McGraw-Hill Book Company Inc.

Hara, Captain Tameichi, Saito, Fred & Pineau, Captain Roger, *Japanese Destroyer Captain.* 1961: New York. Ballentine Books.

Jenkins, Dale, *Midway, the American Attack: First Stage.* Thesis – To the Author, 1 September 2017.

Lord, Walter, *Incredible Victory.* 1967: New York. Harper & Row.

Lundstrom, John B., *Black Shoe Carrier Admiral: Frank Jack Fletcher at Coral Sea, Midway and Guadalcanal.* 2006: Annapolis. Naval Institute Press.

Miller, Thomas G., *The Cactus Air Force.* 1969: New York. Admiral Nimitz Foundation.

Morison, Professor Samuel Eliot, *History of the United States Naval Operations in World War II, Volume V: The Struggle for Guadalcanal.* 1951: Boston, Little Brown & Co.

O'Reilly, Patrick & Sedes, Jean-Marie Jaones, *Noirs et Blanc: Trois Anneés de Guerre aux Les Salomon.* 1949: Paris. Editions du Monde Nouveau.

Peattie, Mark A., *Sunburst: The Rise of Japanese Naval Air Power, 1909-1941.* 2001: Annapolis. Naval Institute Press.

Prados, Dr John PhD, *Islands of Destiny: The Solomons Campaign and the Eclipse of the Rising Sun.* 2012: New York. NAL-Caliber.

Reynolds, Clark G., *Admiral John H. Towers: The Struggle for Naval Air Supremacy.* 1991: Annapolis. Naval Institute Press.

Roskill, Stephen Wentworth, *The War at Sea, Volume Two.* 1957: London. HMSO.

Santelli, James S., *Marines in the Recapture of the Philippines.* 1965: Washington D.C. Historical Branch, HQ USMC.

Sherrod, Robert, *History of Marine Corps Aviation in World War II.* 1952: Washington D.C. Combat Forces Press

Smith, Peter Charles Horstead, *Jungle Dive Bombers at War.* 1987: London. John Murray.

_____, *Douglas SBD Dauntless.* 1997: Ramsbury. The Crowood Press.

_____, *Midway Dauntless Victory: Fresh Perspectives on America's Seminal Naval Victory of World War II.* 2007: Barnsley. Pen & Sword Maritime.

Stafford, Edward Peary & Stillwell, Paul, *The Big 'E': The Story of the USS Enterprise.* 1962: New York. Random House.

Weisheit, Major Bowen Pattison, *The Last Flight of Ensign C. Markland Kelly, Junior, USNR: with a New, Corrected Charting of the Flight of VF-8 from USS* Hornet *During the Battle of Midway.* 1993: Annapolis, MD. Self-Published.

White, Alexander S., *Dauntless Marine: Joseph Sailer Jr Dive-Bombing Ace of Guadalcanal.* 1996, Fairfax Station, Va. Pacifica Military History.

Index

INDEX

INDEX

INDEX

Mitsubishi A6M4 Zero ('Zeke') -
  fighter 26, 32-34, 36, 38-39, 42-43,
  48, 62, 65-67, 80, 84, 101-102, 106,
  123, 126, 143-144, 161-165, 194
Mitsubish F1M2 'Pete' Floatplane 107
Mitsubishi G4M 'Betty' bomber
  16, 192
MO, Operation 24-25
Mochadzuki, Japanese destroyer 96
Mogami, Japanese heavy cruiser 67-68,
  74, 162
Mohan, Private T L 89
Mohler, AAM3c William Ripley 59
Monahan, RM3c Eugene James 87,
  112, 116
Montensen, ARM1c Clyde S 56
Moore, Flying Officer Alexander 133
Moore, Lieutenant Benjamin
  Eugene, Jr. 55, 64, 71, 73, 125
Moore, Corporal John A 47
Moore, Sea1c John Arthur 41, 47, 69
Moore, ARM2c Oral Lester 56, 125
Moore, Second Lieutenant Thomas
  Carlyle, Jr. 47, 89, 92
Moffett, Admiral William Adger 5
Monaghan, US destroyer 12
Morison, Professor Samuel Eliot 114,
  118, 217
Morris, US destroyer 128
Morris, Sergeant Donald Martin 190
Morozumi, General Gyosaku 193
Moss, Lieutenant Abraham Hugh 104
Moyers, Ensign Hank 158, 164
Mucci, Lieutenant Colonel Henry 189
Muda, Colonel Toyhorei 135
Mudge, Major General Verne
  Donald 182
Muntean, RM3c Samuel Andrew 54
Murakumo, Japanese destroyer 95
Murasame, Japanese destroyer 94
Mutsu, Japanese battleship 107
Myōkō, Japanese heavy cruiser 96,
  107, 119
Munro, Flight Sergeant John Keith 133

Murray, Rear Admiral George
  Dominic 119
Murray, ACRM James Francis 13, 18,
  54, 64
Musgrove, ARM3c Desmond
  Christopher 30
Musashi, Japanese battleship 117, 154
Mustin, US destroyer 127

Naganami, Japanese destroyer 98
Nagano, Admiral Osami 24
Nagara, Japanese light cruiser 63
Nagara Maru, Japanese transport 102
Nagata Maru, Japanese auxilliary
  vessel 17
Nagumo, Admiral Chuichi 24, 50, 79,
  106, 110, 118, 121, 123, 201,
  203, 205
Nakajima A6M-2 'Rufe' seaplane
  fighter 93, 97
Nakajima B5N 'Kate' torpedo bomber
  27, 33-34, 43, 60, 115
Nako Maru, Japanese transport 102
Nalls, Ensign John Van Buren, Jr. 49
Natsugumo, Japanese destroyers 95
Naval Aircraft SBN-1/2 dive bomber 6
Neely, Ensign Richard Franklin 29, 41
Nelson, RM2c Harrold William, Jr. 13,
  18, 29, 54
Nelson, RM3c James Warren 122
Nelson, Captain Roscoe Maughan 105
Neosho, US oiler 27, 31-32
Newell, Lieutenant James Harold 29
Newman, Lieutenant Melvin Rollie 98
Newman, Commander Roscoe Lee 166
New Orleans, US heavy cruiser 45
Newton, Rear Admiral John Henry 9
Newton, Ensign Oran, Jr. 93, 112
Nickerson, Ensign Henry John 57,
  65, 74
Nickey, Sea1c George LaDanyi, Jr. 57
Nichol, Lieutenant Commander
  Bromfield Bradford 10
Nichols, Corporal Robert Ernest 81

INDEX

INDEX